Australian Politics

2nd Edition

by Dr Nick Economou and Dr Zareh Ghazarian

Forewords by Linda Burney MP, Michelle Grattan AO, and John Howard OM AC SSI

for dummies®

A Wiley Brand

Australian Politics For Dummies®, 2nd Edition

Published by
John Wiley & Sons Australia, Ltd
42 McDougall Street
Milton, Qld 4064
www.dummies.com

Copyright © 2022 John Wiley & Sons Australia, Ltd

The moral rights of the author have been asserted.

ISBN: 978-0-730-39542-3

 A catalogue record for this
book is available from the
National Library of Australia

Cover image: © Alex Cimbal/Shutterstock

Typeset by SPi

Contents at a Glance

Table of Contents

Foreword

Although the Australian nation may have only come into existence as a federation in 1901, it is one of the oldest continuous democracies, of which I was given the great privilege of being its prime minister between 1996 and 2007. The prime minister is but the first among equals in those countries such as ours that embrace the Westminster system. However, the Australian version of the Westminster system has some special home-grown features. Indeed, Australia has been a pioneer in many democratic practices, such as the secret ballot and granting women the vote in parts of Australia well in advance of other nations. Our system of government took the best traditions, institutions and practices of Britain, with some elements from the United States, and combined them in a distinctly Australian way to make it the greatest country in the world. There are, however, some unique features of our political system that require explanation.

I was first elected to parliament in the double-dissolution election of 1974, in which all seats of parliament were contested (as opposed to a regular election in which only half the Senate seats are up for election). This election was also held less than 18 months after the 1972 election, in which Prime Minister Gough Whitlam had won a majority in the House of Representatives but not in the Senate. Seeking an early election, with the Senate having blocked six government bills, the prime minister advised the governor-general Sir Paul Hasluck — the representative of Queen Elizabeth II —to dissolve both houses. This made every seat in parliament vacant. After being sworn in, my first experience on the floor of parliament was the only ever joint sitting of all members of parliament from both houses. The following year, I witnessed the most significant constitutional crisis in Australian history. The Coalition blocking supply in the Senate was followed by Gough Whitlam's refusal to call an election, resulting in the governor-general Sir John Kerr dismissing the prime minister in order resolve the impasse.

This book helps to explain our political system. Authors Dr Nick Economou and Dr Zareh Ghazarian provide a direct and straightforward explanation of how politics works in Australia. They are both leading researchers and commentators in Australian politics. It sometimes troubles me that many of the achievements of democratic government in our country are not as fully understood as they could be. The remarkable stability and social cohesion we sometimes take for granted in Australia owes a great deal to the effective functioning of our democracy.

John Howard, OM AC SSI
Prime minister of Australia, 1996–2007

Foreword

The COVID-19 pandemic reminded us of the influential role government plays in our lives. It also demonstrated the important function of citizens in shaping the government and its decisions. This requires us to be informed: to understand not just the issues, but the rules and the players.

Over the period of 120 years since federation, we've had 30 prime ministers and 46 elections. Yet, for all the rough and tumble of our politics, we've still managed to sustain a working democracy.

Like most governments around the globe, the legitimacy of the Australian political system hinges in large part on its citizens placing their faith, confidence and trust in the system and the institutions, while applying an unrelenting vigilance and scrutiny of those holding the levers of power.

Political systems must demonstrate to the citizenry, on the whole, that it works for them. The *how* and *who* have evolved over time with changing community values and attitudes. For example, when women in Australia were granted the right to vote in 1902, First Nations were excluded. It wasn't until 1962 that First Nations people were given the option to vote in federal elections, and not until 1984 that First Nations people were compulsorily enrolled. In Australia, we have sought to strike a fine and often blurred balance between guarding the fundamentals of the system and providing for constant tinkering to adapt to modern times.

In light of this, the successful 1967 referendum to amend the Australian constitution enabled the Commonwealth to make beneficial laws with respect to First Australians, as well as to count us in the census. More broadly, however, and as a political exercise, it provided an historic case study of Australia's political system adjusting to meet the new and changing values and attitudes of its citizenry.

But as the '67 referendum also demonstrated, it is a two-way street: the system allows for change, but the citizenry must act upon it. The system did not simply adjust itself in 1967. The referendum was the result of a decades' long community campaign from grassroots activists to precipitate structural change.

Citizens have a duty to remain vigilant and to ensure that governments serve the interests of its people. And this means keeping informed.

When we turn on the television, listen to the radio, or scroll through social media, it can seem as if much of what is happening in politics is a lot of theatre, conflict and grand standing. And yet the hot button issues of the parliament form just a thin layer of the work and business of government. The vast majority of laws of the parliament are passed with bipartisan support and little controversy. So much of our life is impacted either directly or indirectly by government: from who collects our waste, to how much it costs to take the train, to buying affordable medications from the chemist. Whether we like it or not, all of us have an active interest in the operations, deliberations, and, ultimately, the election of our governments.

The COVID-19 pandemic prompted all of us around the world to re-examine the relationship between citizens and governments and the competing interests of individuals and communities, lives and livelihoods. The stakes are so high and yet disinformation continues to pervade and hinder these deliberations. There's never been a more critical time to remain properly informed.

Whether you're deciding how you want to cast your vote, or whether you want to flaunt your political credentials at your next dinner party, *Australian Politics For Dummies* provides a simple yet comprehensive guide to the Australian political system and its historical origins, the core principles that underpin it, its critical components, the role of political parties, the function of citizens, and the hot button issues of our time.

Hon Linda Burney MP
Member for Barton, New South Wales

Foreword

Democracy has been having a hard time of it in many parts of the Western world in the last few years.

Dislocation and insecurity, flowing from technological advances and economic shocks, have upended many people's lives. The digital revolution and rise of social media have brought great advantages, including much wider access to data and ways for people to have a 'voice' — but they have also produced new inequalities, 'silos' and echo chambers, and coarsened the political conversation.

Social media has led to an explosion of information, but often to more confusion about what is correct or fake. Misinformation spreads as quickly as coronavirus. In Australia and elsewhere the media has polarised, and become more shrill.

For many people, a sense of community has been lost. Individuals and families are under extra stress. Being excessively 'connected', a feature of contemporary society, perversely can lead to some people becoming unable to cope, and feeling alone.

In some countries, populist movements and leaders have exploited perceptions of powerlessness, to fuel resentment of 'elites' and to fan the decline in trust in political institutions and more conventional leaders.

The build-up of cynicism over recent years, within both the political class and the populace, is corrosive. It weakens the chassis and the engine of the vehicle that is democracy. We see it in Australia, although not as badly as in some democracies.

Too often, our politicians regard their trade as a game of tactics; their debates turn into slanging matches, lacking any respect for the other side's point of view. Moreover, our parties have become hollowed out, which narrows the recruitment pool for our parliaments.

We are blessed in Australia with compulsory voting. It might be flawed in theory — surely we have the right to decide not to vote, it can be argued — however, in practice it delivers some gold, because it pushes our politics away from the extremes. Even so, too often members of the public simply turn off politics, regarding it and its practitioners with indifference or disdain.

Yet, despite the frustrations, it is vital we retain faith in our democratic institutions and those who participate in them. Ideally, that means becoming involved, even to a small extent. Vitally, it means keeping informed — understanding not just what's happening at a particular time but also the system itself, its parts and gears, so we can exercise a vote based on informed judgement. As the authors of this book say: 'Knowledge is power, and knowing how the system works gives you the power to understand and influence the decision-making processes of the country.'

Our system is complex, because of the nature of the federation, with its divided and shared powers. At the national level, the bicameral federal parliament, with its very powerful upper house, makes the legislative process often protracted and uncertain.

Australian Politics for Dummies, 2nd edition, written by academic experts Nick Economou and Zareh Ghazarian, is a valuable resource for both specialists needing to access facts quickly, and the general reader wanting to grasp the whole as well as the detail. It combines rigour with bite-sized convenience.

Michelle Grattan, AO FASSA
Chief political correspondent at *The Conversation*

Introduction

Welcome to the second edition of *Australian Politics For Dummies!*

One of the most exciting things about politics in Australia is that it's accessible. Finding an Australian who doesn't have an opinion on politics is difficult; what's more, the people of the nation decide who gets to govern, thanks to regular elections.

Australia's system of government borrows elements from the British and American models, so is sometimes called a hybrid system. Throw some Australian ingenuity into the mix and what you have is a system of government that is unique.

Knowledge is power, and knowing how the system works gives you the power to understand and influence the decision-making processes of the country. Remember, the most important feature of politics is *you*. So, understanding and getting active in politics is the key to influencing decisions and, ultimately, shaping your community, your country and potentially the world.

About This Book

The Australian political system often appears complex and confusing. With so many levels of government, keeping track of who's responsible for what can be a bit tricky. Similar to other countries, Australia also focuses heavily on its leading politicians, sometimes overlooking the important contributions made by those without such high public profiles.

This book aims to help you understand the Australian political system by examining its key features. You can learn about important aspects such as how government is structured, the rules that governments must follow and the importance of political parties. You can also gain an insight into who the important players are in the system and how crucial they are in deciding government policy.

Australian Politics For Dummies also gives you the power to understand the voting system, one of the most important aspects of politics. You get to see how the outcomes of elections are often influenced by the voting system. So, understanding the system enables you to understand election outcomes and make your vote more effective.

By exposing you to the innards of political systems, this book removes the veil of confusion and complexity from Australian politics. It arms you with the knowledge to understand and become even more active in your democracy.

This book is written as a reference that you can pick up whenever you need to check on the key features of Australian politics. It explains the jargon that's often bandied about. It helps you quickly answer your questions on Australian politics through its table of contents, index, sidebars, cross-references, icons and glossary. These elements mean you can find the answers to your questions without having to read the book from cover to cover, although you can do that as well if you want.

To help you get the information you need as quickly as possible, this book also uses several conventions:

>> **Bold** words make the key terms and phrases in bulleted lists jump out and grab your attention.

>> *Italics* signal that a word is an important defined term.

>> Monofont is used to signal a web address.

>> When this book was printed, some web addresses may have needed to break across two lines of text. If that happened, rest assured that no extra characters (such as hyphens or spaces) are used to indicate the break. So, when using one of these web addresses, just type in exactly what you see in this book, pretending that the line break doesn't exist.

>> Sidebars, text separated from the rest of the type in grey boxes, are interesting but slightly tangential to the subject at hand. Sidebars are generally fun and optional reading. You won't miss anything critical if you skip the sidebars. If you choose to read the sidebars, though, we think you'll be glad you did.

Foolish Assumptions

Politics is often seen as something that 'other people' do. But, in reality, it's something everyone's part of. Politics concerns almost everything in society, from who gets to run the country, the state and the local council, and what they can and can't do, to how often you get to vote for them, to how often you can water your garden. We're guessing your interest fits somewhere within that spectrum!

This book is written for anyone interested in Australian politics. It's a great resource for those without any prior understanding of the system, as well as those with a more advanced knowledge of Australian politics. And, if you *are* absolutely new to politics, this book will bring you up to speed, fast.

Icons Used in This Book

A picture says a thousand words. Indeed, in the case of these icons, they may actually save you reading a thousand words. Throughout the book are little round pictures that point out information and things you should remember about Australian politics. They're handy to highlight some interesting — and some crucial — facts about Australian politics.

REMEMBER

This icon highlights vital information that you shouldn't forget. Without taking heed of this information, you may not be able to get a full account of Australian politics.

TECHNICAL STUFF

This icon highlights information that's a bit more complex than usual. But don't worry — the information with these icons is not crucial in understanding the political system.

TIP

This icon denotes a piece of advice about the subject matter being discussed that helps you to learn more.

VOTE 1

This icon highlights interesting political facts. They're case studies, anecdotes and other bits of trivia that add to your understanding of Australian politics.

Where to Go from Here

The beauty of this book is that you have the choice about how you read it. Feel free to read it cover to cover, but you can also skip from chapter to chapter if you wish, or even from section to section. Simply find the chapter or section you're interested in, and jump in:

>> If you'd like to know more about the building blocks of Australian politics, head straight to Chapters 1 and 2. These help you to identify the key features of the system and also have an understanding of the important debates going on.

>> Chapters 3 to 7 examine how government is structured in Australia. Here you can delve more deeply into the critical components of the system and how they work together to create a unique system — one that's designed to represent you.

>> If you're looking to get your head around all the different political parties in Australia, jump to Chapters 8 to 12. You find out here how Australia's party system emerged and what role political parties — both major and minor — play.

>> Perhaps you're most interested in your power as a citizen to elect governments — in which case, Chapters 13 to 15 are for you. Examining the voting system, as well as the various parts of the election process, enables you to see how important elections are to Australia's system of government.

>> If you want bite-sized chunks of information, check out the final part in this book. Its four chapters list the ten politicians who made an impact, the ten speeches worth listening to again, ten acts of political bastardry and ten women who have made history in Australian politics. Get to know some of this delicious detail and you can name-drop like a pro at dinner parties.

Remember to use the tools we've supplied also — the table of contents and index enable you to flick to the exact information you want, and the handy glossary of terms at the back of the book is invaluable for sorting out the political jargon and official terminology.

1

Politics:
You're in It

Find out about the importance of politics in society, as well as *your* role in it and your power as a voter to decide on the future of the nation.

Discover the building blocks of Australian politics and examine the issues that have featured in, and continue to dominate, the Australian political debate.

Identify the key players and arguments of the great debates — the unions, immigration, reconciliation, the environment, climate change, globalisation . . . the list goes on.

IN THIS CHAPTER

» Exploring the difference between politics and government

» Coming to grips with Australia's voting system

» Understanding the three levels of government in Australia

» Getting to know the key players in Australian politics

» Checking out interest groups

» Looking at what makes a politician

» Realising you can't ever be outside politics

Chapter **1**

Australian Politics: The Basics

olitics is everywhere. Throughout history, humans have grappled with understanding politics. In fact, it's one of the oldest concepts studied. Politics moulded the most ancient civilisations and plays a crucial role in the running of modern society. The world would be a very different place without it.

In this chapter, you get a quick tour of the basics in Australian politics and tackle the time-honoured question, 'What is politics?' You also get to kick around the reputation of those who seek to become politicians. (In fact, you get to see how becoming involved in politics is a very noble pastime, despite the way politicians' reputations tend to be besmirched by commentators.)

Also in this chapter, you find some of the key features of the Australian system, all of which we cover in greater detail later in the book. Included in this chapter are quick introductions to some of the major organisations through which citizens try to engage with the political system, including political parties, interest groups and protest movements.

What Is Politics?

Elections! Leaders! Policy! Government! To most Australians, politics can be any one or all of these things. But, technically, the study of politics is the study of power. Political scientists tend to assume that the struggle that occurs between people and between associations to win power constitutes politics.

Power is a difficult thing to define, but, in a country such as Australia, the idea that someone has power is often equated with the idea of government. A powerful person may be the prime minister, given that he or she is the person who heads a government. A government minister may be thought of as powerful by having the right to make decisions on policy and having a department of public servants to carry out that policy.

The elusive nature of power is often revealed when ex-ministers and even former prime ministers talk about their time in office, lamenting that they wanted to achieve so much more than they did. Often, the blame for thwarted ambition is laid at the feet of politics.

AREN'T POLITICS AND GOVERNMENT THE SAME?

Many people think politics and government are the same thing, but they're actually quite different.

Government refers to the way a community administers its own affairs. It is also a reference to the institutions and structures used by members of the community (in a modern democracy, the body of elected representatives) to make decisions on matters of policy and have those decisions carried out. So, government involves parliaments as the places where decisions are debated and made, and public service departments that convert political decisions into actual administration.

Politics, on the other hand, is the product of the struggle that occurs between individuals, organisations and even governing institutions for influence over decisions that are made.

TECHNICAL
STUFF

The ancient Greeks understood politics to be the product of *democracy* — the idea that citizens should be able to govern themselves. The interaction of ideas and arguments as part of decision-making was seen as being the stuff of politics. The ancient Greeks also had a word for a person not interested in public affairs — *idiot*.

Compulsory Voting

For most Australian citizens, politics is also equated with democracy. In this case, democracy is actually *electoral democracy* — that is, the will of the people expressed by way of an election. In this process, voters elect representatives to the *legislature*, the generic word for parliament, where governments are formed.

The Australian national parliament is made up of two chambers — the *House of Representatives* (or lower house) and the *Senate* (or states' house or, indeed, the upper house).

As a political writer once pointed out, participating in elections is the closest most people come to politics in their lives. This is a bit distinct from government, however, because government affects everyone's life every day through the provision of services as a result of government policy. In this way, politics does have an impact on everyone's life every day, whether they think about it or not.

In any modern electoral democracy, voting is seen as an important human right. Australia has an interesting take on voting. In addition to being a right, voting is actually a duty of citizenship. Australia has compulsory voting. You get to explore the intricacies of compulsory voting in Chapter 13.

REMEMBER

Compulsory voting means all Australian citizens must take an interest in politics. Opting out isn't an option — not turning up to an election is against the law!

A Lot of Government

As the saying goes, 'the more the merrier', especially if you like elections. Australia has many elections because it has a lot of government. For a nation of just over 25 million people, Australia has an abundance of politicians hard at work in their national and state parliaments, and their local town halls and civic centres.

Australia has three levels of government:

>> Federal government (that's the government going on in the national capital of Canberra)

>> State government (based in the capital city of each state but overseeing the whole state)

>> Local government (in cities and shires across each state)

Each level of government has its own rules that determine how much time elapses between elections. Some states have fixed four-year terms; others have variable four-year terms. The federal government is elected for a three-year term, but early elections can and do happen. Each state's local government election system varies, with some states having compulsory local elections.

In short, Australians are constantly involved in elections. The variety of elections is matched by the variety of electoral systems, with permutations and outcomes that could give Pythagoras a headache (more on that in Chapter 13). The reason Australia has this array of government is because it is a federation.

Federations involve dividing the power to govern between national and state governments. Each level of government has the legal authority to make policy and enact laws in particular areas, thanks to the existence of constitutions. *Constitutions* are legal documents that establish the legal authority of government and the powers that government can exercise.

VOTE 1

In Australia, the state governments came first. The national government — often referred to as the federal government — came along later. Indeed, the federal government was created by the states (originally called colonies), which gave the new national system of government specific powers, while retaining some powers themselves. We cover the division of powers between the federal and state governments in Chapter 3.

Governing the nation

National governance is the concern of the federal government, which has its parliament in Canberra, in the Australian Capital Territory (the ACT). The Australian Constitution, the document that outlines the way Australia is run, was drawn up by the federating colonies in the 1890s, and ratified by the British parliament in 1900. The first meeting of the federal parliament occurred on 1 January 1901 in the Royal Exhibition Building in Melbourne.

The federal government can only exercise power in those areas of responsibility outlined in the Constitution. This includes powers over defence, quarantine, immigration, currency, external affairs, marriage, foreign corporations, foreign policy, and importing and exporting (especially of strategic minerals).

The federal government also has substantial power over finances, including the payment of money to the states. During World War II, the federal government legislated to establish a monopoly over the levying of income and company tax. This makes the federal government the dominant level of government in federal–state financial relations. When you pay your income tax, your money goes to the Australian Taxation Office, which acts on behalf of the federal government.

The head of parliamentary government in federal politics is the prime minister. The Queen's representative is called the governor-general. Chapter 3 covers the roles involved in Australia's system of constitutional government in detail.

Governing the states

After 1 January 1901 — the date of Federation — the six Australian colonies became six states: Victoria, New South Wales, Queensland, South Australia, Western Australia and Tasmania. These are known as the *original states* and are guaranteed a minimum of five seats in the federal parliament's House of Representatives, and an equal number of senators in the Senate (today, 12 senators each).

REMEMBER

Each state has its own constitution, parliament, legal system, governor and head of parliamentary government, known as the premier. Each state is responsible for its own electoral system.

TECHNICAL STUFF

In theory, any governmental power not mentioned in the Australian Constitution is a power exercisable by the states. Technically, these are called *residual powers*. Don't think that residual means somehow less important. These residual powers mean the states are responsible for the delivery of health policy, primary and secondary education, land use and planning, law and order, and transport.

Administering the territories

In addition to the six states, Australia has two territories — the Northern Territory (with its capital city of Darwin) and the Australian Capital Territory (the territory created under the Constitution with the capital city of Canberra).

The territories don't have the same constitutional status as the states. In fact, they're administrative units of the federal government. In the 1980s, a law passed by the federal government gave self-government to the territories. This change means they now have their own parliaments, their own head of parliamentary government (known as the chief minister) and their own representative of the Queen (called a chief administrator).

VOTE 1

The territories are governed like states and deal with local issues. The Northern Territory, for example, has a very large Aboriginal population and so Indigenous affairs is an important matter for the government. It must be remembered, however, that the power of the territories is subordinate to the federal government.

Roads, rates and rubbish: Local government

Local government is sometimes thought of as the third level of government, but this concept is a little bit misleading. Local government is actually an administrative power of state governments, and councils are subordinate to the state parliament.

You may have heard that local government in Australia is interested in the three Rs — roads, rates and rubbish. The levying of rates and maintenance of local services, including roads and waste management, do figure prominently in local government. However, councils also deal with important planning matters and can have a big influence in areas relating to climate change policy and action. Disputes between councils and state governments can break out, especially over planning decisions relating to major development projects.

Each state's local government arrangements tend to be different, especially when it comes to how local councils are elected. Local politics tends to be the domain of independent politicians, although in some states the political parties can play a major role.

From Government to Politics

Politics is the result of the struggle for power. In democracies such as Australia, the battle to win executive power involves a struggle to win control of the legislature (parliament). This struggle plays itself out via elections.

In theory, democracies are about *popular sovereignty*, which is jargon for saying 'the empowerment of individual citizens to run their community' (also known as society). This, of course, is the basis for democratic government.

In the modern world, communities have become increasingly large and more complex. Whenever government is discussed, it's usually in the context of talking about governing the nation. Of course, in a federal country such as Australia, governing the states is also a factor of government.

Australia as a nation, or the Australian states when considered individually, is a large and complex community. Despite the theory of popular sovereignty, the reality is that the ability of a person to have an impact on the governing process is severely limited by the size of government. As a result, individual citizens seek to affect government through groups. In understanding politics, two sets of groups are particularly important — political parties and interest groups.

Political parties

Don't raid your pantry for chips and dips, because we're not talking about political shindigs here. Political parties are the basic building blocks of politics. All political systems have political parties.

REMEMBER

A *political party* is an association of people coming together for the express purpose of recruiting candidates for elections and backing these party-endorsed candidates with resources to help them fight the election campaigns.

The basic assumption is that political parties contest elections with the intention of winning them (that might mean winning a majority of the vote cast or, more likely, winning a majority of seats in the legislature). The point of winning elections is that this win is the precursor to winning executive power (that is, winning government).

Parties can be organised in many different ways and have different approaches to how they debate policies and so on. One of the key features of modern parties, however, is that they are disciplined. What this means is that, in exchange for endorsing candidates, parties expect loyalty from their endorsed candidates when they win seats in the parliament. Check out Chapter 8 for more on the party system.

VOTE 1

The dominance of disciplined party politics has led some political commentators to describe government as being *party government*. Government in Australia is invariably determined by the electoral victory of a political party or perhaps a combination of parties (known as a *coalition*).

The major parties

As with nearly every electoral democracy, Australian politics is dominated by two political parties. In Australia, these are

» The Australian Labor Party (also known as the ALP, Labor or the Labor Party)

» The Liberal Party of Australia (simply known as the Liberal Party or the Liberals)

Nearly every member of an Australian parliament, whether the national parliament or the parliaments of the states and territories, belong to either the Labor Party (see Chapter 9) or the Liberal Party (see Chapter 10). These two parties command the largest share of the vote cast in Australian elections (anywhere between 75 and 90 per cent between them), win the majority of parliamentary seats and have large memberships. Because of this, they're often referred to as the major parties in the Australian system.

The minor parties

Many more political parties exist than just Labor and the Liberals (refer to the preceding section). What's more, some parties other than the Labor–Liberal duopoly can win seats in the national parliament and the state parliaments, especially where a favourable electoral system is used. One party — the National Party — can even win seats in an electoral system dominated by the Labor and Liberal Parties. Chapter 11 gives you the details on the National Party.

TECHNICAL STUFF

The parties outside of the Labor–Liberal duopoly are understood as minor parties. One political scientist estimates that more than 100 minor parties have registered to contest federal elections since 1949, although only a handful have ever won seats in the national parliament.

Examples of electorally successful minor parties since 1949 include the Democratic Labor Party (DLP), the Australian Democrats, the Nuclear Disarmament Party (NDP), the West Australian Greens, the Australian Greens, One Nation, Family First, and the Palmer United Party (see Chapter 12 for a rundown of minor parties). These parties are diverse in their philosophical outlooks, and their electoral successes have mostly been in winning seats in the Australian Senate. This is a direct consequence of the system of *proportional representation*, used as the electoral system for this chamber. See Chapter 5 for more on the Senate and Chapter 13 for information on the different voting systems.

A two-party system?

The Australian party system is sometimes described as a *two-party system* because of the dominance of the Labor and Liberal parties. The fact that many other parties exist tends to be obscured by the way both Labor and Liberal dominate the election contest. However, even in lower house elections, using preferential voting, observing a third political party at work is possible. With a band of electoral support concentrated in the Murray–Darling Basin, the National Party (formerly called the Country Party) wins seats in both the House of Representatives and the Senate.

The National Party tends to work cooperatively with the Liberals, even though they can be rivals at election time. Federally, the Liberal and National Parties have always governed in coalition. Coalitions have also often been formed in states such as Victoria, New South Wales and Queensland. For this reason, the media sometimes uses the term *coalition* when speaking about a government with the Liberal leader as prime minister.

VOTE 1

Before campaigning begins, the Liberal and National Parties come to an agreement about what positions they'll hold when in government. At the federal level, the Liberal leader will be the prime minister, while the National Party leader is given the position of deputy prime minister, with other National members of parliament (MPs) also getting ministerial positions. See Chapter 11 for more on the coalition agreement.

Interest Groups: Fighting for Causes and Advancing Interests

Interest groups are, well, very interesting because they're another form of organisation that allows citizens the opportunity to interact with politics. If political parties seek to win executive power, interest groups can be understood as organisations that seek to exert influence on the party or parties that win executive power. (Or, to put it another way, interest groups try to exert influence on the government of the day.)

Another aspect of interest groups is that they're usually registered associations that adhere to a constitution, elect executive positions and formulate policies, just like political parties. Some members even go on to become politicians.

Interest group politics is usually closely associated with government. In particular, it has an important role to play in the formation of policies and programs (also known as *public policy*).

Interest groups come in all sorts, and it's possible for them to employ a variety of tactics to try to have an impact on the governing process. See Chapter 8 for more on the influence of interest groups. For all the possible types of interest groups that could be described, two broad categories can be identified — promotional and sectional.

Promotional interest groups

The *promotional interest groups* are those that pursue broad causes. This includes environmental groups, community groups and associations trying to address social and/or cultural matters (such as an ethnic community council) and perhaps even controversial matters such as abortion (for example, the Right to Life Association or the NSW Pro Choice Alliance).

Promotional groups are also sometimes discernible by the way they seek to affect the political process. Promotional groups tend to be associated with campaigns designed to have an impact on public opinion. Promotional groups use public events such as election campaigns to press forward their agendas. They may also seek to use protest activity and publicity stunts with a view to drawing attention to their causes. The theory behind this approach is that promotional groups use public opinion as a lever on government, on the assumption that governments respond to campaigns that can demonstrate public support for the interest group's agenda.

VOTE 1

Promotional groups have an approach to attracting membership not dissimilar to that of political parties, in that membership is open to anyone, provided they subscribe to the ideals and agendas of the group.

Sectional interest groups

Sectional interest groups are those groups that have a close relationship to the economy. Such groups arise on the basis of the potential power they may have over economic policy, given their contribution to economic activity. These groups don't have an open membership. Rather, membership is confined to those people who are part of the economic activity being represented. This category includes trade unions, professional groups such as the Australian Medical Association, business groups and what are called producer groups.

These groups may resort to publicity stunts or disruptive behaviour to get their point across. The more powerful sectional groups, however, are those that can interact with government behind closed doors. It's not uncommon for governments to actively seek out these groups to consult with them on policy options or to ask for feedback on current policies. The power and influence of these groups tend to be a reflection of the power of the economic activity in which they're engaged.

Trade unions and politics

Trade unions are sectional interest groups, representing workers in particular industries, but their impact on Australian politics goes far beyond simply trying to exert influence over the government of the day. For one thing, the trade union movement has a close relationship with the Australian Labor Party (see Chapter 9). The unions helped create the ALP and, even to this day, unions often affiliate with the party, and have a role to play in the running of the party and the creation of party policy.

The role of unions in the Australian economy and society is one of those debates people never stop having in Australian politics (see Chapter 2 for more). The reason for this is partly because of the political situation, but also partly because of the role unions have traditionally had in the nation's industrial laws.

Professional groups

As the name suggests, professional groups tend to be concerned with representing the interests of usually highly skilled and/or highly educated professionals. These associations may lobby government on policy matters, or they may sometimes be consulted by government on how policies may change.

One example of a professional interest group is the Law Council of Australia, which is the representative body of legal practitioners in Australia. The Australian Medical Association (AMA) is another example of a professional interest group. The AMA is seen as one of the most powerful professional groups in Australia because it represents doctors. The AMA is active in the political debate, especially on issues concerning health policy.

Business groups

Business groups also try to affect the economic policy debate. Business interests tend to be associated with the Liberal Party (see Chapter 10), but the relationship between the groups and the party is nowhere near as direct as that between unions and the ALP. For a start, Liberal Party rules don't allow for groups to affiliate with the party. Second, business interest groups realise that, sometimes, they have to deal with Labor governments and that being seen to be too close to the Liberals may impair their ability to lobby government.

Divisions within the business community also exist. The interest of big business owners and leaders may not be the same as those of small business owners. Export-oriented business groups may want very different policy outcomes from government than groups oriented towards the domestic market, for example.

Whether an individual firm (especially a really big company) constitutes an interest group in its own right is debatable. The alternative view is that all communication to government needs to come from a broader association of groups. Clearly, business interest group politics are diverse and complicated.

Producer groups

Farmer groups are also very important players in Australian politics, not least because of the historical contribution agriculture has made to Australian economic development since colonial times.

As with business groups and their relationship with the Liberal Party, producer groups tend to be close to the non-Labor parties generally, and the National Party in particular (see Chapter 11) — although, like the Liberal Party, National Party rules don't allow for the affiliation of external groups.

VOTE 1

Producer groups may also include associations representing mining companies (such as the Minerals Council of Australia). Once again, the power and influence of these groups are a reflection of the importance of the activities of their constituents to Australia's economic wellbeing. Governments — whether Labor or coalition — consult with producer groups as part of the policy-making process.

Umbrellas and peaks

Governments can find it difficult to deal with a proliferation of diverse sectional interest groups, not to mention the onslaught of promotional groups. Interest groups understand this, and many of them seek to coalesce into broader representative bodies that try to utilise a single association to talk on behalf of many constituent groups. These associations are sometimes called *umbrella organisations* (because they try to cover all of the demands of their constituent groups) or *peak bodies* (because they represent the highest advocacy group on behalf of their constituent interest groups).

Umbrella and peak groups are usually distinguishable by their nomenclature, which very often has the word *council* in it. The Australian Council of Trade Unions (ACTU) is a classic umbrella organisation for the trade union movement, the Australian Council of Social Service (ACOSS) is a national peak body for the nation's welfare advocacy groups and the Minerals Council of Australia (MCA) is an example of a business-oriented peak body.

Understanding Politicians

Most people equate being a politician with being a member of parliament. Members of parliament clearly are professional politicians, but others may be considered to be politicians as well, including those who lead interest groups. In fact, anyone who interacts with the governing process may be thought of as a politician.

Who becomes a politician?

A politician is anyone who engages in politics. The answer to 'Who becomes a politician?' in a democracy is 'Anyone.' Not everyone can become a member of parliament, however, although in a democracy few barriers should exist to running for public office.

Those who become a member of parliament are those who win elections, and this process invariably involves the political parties. Getting the endorsement of a political party is usually the first important step towards winning a seat in parliament.

Of course, it's quite possible for people to run for parliament who aren't in political parties. These people are known as independents, and sometimes they can and do win parliamentary seats.

TECHNICAL STUFF

What sort of people get themselves involved in party politics and the battle to win seats in parliament? Studies have shown that the sort of person most likely to get into parliament has a past record of involvement in community affairs, perhaps having had a go at running for or serving on a council, or having worked for an interest group. In more recent times, the background of parliamentarians includes having done some political work in the past as an electoral secretary for an MP, as an adviser to a politician, or as a research officer for an interest group such as a trade union or a producer group.

A 'boys' club'?

For much of the nation's history, politics was an almost exclusively male affair. Women were able to vote in federal elections across the country from 1902 onwards, but the first woman wasn't elected to the national parliament until Enid Lyons won the Tasmanian seat of Darwin in 1943. Julia Gillard is Australia's only female prime minister and she didn't ascend to the position until 2010.

POLITICIAN: IT'S NOT A DIRTY WORD

The term *politician* is sometimes used somewhat negatively to denote someone who perhaps ruthlessly seeks power (sometimes the media also uses the term *Machiavellian* to describe such a person), or who is overly pragmatic, or who is prepared to corrupt their principles to achieve power and maybe even take bribes.

The besmirching of the reputation of people who interact with the political process in this way is one way of looking at politicians. The other way is to see such people as those who are willing to be active in their community and take up the opportunity that democracy allows to try to influence the affairs of their community.

From the 1980s up until the 1996 election, women made up less than 10 per cent of the total number of federal parliamentarians. However, by 2021, this proportion had risen to 38 per cent of federal parliament.

The power to influence the gender balance of the parliament rests with the political parties, for it is they who endorse the candidates electors will vote for. The two major parties have both committed to achieving a more equal gender balance, although they take very different approaches to doing so.

As explained further in Chapter 9, Labor has the more rigid and centralised organisation, and it has committed to an 'affirmative action' policy. This means, since 1994, Labor has set quotas and targets for the percentage of women in its federal caucus. The Liberal party is more committed to the idea of candidates being selected 'on merit' and the power to select candidates is held by the local branches. Labor tends to have more women in its parliamentary ranks than the Liberal party, but the overall proportion is rising.

Even though the male majority is nowhere what it was in previous times, many people — both inside and outside of government — continue to see politics as a 'boys' club'. These issues came to the fore in early 2021 (see Chapter 2 for more on this).

Heavy hitters: Interest group politicians

Members of parliament are obviously involved in politics and are most readily identified as politicians. Interest group leaders, too, stand out as political actors.

Some interest group leaders become immediately obvious when they lead major public campaigns. Before he was a senator, Dr Bob Brown from Tasmania was most famously recognised as a leader of the conservation campaign to stop the

Franklin River dam. (Check out Chapter 12 for more on Bob Brown and the Australian Greens.)

Leaders of sectional interest groups are also political heavy hitters, especially if they represent powerful economic activities. These leaders are sometimes hard to notice in public (their influence tends to be exerted behind closed doors), but they can be observed in action in media treatment of policy debates, where sectional interest group leaders are asked for their opinion on the direction economic policy should take. (Chapter 15 discusses the media's influence in politics in detail.)

Politics: You Can't Escape It

You can't get away from politics, just as you can't get away from government. Government can have an impact on nearly every aspect of a citizen's life, thanks to the extensive role that public policy has in providing services ranging from health and education through to transport, planning, and law and order.

REMEMBER

With its system of compulsory voting reaching down even as far as local government in some states, the Australian system requires that everyone over 18 years of age participates in politics. You can't avoid it (unless you want to get a fine).

Chapter **2**

Hot Topics in Australia: The Political Debate

D ebates about policy are fundamental to politics. Democracies are supposed to revolve around debates on issues ranging from the very basic ('What sort of tax cut will I get?') through to the very complex ('What does it mean to be an Australian citizen?'). Political debate can also be undertaken through many different forums. The parliament is the most obvious place where policy is debated, because the parliament is where government is formed. Debate can also be carried out very extensively in the media (see Chapter 15).

Parliamentary exchanges and media debates are the primary public realms where politics is debated. Political discussions can occur in private realms as well, although Australians are renowned for their rather more private approach to politics than, say, some European societies, where people are very demonstrative about their political beliefs and party alignments. A dinner party in an Australian household is more likely to undertake a robust exchange of views about sport (especially football) than to talk about politics.

This chapter examines some of the political debates that have been central to Australia's political development, and those that continue to resonate, as well as some of the philosophies behind them.

Apathetic or Engaged?

Claims that Australians are apathetic when it comes to politics usually come from studies of what Australians know about their constitutions and electoral systems (sometimes called the study of civics). These studies find low levels of sophisticated understanding of the Australian system (and have led to increased focus on the teaching of civics and citizenship in Australian schools). Part of the reason for this reduced understanding, of course, is that the Australian system is actually a bit difficult to understand because of its complexities.

The fact that Australia has compulsory voting may also contribute to the apparent lack of deep understanding of the system. If you're required by the law to be part of the system, it may be argued, the incentive to understand that system is reduced.

VOTE 1

Are Australians really apathetic when it comes to politics? Participation rates in Australian elections indicate that people are quite happy to be part of a system based on compulsory attendance. On average, over 95 per cent of eligible voters attend federal and state elections. Of course, this could simply be the consequence of the compulsory system (it's easier to vote than to pay a fine). Interesting to note, however, is that, in some states where voting in local elections is compulsory, the attendance rate is only 75 per cent. People participate in state and federal elections not only because they have to, but also because they want to.

Awareness of issues

Australians may have a rudimentary understanding of the complexities of the constitutional arrangements and different electoral systems in use across the country. On the other hand, however, Australians are renowned for their awareness of the issues being debated in Australian politics. What's more, political scientists have plenty of evidence to show that Australian voters are very capable of separating state issues from federal matters, and voting accordingly. In fact, the Australian voter is a lot more sophisticated than some commentators would have you believe.

This interest in politics is partly the consequence of compulsory voting. Knowing that participation in an election is required, Australians in general keep well up to date on the matters that make up national and state political debates. Politicians and the media take great interest in the community's awareness of policy debates, with political parties and news organisations constantly conducting opinion polls that gauge everything from how voters intend to vote at the next election through to what issues they see as being important and how they prioritise those issues.

IDEOLOGY AND PHILOSOPHY

Both ideology and philosophy are thought to play an important role in politics, although commentators hotly debate exactly what *ideology* means.

Philosophy, of course, is as much about the human condition as anything else, and the views that people hold about politics reflect in no small way their personal philosophies about community, individuals and so on. Many politicians, too, like to talk about the influence of philosophy on their reasons for going into politics. Philosophers are also important in helping a community define ethics. Ethics are seen as being really important in government, particularly as an ethical approach to politics helps people identify the difference between behaviour that contributes to the good of the community and behaviour that might be seen as corrupt.

Ideology, meanwhile, is a word constantly bandied around in discussions of politics. *Ideology* is generally understood as firmly held views and core beliefs. Quite often, commentators and politicians use the word to describe what they stand for or what their political parties believe and stand for — hence the constant use of the phrase *party ideology* when discussing the approach of the Labor or Liberal parties to debates about philosophies or policy ideas.

The 'isms' in politics

Australian politics tends to be very pragmatic, with less interest in ideology and philosophy, and more interest in practical approaches to issues that will eventually result in policy outcomes. Issues, rather than ideology, are the real drivers of Australian politics. Some of the big ideological and intellectual traditions of political debate are recognised by the 'ism' attached to their labels.

Socialism

The ideology of socialism is often associated with the beliefs of the Australian Labor Party (ALP — refer to Chapter 1 for a brief description of the ALP and see Chapter 9 for the full lowdown). Technically, *socialism* refers to the common ownership of property. This means that the economy is owned by government on behalf of the community. In some countries (Britain in the 1950s being a classic example), governments may take ownership of previously privately owned businesses. This practice is called *nationalisation*.

IS LABOR A SOCIALIST PARTY?

TECHNICAL STUFF

Labor hasn't ever really been socialist in the technical sense of the word, although a lot of commentators associate other Labor concerns about having legal protections for workers and extending welfare to people as examples of socialism. These are not actually examples of socialism either. Rather, the idea that wealth should be redistributed and that some of the more exploitative aspects of capitalism should be moderated through industrial law and so on is technically understood to be *social democracy* rather than socialism.

The ALP is often associated with socialism because, between 1922 and 1981, the party had a specific Socialist Objective in its policy platform (see Chapter 9) and, in 1947, a Labor government tried to nationalise the banks. This attempt ended up in the High Court, which declared the government's legislation to be illegal. In short, the High Court found that Section 92 of the Australian Constitution doesn't allow for nationalisation to occur.

Liberalism

Liberalism, funnily enough, is associated with the Liberal Party (refer to Chapter 1 for a brief description of the Liberals and see Chapter 10 for more detail). *Liberalism* is less an ideology and more a philosophy, however, and is based on the idea of individual liberty. In particular, liberals worry about the capacity for government to impinge on individual freedoms. This is based on the idea that the individual, rather than the collective, is the more appropriate basis for society, although many liberal philosophers, such as John Stuart Mill, saw the need for a collective approach to society.

Many different types of liberal philosophy exist, but two camps have been important in Australian politics:

>> **Welfare liberals:** The welfare liberals are committed to individualism but see an important regulatory role for governments to ensure that everyone in a 'good' society has access to equal opportunity. These liberals support the idea of state-based education, state assistance for industry and a welfare system — in fact, they're not vastly different in their outlook from social democrats in the Labor party.

>> **Market liberals:** The market liberals are much less comfortable with the idea of state intervention in the economy and are strong advocates of the importance of the marketplace in economic and social affairs. These liberals tend to see welfare payments as distortions of the marketplace. Some of the more radical liberals even argue the case for governments to stay right out of the affairs of individuals on matters such as sexual choice or behavioural choices.

The Liberal Party has large numbers of people who subscribe to one or other, or even a combination of both, of the major themes in liberal thinking. As with their Labor counterparts, these Liberal Party liberals tend to be pragmatic in their approach.

Conservatism

The Liberal Party also has a large number of conservatives. *Conservatism* is also something of a philosophy rather than an ideology, mainly because it's based on rather pessimistic outlooks on the nature of humanity. Conservatives worry about the declining moral fibre of society, as well as fearing the revolutionary capacity of mob rule (a rhetorical flourish usually directed at socialists). Conservatives advocate the importance of venerable institutions such as the church and the monarchy for their capacity to civilise society.

Pragmatism

Politics in liberal democratic states such as Australia, it's argued, tend to be pragmatic rather than ideological. The political debate tends to be characterised by much less rigidity in approaching arguments and a willingness to borrow from a range of ideas and philosophies in order to formulate policies in a bid to attract the support of electors.

Pragmatism is usually associated with the processes of dialogue across the community in a bid to form a broad consensus about what policies ought to be pursued. Negotiation and bargaining can be part of this political process as well. In pragmatic political systems, the major political parties have almost as many things they agree on as they have points they disagree on.

Australian politics is famously pragmatic. It's often described as being about the politics of the centre, which means that the electorate is seen as being less interested in philosophy and ideology, and more interested in practical policy programs that deal with education, health, taxation and the economy.

Ouch! Touching the hip-pocket nerve

Former Prime Minister Ben Chifley once described the Australian electorate as being motivated by the 'hip-pocket nerve'. This phrase refers to an assertion that the modern voter has become so used to the major political parties confining themselves to debates about economics and the provision of services that voters respond to the debate by asking, 'What's in it for me?' — the very basis of pragmatism, indeed.

VOTE 1

LEFT, CENTRE, RIGHT?

Talk of Left, Centre and Right may sound like a dance move, but the terms are actually part of the specialist language used by people who work in politics for a living. While they understand this language, it mystifies those who don't share in the jargon.

To people in politics, the meaning of these terms is clear. The Left is usually associated with collective working-class politics such as that of trade unions and trade union–based parties, and with ideas such as socialism. The *Right* is usually associated with individualism, property ownership and a suspicion of socialism. The *Centre* is usually associated with pragmatism.

The terms derive their origin from France just before its political revolution. Just before he was deposed, the French king, Louis XVI, created a parliament (derived from the French word *parler*, to talk), in which representatives from the peasantry and the aristocracy would be elected and discuss affairs of state. The peasant representatives sat to the left of the presiding officer, and the aristocracy to the right — and voilà: there you have the Left and the Right, and, of course, the Centre follows logically.

This labelling might be a bit unfair to those in Australian politics who try to bring a wider range of issues to the debate than simply how big a tax cut or how much government assistance is on offer. Australian political history is also peppered with moments of great philosophical import. These have been particularly in evidence in debates about immigration, the importance of the environment, the need to reconcile Indigenous and non-Indigenous Australians, equality for women, and Australia's role in the world. In such instances, philosophy and debates about visions for the future have played their part.

Things We Never Tire of Talking About

In among the plethora of issues that have become prominent over the years, a number of matters have been the subject of fierce debate. Though these debates aren't the sole preserve of politicians, they've resulted in all sorts of policy decisions since the arrival of the convention of Responsible Government (see Chapter 4 for more on Westminster conventions such as this) to the Australian colonies in the mid-1850s, and certainly since Federation.

Tariffs

A *tariff* is a tax levied on imports. Tariffs may be levied as a way of raising revenue, but in Australia they've been used primarily to protect local industry by making imported commodities more expensive than locally produced items.

This rationale was one of the hottest topics surrounding the Federation Movement (see Chapter 3 for more on Federation and the topic of tariffs), and it's still part of the policy debate today (these days referred to as *Industry Policy*).

Industry protection has been a long-standing feature of the Australian political debate. Advocacy of the need to protect local industries was strongest in Victoria and South Australia, with manufacturing an important part of the economies of both states. Tariffs had a political dimension as well. Local business owners were advocates of protection, as indeed were local trade unions whose members worked in protected industries.

The imposition of protective tariffs was an article of faith in Australian economic policy until 1974, when a massive cut to tariffs (25 per cent) indicated a shift in thinking. Since the 1980s, tariffs have been deliberately reduced as part of the need to globalise the Australian economy. Economists argued that tariffs encouraged inefficient industries and cost the consumer. Exporters argued that the imposition of tariffs by Australia was leading to retaliation against Australian exports.

Today, industry protection continues to be wound down. This has had dramatic consequences, especially for the nation's car-manufacturing industry. Between 2016 and 2017, Ford, Toyota and Holden all closed down their vehicle production lines in Australia.

The role of the unions

Trade unionism — the idea of forming an organisation to collectively represent the rights of workers — has been a part of Australian politics since the mid-1850s. The influx of free settlers with the gold rushes helped bring British-style unionism to Australia. When gold mining in Australia went from small-scale alluvial digging to large-scale corporate mining that required miners to become wage and salary earners, the process of entrenching the unions in the Australian industrial landscape began. A similar process was at work in the labour-intensive rural industry (shearing in particular) and this led to the formation of big unions such as the Australian Workers' Union (AWU) that still exist to this day. The political consolidation of trade unionism didn't stop there. Following a series of defeats in strikes held in the 1890s, a number of unions decided to create a political party to contest parliamentary elections — the Australian Labor Party.

The formation of the ALP led to an increased effort on the part of business interests to form political parties that could counter the unions. This competitive dynamic between unions and business for influence over policy-making was established as early as 1891 (when the ALP was first created) and remains in the party system to this day.

The role of unions in the Australian economy and society was more than just a political phenomenon, however. Seeking ways to reconcile workers and their bosses became a part of the legal process. Each colony established courts to try to resolve industrial disputes and, when the Australian federation was created, a national system of arbitration and conciliation was also established. The tenor of the legal approach was established in 1907 through a ruling by an industrial judge who would later go on to be a High Court justice. In the Harvester case before Justice Henry Bourne Higgins, the court found that Australian industrial law would be based on the principle of 'a fair day's wage for a fair day's work'.

REMEMBER

HISTORY REPEATING

After its election success in 2004, John Howard's Liberal–National coalition government introduced the Work Choices legislation in a bid to freeze unions out of the industrial relations system. In the 2007 election, the coalition lost government and Howard lost his seat — largely due to voter backlash against this legislation and a promise from Labor leader Kevin Rudd that Labor would abolish it if they won government.

Labor, too, has been guilty of over-reaching on this matter. In 1983, former union leader Bob Hawke became prime minister, and Labor embarked upon a period in government where the unions appeared to have strong influence over policy outcomes. By 1996, the voters had had enough of Labor and the unions, and elected the Liberal–Nationals to power.

The battle between unions and business — an integral part of Australia's political history and replicated in the Australian political party system — is as intense a matter in contemporary Australian politics as it has ever been.

VOTE 1

Ever since Federation, unions and business have grappled with each other in the realms of industrial law and politics. The involvement of the political parties over the years has resulted in some extreme outcomes. In 1929, for example, Nationalist Prime Minister Stanley Melbourne Bruce proposed to freeze unions out of industrial law. In the federal election that year, the Nationalists lost government and Bruce lost his seat.

Immigration

Immigration is another red-hot political topic with origins going way back to the 1850s. The discovery of gold in 1851 helped convert the image of the Australian colonies from being penal colonies to suddenly becoming a land of opportunity. Among the flood of free settlers who came to Australia looking for gold was a large number of Chinese. The presence of people from Asia caused concern in the colonies. In New South Wales, there were instances of violence perpetrated against Chinese diggers and a major race riot occurred at Lambing Flat. Victoria, meanwhile, passed laws prohibiting Chinese migration (although Chinese diggers got around this by landing at Robe in South Australia and walking overland to the western Victorian diggings through the largely deserted Mallee region).

VOTE 1

Immigration concerns were also to the fore during the Federation Movement (see Chapter 3). The promise of a national parliament capable of enacting national laws to prevent the migration of non-British people was one of the few things about federation that interested the unions and the newly formed Labor Party during the Federation Movement. Indeed, the enactment of what became known as the White Australia policy was one of the first pieces of legislation passed by the new Australian national parliament.

POLICY OF WHITE NOT ALL RIGHT

Australia's abandonment of the White Australia policy really commenced in the 1960s as part of its role in the wars against communism in Vietnam, Cambodia and Laos. However, the real sign that the policy had been abandoned occurred in 1976, when the Fraser government accepted a large influx of Vietnamese 'boat people' fleeing communism in their country, and Cambodians fleeing the murderous communist regime there. The argument was that, as Australia had directly contributed to the Indochina War, it had a moral responsibility to accept its refugees.

The White Australia policy remained in place officially until it was finally declared redundant by the Whitlam government in 1973. The main aim of the policy was to prevent Asian and African migration, although, between 1901 and 1944, it was also used to prevent migration from any European nation other than Britain. This is not to say that no migration occurred from European nations other than Britain. German migration had been part of the opening up of South Australia, and a major influx of Italians occurred around World War I, with many harvesting sugar in Queensland and opening up the Riverina region in New South Wales for irrigation.

Despite this, the official view was that Australia was British. This changed after World War II, when the Chifley government decided that, to boost Australia's ability to defend itself in the future, it had to immediately boost its population. The post-war migration program began first with an influx of refugees from northern and central Europe and then, later, from southern Europe. This huge influx of people resulted in a situation today where nearly 40 per cent of Australians claim an ancestry from somewhere other than Britain.

The immigration debate in Australia has been subject to some subtle shifts. In the period after World War II, immigration was argued for on the grounds of security (Australia had to 'populate or perish', as the slogan went). In the 1960s, it became an economic argument — immigration, it was claimed, had provided the basis of Australia's economic wealth and prosperity. The recession in the 1970s undermined this argument and saw a rise in popular resentment of immigration. By the 1980s, a new moral argument about the importance of Australia being a place of asylum for refugees emerged (although most migration was still for economic reasons or as part of the family reunion program).

MULTICULTURALISM: WHEN DID IT START?

The term *multiculturalism* refers to the diversity of cultures and languages found within Australian society. The Whitlam Labor government (1972–1975) made moves to incorporate multiculturalism as a social policy during its short stint in office. However, the first national policies on multiculturalism were implemented by the Fraser government in 1978. Multiculturalism has been a policy of federal governments ever since, and it has arguably also become part of Australia's social fabric.

The topic of immigration can cause as fierce a debate today as it did in the 1850s or the 1890s or the 1940s. These days, the debate has become entangled with concerns about border security. The notion that Australia has an obligation to people displaced by war has been overtaken by concerns about the security and health implications of unauthorised arrivals. As it was in colonial times, debates about immigration can be highly charged with emotion.

Reconciliation

The history of relations between white settler Australia and Indigenous Australia has been a difficult one indeed, tending to make the politics of creating public policy on Aboriginal affairs (as Indigenous issues used to be called) extremely difficult and extremely contentious. The controversies that emanate from this topic go way beyond disagreements about the best policy options that should be put in place.

To this day, Australian historians and social commentators argue about the colonisation of Australia and what happened to its Indigenous peoples with a vehemence rarely seen in other debates. The positions adopted by the debaters can be quite robust, with some equating Australian white colonisation to a form of genocide of Indigenous Australians and destruction of their culture, and the other side of the debate rejecting such claims as examples of a 'black armband' view of history, a title that tends to scoff at the opposing view as being bleeding-heart liberalism.

TECHNICAL STUFF

In public policy terms, this debate has been complicated by shifts in governmental responsibility for Indigenous Australians. From the beginnings of white settlement, responsibility for Indigenous people lay with the colonies, and this was retained at Federation so that the matter was left to the states. Then, in 1967, following a campaign to recognise the full citizenship rights of Indigenous Australians that was supported by both the Labor and Liberal parties, Australians voted overwhelmingly in a referendum to alter the wording of Section 51 of the Constitution. In technical terms, the Commonwealth then acquired concurrent responsibility for Indigenous Australians along with the states.

In more recent times, this area of policy has been subjected to greater intervention by federal governments. The first major federal foray into this field was the Whitlam government's recognition of Indigenous land rights, when the title for a large piece of Crown land in the Northern Territory that was formerly a cattle station was handed back to local Aborigines. Land rights has been a major issue ever since, including a major battle between the political parties over the issue of native title that occurred in the 1990s.

Many other issues about the rights of Indigenous Australians have also been debated. Indigenous Australians are among the poorest members of the Australian community, and so health and welfare policies emanating from Canberra often have to address the needs of Aboriginal and Torres Strait Islander peoples specifically. These concerns led to targets aimed at 'closing the gap', originally outlined by the Kevin Rudd Labor federal government in 2008 and then redefined by the Scott Morrison Coalition government in 2020.

REMEMBER

In the 1980s, the federal Labor government decided it would experiment with a limited form of Indigenous self-government and introduced the Aboriginal and Torres Straits Islander Commission (ATSIC). The Howard government, elected in 1996, abolished this body and also implemented the Northern Territory National Emergency Response, more commonly referred to as the Northern Territory 'intervention', before the 2007 federal election, which was continued by the Rudd and Gillard Labor governments.

In the late 1980s, Prime Minister Bob Hawke floated the idea of a treaty with Indigenous Australians. The idea was scotched by Labor premiers. When he was prime minister, between 1991 and 1996, Paul Keating instigated a commission of inquiry into the practice of Indigenous children being taken from their families and placed with white families or in institutional care. The report that resulted from this inquiry, *Bringing Them Home*, again fired political debate, with marchers around the country demonstrating their support for Indigenous Australians, such as in the Walk for Reconciliation, which saw more than 250,000 people walk across the Sydney Harbour Bridge in 2000 (see Figure 2-1).

Women in politics

Australian politics is sometimes described as a 'boys' club' — a reference to the fact that the overwhelming majority of people who are or have been members of parliament have been men, and that the issues important to women are often sidelined or ignored. Even in these supposedly more enlightened and feminised times, women make up only less than 40 per cent of the total number of federal parliamentarians.

FIGURE 2-1:
The Aboriginal and Australian flags, side by side, during the Walk for Reconciliation across the Sydney Harbour Bridge in 2000.

The low rate at which women win places in the parliament contrasts with Australia's fairly strong record of giving women the vote. South Australia gave women the vote in 1895, and nationally women were given the right to vote at the second federal election, held in 1903. Victoria was the last state to allow women to vote when it changed its rules in 1908. Australia led other liberal democracies in extending suffrage (the ability to vote) to women. For example, in the United States, universal suffrage was granted in 1920. The United Kingdom lagged further, with all women being given the right to vote in 1928.

Along with the right to vote usually came the right to nominate for and sit in parliament. (This was granted to women nationally along with the right to vote in 1902, making Australia the first country in the world to grant this.) The rate of success of women winning parliamentary seats wasn't great, however. Edith Cowan was the first woman to be elected to an Australian parliament when she was elected to the Western Australian lower house in 1921. The first women to be elected to the federal parliament were Dorothy Tangney (Labor, to the Senate, from Western Australia) and Enid Lyons (United Australia Party, to the House of Representatives, from Tasmania) in 1943.

It wasn't until 1976 that Margaret Guilfoyle became the first woman to be sworn in as a member of a federal Cabinet and, in 1990, Carmen Lawrence became the first ever female premier of a state (Western Australia). In 2007, Queensland's Anna Bligh took over as premier of the state mid-term and, in 2009, became the first female party leader to win a state election. Following this in June 2010, a

Labor Party leadership challenge resulted in Julia Gillard becoming Australia's first female prime minister.

The gender balance is gradually tipping towards greater female representation than in the past, but as this sketch of Australian politics shows, the advances in female representation have been quite recent and are still a long way from equality. Scholars have suggested a number of reasons for this situation, ranging from the way the internal politics of the political parties have tended to be dominated by men, all the way through to the importance of changes in community attitudes towards the role of women in society and the focus given to issues important to women.

The continuation of Australian politics as being a 'boys' club' was starkly highlighted by events in early 2021, when accusations of rape, sexual harassment and assault, and inappropriate behaviour by male politicians and staffers came to light. The Morrison coalition government was accused of being slow to act on these accusations and talk with the women involved, but later responded with a cabinet reshuffle, promoting five women and introducing a new Minister for Women.

Great and powerful friends

How interested are Australians in foreign policy? The general view is that Australian political debates are more usually concerned with domestic issues and leave the complex world of foreign policy to the experts. On occasion, however, popular opinion has played a critical role in policy decisions. The electorate has also tended to hold some fairly strong basic views about foreign policy, influencing the development of the particular approaches of the political parties.

The importance of 'great and powerful friends' is one such principle. These words were actually uttered by John Curtin, Australia's prime minister during World War II, when the Australian government was about to shift its foreign policy focus from Britain to the United States of America. The reason for this shift was simple enough. Britain, struggling to withstand the onslaught from Germany in Europe, was in no position to extend defence to its former empire in Asia and the Pacific, where Japan was expanding. As part of its strategy to defend itself against Japan, Curtin announced that Australia would align itself with America.

This stand triggered a period of close relations between Australia and the United States, a relationship that enjoys general support among the Australian electorate. Both the relationship with the US, and the notion that Australia needs to align itself with a like-minded great power to ensure its defence, have been long-standing themes in Australian foreign policy.

Australia was a willing participant on the side of the British Empire in the Great War (World War I), yet a proposal by then Prime Minister Billy Hughes to introduce conscription was defeated at a national referendum. Curtin could talk of the United States as a friend, but even as late as the 1960s Prime Minister Robert Menzies was described as being 'British to his bootstraps'.

During the war in Vietnam, an Australian prime minister declared to US President Lyndon Baines Johnson that the country was 'all the way with LBJ', yet by 1969 massive anti-war demonstrations were being held in Melbourne, Sydney and other state capitals (see Figure 2-2). In 1972, a Labor government promising to end Australia's involvement in the war was elected.

FIGURE 2-2:
Protestors face police at an anti-war demonstration in Canberra, 1970.

When the United States went to war against Iraq as part of its 'war on terror', Australian Prime Minister John Howard declared Australia's willingness to be part of the 'coalition of the willing'. After the 2007 election of Labor's Kevin Rudd, however, the policy became one of finding ways to get out of Iraq.

New Things We're Talking About

Current political debate also deals with new (or revived) issues. Some matters seem to have been around forever, yet many of these debates still revolve around the need for governments to create policy to address them.

COVID-19 and the pandemic

At the start of 2020, the first case of novel coronavirus was confirmed in the Australian state of Victoria. The speed in which the coronavirus spread had a major impact across the globe. In addition to the social and economic challenges, the pandemic also highlighted debates about the role and power of state and national governments in Australia. Those who had forgotten were reminded just how powerful state governments are in the Australian system, particularly in areas relating to health policy — and especially when the states started to lock down their communities and close off their borders.

The rollout of measures such as social distancing policies and the coronavirus vaccination program gave rise to the term 'COVID normal'. This term began to be used to refer to the way in which people could continue to live their lives during the pandemic, while governments allocated billions of dollars in measures designed to mitigate the economic disruption caused by the pandemic.

The environment and climate change

The environment and climate change has emerged as one of the major issues debated across the world in comparatively recent times. Concerns about the environment and climate change have now become a dominant feature of Australian politics.

One of the first examples of environmental politics was the campaign to save Lake Pedder in Tasmania from being dammed in the early 1970s (a battle that was lost). But it was the battle between conservationists and the Tasmanian government over the proposed damming of the Franklin River in the Tasmanian west coast wilderness that affected the national election campaign in 1983 (see Figure 2-3).

FIGURE 2-3: Franklin dam protestors at the Liberal Party federal election campaign opening in Victoria in 1983.

A year later, the newly elected Hawke government passed legislation designed to stop the Tasmanian government from building a hydro-electric scheme on the disputed river. The High Court upheld this law, and the precedent for the federal government intervening in state management of environmental matters was set.

Since the Franklin campaign, the environment has featured in policy debates at nearly every election. The nature of the debate has changed over the years. Initially about conservation of wild rivers and disputed forest areas, the debate then began to tackle the matter of ecological sustainability. Under this heading came other issues, including the concern about the impact of industrial pollution and worries that the production of carbon dioxide as a result of burning fossil fuels is altering the world's climate.

VOTE 1

GREENING AUSTRALIA

The campaign to save Lake Pedder in Tasmania led to the creation of the United Tasmania Group (UTG) in 1972. The UTG is widely regarded as being the first green (environmental) political party in the world. No doubt the fact that Australia can boast about having the first green party makes other countries green with envy.

Today, climate change is arguably the most important environmental matter being discussed by governments. Its impact on Australian politics has been dramatic, with the failure to deal with this matter — or deal with it in a manner deemed appropriate by voters — contributing to the fall of no less than four prime ministers between 2007 and 2016. One of the interesting things about the environment debate has been the way it has gone from being about local land-use disputes to now being a major issue debated by the world's governments in a bid to find a multilateral solution.

Climate change and water

For years environmentalists have warned that, as one of the driest continents in the world, Australia would need to rethink its approach to water. And rethink it did, with the onset of drought coupled with rising scientific arguments that climate change is occurring across the globe and making dry countries such as Australia even more vulnerable to water shortages. The response from the political community has been to put water at the centre of the policy debate.

Water is actually a very difficult issue for the Australian political system to deal with. Quite apart from the debate that rages between those in politics who believe that climate change is occurring and those who don't accept the argument (or that it is caused by humans), trying to do something about water involves a variety of interest groups as well as a number of political authorities.

If nothing else, the attempts to develop effective policy over water resources highlight how difficult the politics of policy-making can be. Politicians have to try to reconcile different interests and different demands on the resource. Legally, they have to deal with six state governments, a federal government, many local governments and a host of water-use authorities. Trying to coordinate all of these interests and agencies in a bid to make national policy is proving to be very difficult. Indeed, it's not easy being green.

VOTE 1

IF THE RIVER RUNS DRY?

The Murray–Darling Basin is a massive area of Australia through which two major rivers run. The rivers flow through four states, and have countless towns, irrigation and farmers dependent upon them. At the end of the system is the city of Adelaide, which is also dependent on the rivers for its water. Managing the basin has been a problem politicians and policy-makers have been trying to deal with since Federation. The latest round of concern about the rivers has become more acute with the persistence of drought. Ecologists warn that the system will collapse and die if something isn't done to address some of the problems of wasteful usage and poor water management.

The republic

Although the poet and writer Henry Lawson first floated the idea of an Australian republic detached from its former British colonial masters as far back as the 1890s, the modern debate about Australia becoming a republic probably owes its origins to the way Governor-General Sir John Kerr intervened in a constitutional crisis involving a Labor government, a Liberal–Country Party opposition and a dispute in the Senate, back in 1975 (see Chapter 5 for all the gory details). The fact that the Queen's representative was able to intervene in a political affair led some to think the time had come for an overhaul of the Australian Constitution, starting with Australia's relationship with Britain.

The debate also probably owes something to the cultural and demographic change to the Australian community in the post–World War II era. Once a solidly British community, Australia had evolved into a multicultural community whose ancestors had come from a variety of places. With the centenary of Federation looming in the late 1990s, some political commentators decided that the time was now right to ask the Australian people if they were ready for Australia to become a republic.

VOTE 1

Those who simply wanted to detach Australia from Britain and have an Australian head of state advocated what was known as a *minimalist* change to the Constitution. Defenders of Australia's British cultural heritage opposed this move and began to rally in defence of the British monarchy. Into the mix came a third group of radical republicans. This group wanted not only a thorough overhaul of the Constitution, but also a directly elected head of state.

This point is where the move for a republic was defeated. The minimalist republicans and the radical democratic republicans were fundamentally at odds with each other. The mutual antipathy was most evident at the Constitutional Convention convened in Canberra in 1998 to discuss the matter and try to get a republican model ready for Australians to vote for in 1999. The failure of the republican push was completed at the 1999 referendum, where an overwhelming majority of Australians answered no when asked if they wanted to change the Constitution to achieve a (minimal) republic.

Despite these failures, debate on whether Australia should become a republic remains alive — although support is dropping. A 2021 poll found only a third of Australians support Australia becoming a republic. The organisation the Australian Republican Movement continues to campaign and propose potential models for change in this area.

Globalisation

Globalisation can mean many things, but to Australian policy-makers its primary meaning relates to international trade and Australia's integration into a global economy. This represents a shift from the period after World War II, when the use of tariffs and other forms of industry protection were designed to orient the Australian economy towards domestic consumption.

The Hawke government in the 1980s argued that protectionism was inefficient, and began the process of globalisation by floating the Australian dollar and reducing industry protection. The Howard government continued these policies and further encouraged the country's economic specialisation as an exporter of minerals and energy, especially to the People's Republic of China and India.

Economists argue that Australia's embracing of globalisation has contributed to its prosperity, but political dissidents have emerged along the way. The defeat of the Keating government in 1996 was attributed to the Prime Minister's deep commitment to globalisation. Then, when the newly elected Howard government appeared to be going along the same policy path, a politician called Pauline Hanson appeared and, with her new political party One Nation, criticised globalisation as being the cause of unemployment and the economic collapse of sections of rural and regional Australia. (See Chapter 12 for more on One Nation.)

REMEMBER

Hanson's foray into the political debate was all the more controversial because of her attack on immigration and the policy of multiculturalism, which she described as 'divisive'. One Nation performed very strongly in a state election in Queensland in 1998, and won 10 per cent of the vote in the 1998 federal election. This wasn't a strong enough vote to win many parliamentary seats, and Hanson slowly faded from the political scene. In 2016, however, Hanson led her party's return to the national parliament when it won four seats in the Senate.

Nation building

In 2008, the world's financial institutions began to collapse. Then the world's stock markets collapsed, and suddenly the international economic community was gripped with fear about a new Great Depression descending on the world economy — the global financial crisis (GFC).

The Australian government at the time — the Rudd government — instituted a policy of using government resources to stimulate the Australian economy. As part of this program, the government announced its Nation Building program. Aiming to combine government expenditure in the areas of health and education, the government argued that building programs in both sectors would help boost infrastructure. The government also sought to encourage the various state governments to work with the Commonwealth on these projects. Nation Building also aims to provide federal assistance to the states in their development of transport projects.

These initiatives replicate attempts by previous governments to coordinate their public expenditure programs. The really innovative bit about Nation Building, however, was the government's program of revitalising Australia's communications network to provide broadband internet access to all households and businesses. This project had been planned ahead of the GFC and so represented an idea that predated the demand on the government to provide a boost to the Australian economy.

The coalition governments that have held power since 2013 have in some ways continued this 'nation building' approach in times of economic uncertainty. Along with other measures introduced during the COVID-19 pandemic, the federal government provided incentives to support the construction industry.

Complex Issues, Simple Choices

The political debate in Australia is extensive and can be quite complex.

Modern democracies provide the opportunity for citizens to feel they've participated in the process of policy-making. The idea of democracy is that government occurs for the people, by the people. The trouble is, very few modern democracies allow their citizens to directly determine policy by way of referendums or a mass vote of citizens at a forum. In modern democracies, the power of the people when it comes to policy is an indirect power. It's exercised by the representatives chosen by voters to go to legislatures (parliaments) and formulate policy on their behalf.

VOTE 1

In this process, citizens indirectly participate in a really complicated and multifaceted debate about a range of policies. The election process, however, requires that citizens make simple choices, usually between candidates running for election.

Elections are an ideal time to remind politicians of one of the key functions that political parties play in democratic systems. The political parties are at the heart of simple choices. They simply put up candidates and ask voters to vote for them. But behind the act of putting up candidates is another important function whereby parties debate policy options within their organisations, filter those things that the party stands for and include these in the rationale as to why voters should vote for them.

In other words, the political parties are integral to the process where citizens are asked to make simple choices about complex issues. The political parties' traditions and policy manifestoes, therefore, become the clearing-house for policy ideas. Voters then simply choose which party they wish to vote for. The debate over policies that goes on within the political parties becomes just as important as the debate that goes on between parties.

2

The Australian System of Government

Understand how the Australian system of government is structured, including how government decisions are made and how you can more effectively seek to influence those decisions.

Examine how the Australian Constitution was influenced by American politics, as well as how the British tradition lives on in our unique hybrid system of government.

Work out the role of parliament, its players and how governments operate.

IN THIS CHAPTER

» Understanding that federal and state governments have their own constitutions

» Examining what led to Federation

» Looking at state representation

» Exploring Australia's constitutional government

» Acknowledging the unwritten aspects of constitutionalism

Chapter **3**

One Country, Many Rulebooks

The Australian system of government is based on a complicated combination of written rules and unwritten conventions. In this chapter, we explore the Australian system of government by looking at the rulebook — or, more accurately, at all the rulebooks, because Australia is a federation and each state has its own foundation document. The rulebook of government is known as a *constitution*.

We also examine how Australia's federation came about, and how the states and territories are represented in the federal government, as well as the importance of those unwritten conventions.

Australia Is a Federation

The very first critical point you need to grasp in understanding how Australia is governed is to remember that Australia is a federation, which means that the power to govern is shared between the national government and the six state governments. The division of governing powers between the national government and the states is outlined in a core legal document — the Australian Constitution.

The Constitution and power-sharing

The Australian Constitution allows for power-sharing between the states and the Commonwealth, as follows:

>> **Exclusive powers:** The Australian Constitution outlines the powers given by the federating states to the new national government. These powers are called *exclusive powers*, in that the federal government can exercise power over them without referring to the states.

>> **Concurrent powers:** The Constitution also has some powers that are shared with the states, including responsibility for the levying of taxes, management of Indigenous issues, and the formation and regulation of industrial relations laws. These shared powers are called *concurrent powers*.

>> **Residual powers:** Anything not mentioned in the Australian Constitution is considered to be a *residual power* and becomes the concern of state governments.

The constitutions as rulebooks

The Australian Constitution and the constitutions of the states are also important in that they provide the legal authority for the establishment of the national and state parliaments, and the way they operate.

These constitutions also guarantee that the parliamentary chambers will be elected. Importantly (and somewhat confusingly in some ways, because it goes slightly against general public perception), they outline the existence of a body called the *Executive in Council*. Each state, as well as the federal government, has this council, which is technically its official governing body (we describe this body more fully later in this chapter). The constitutions also provide the legal authority for the existence and political independence of the courts.

The Path to Federation

One very good way of understanding the way powers and responsibilities are shared between the national, or federal, government and the governments of the states is to look at the reasons Australia federated. Debates about the need to take a national approach to a number of pressing issues were important in giving the

Federation Movement its impetus. Later, these reasons would be present in the list of powers given to the new national government in Section 51 of the Australian Constitution.

The constitutional conventions

The Federation Movement's development of the idea that Australia could and should become a nation involved a number of conventions. These were meetings of like-minded colonial politicians who discussed what a system of national government would look like (beginning with the National Australasian Convention in Sydney in 1891) and, later, drafted the Australian Constitution (Bathurst 1896, Adelaide 1897 and Melbourne 1897). A series of referendums was held, although the success rate of the yes vote was very patchy, with Western Australia resisting any agreement until the last minute. The draft Constitution was then sent to Britain for ratification by the British parliament.

The delegates who attended these conventions were part of the colonial elite — colonial parliamentarians (with all the colonial premiers present), colonial lawyers and colonial judges. Only one delegate had a union background, and no women delegates and certainly no Aboriginal delegates attended.

The states came first

Before a federal government was established, and before the *Commonwealth of Australia Constitution Act 1900* was passed by the British parliament, government in Australia was performed by the colonies. The front page of the Act is shown in Figure 3-1.

NEW ZEALAND WAS THERE!

At the very first convention, New Zealand considered being part of a new Commonwealth with the Australian states and sent representatives. The New Zealanders obviously didn't like what they saw, for they didn't attend later meetings.

Western Australia, however, was the main problem. The west was dubious about coming into the federation, and was only enticed with promises of a railway connection with the east coast and a water pipe to service the Kalgoorlie goldfields. The prevarications of the west were forever enshrined in Section 3 of the Constitution, which outlined what Western Australia's situation would be if it agreed to join the federation before Her Majesty and the Privy Council declared the Commonwealth to exist.

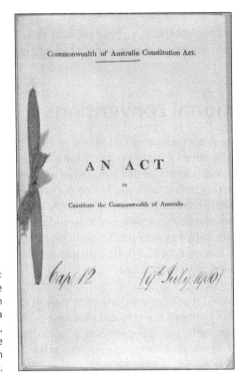

FIGURE 3-1:
The
Commonwealth
of Australia
Constitution Act,
passed by the
British
parliament.

By the time the Federation Movement began in the 1880s, each of the colonies had its own constitution and was responsible for its own government. The colonial constitutions had some features in common, including:

>> A *bicameral parliament* (that is, a parliament with two chambers) with a lower house (called the *Legislative Assembly*) and an upper house (called the *Legislative Council*) that could force the lower house to an election by refusing to pass a budget

>> A governor as the head of government

>> An Executive in Council that entailed the governor meeting with ministers from the parliament to deal with the legislative affairs of the colonial parliament

>> A court system independent of government

>> Application of the conventions of Westminster governance (see Chapter 4), meaning that the premier, rather than the governor, was the real head of government, although this wasn't actually written down anywhere

The need for a national government

The parliamentary systems that each of the Australian colonies had by the 1880s were basically the same as those of today. The six colonies had developed extensively and were like six separate countries. The most obvious manifestations of this structure were:

>> The haphazard development of transport between the colonies that resulted in, among other things, the adoption of different *rail gauges* (the spacing between the rails on a railway track)

>> The imposition of colonial tariffs and taxes against goods produced in the other Australian colonies

>> The development of six separate colonial armies and navies

REMEMBER

The Federation Movement was led by Henry Parkes from New South Wales, whose vision for a national Australian government went beyond simply creating a level of government that could do the things the colonial governments wouldn't or couldn't do. Still, the push for federation was driven by four major policy matters that the colonies were anxious be dealt with nationally — defence, immigration, trade and the need for a national capital.

The defence of Australia

Defence was a key driver of the desire to federate. Put simply, the six colonies were of the opinion that a collective approach would be a more effective way of defending the Australian colonies than the previous practice of each colony having its own army and navy. The variability in the economic capacity of the 'small states' (Queensland, South Australia, Tasmania and Western Australia) to build up their armies and navies was of concern, in that they would be vulnerable in the face of Britain's imperial enemies.

As a consequence, the Australian Constitution outlines not just defence as an exclusive power, but also other areas of responsibility that dovetail with notions of national security, including quarantine, immigration, power over foreign nationals, power over foreign corporations and a power for the national government to make decisions with regard to external affairs.

Immigration and race

The matters of race and immigration were very hot topics in Australia at about the time of the constitutional conventions. Canegrowers in far north Queensland had been enticing itinerant workers from the South Pacific Islands to work on their sugarcane farms, usually for very poor wages. (In some cases, these workers had been stolen from their island homes.) This practice alarmed Australian unions, who were opposed to non-British immigration on the grounds that it would devalue the worth of local workers. Colonial liberals, meanwhile, were appalled at what they thought was a version of slavery.

The push for a national approach to race relations and immigration laws was seen as necessary to force colonies such as Queensland into line. As a result, Section 51 of the Constitution lists immigration as a federal power, and the *Immigration Restriction Act 1901* — the legal basis of Australia's infamous White Australia policy (refer to Chapter 2) — was one of the first pieces of legislation debated in the new federal parliament.

One matter of racial politics remained the preserve of the states, however. When the Constitution was written, the intention was to leave responsibility for Aboriginal Australians in the hands of the states. So Section 51 gave the Commonwealth power to legislate about people from any race other than Aboriginals. This state of affairs remained in place until the Constitution was changed by referendum in 1967.

The tariff and intercolonial free trade

Surely one of the dullest of economic issues, yet an absolutely red-hot topic in the 1890s, pitted the Free Traders of New South Wales against the Protectionists of Victoria. This matter was also behind the first round of a mighty argument about financial relations, especially between these two states. Financial relations between states, and between the states and the national government, is another hot topic that has never gone away (see Chapter 7 for how that debate has panned out in more modern times).

Prior to Federation, each of the colonies levied a tax against imports coming from other colonies. This tax was known as a *tariff*, and was bitterly opposed by Victoria, in particular, because local manufacturers of agricultural and mining equipment found themselves losing market share to British and American manufacturers when other colonial governments imposed a tax on the Victorian-made products.

In the days before income and company tax (these taxes didn't start to come along until World War I), levying tariffs and duties on goods and services was a major source of revenue for the colonial governments.

After the gold rushes, Melbourne had developed into a major manufacturing city. The local politicians — who liked to call themselves liberals because of their adherence to the philosophies of British liberals such as Jeremy Bentham and John Stuart Mill — began to argue that the growth of manufacturing was contributing to the material and cultural prosperity of Australia, and that this boom was a good thing. They then argued that a national policy to encourage manufacturing across Australia, based on the imposition of a protective tariff levied against foreign imports, should be pursued. The Victorian trade unions, whose burgeoning membership worked in Melbourne's factories, agreed.

The Victorian liberals were thus known as *Protectionists*. Their opponents came from New South Wales, where free trade was preferred, especially by those merchants whose wealth came from facilitating British imports. The politicians who sought to counter the Victorian Protectionists were soon called *Free Traders*. The two groups were set to lock horns in the debates about a new national constitution.

The battle between the Protectionists and the Free Traders was in no small way a battle between Victoria and New South Wales. The other colonies weren't disinterested observers, however. On the contrary, the proposal coming from Victorians to do away with colonial tariffs sent alarm bells ringing in the other colonial governments. If such tariffs were abolished, they cried, where would the colonies get their revenue from?

From this debate came some important compromises. First, the small colonies said they wouldn't federate unless they could be guaranteed important revenue sources. The agreement was that the colonies would continue to impose duties on commodities such as land, tobacco and alcohol.

The second part of the agreement was that, in exchange for abolishing interstate tariffs, the new national government would be able to levy national tariffs against international imports if the new parliament agreed to do so. The abolition of intercolonial tariffs was enshrined in Section 92 of the Constitution, which declares that interstate economic activity would be free.

THE COMMONWEALTH'S FUNDS?

The Commonwealth's ability to raise an international tariff meant that it would have a revenue stream at its disposal. As part of the agreement to federate, the smaller states demanded that the new national parliament be given the power to make funding allocations to the states, especially if they were ever in financial trouble. This was enshrined in Section 96 of the Constitution, which states that the federal parliament could make financial grants to the states on any term and condition decided on by the federal parliament.

This seemed to satisfy the small colonies, but one of the Victorian delegates to the conventions and a leader of the Protectionists, Alfred Deakin, warned his fellow delegates of the political dangers of Section 96, saying that, although the new states might be 'legally free', the new constitution actually had the danger of having the states 'financially bound to the chariot wheels of the Central government'. History proved Deakin correct.

A new Australian capital

Delegates from New South Wales and Victoria quarrelled over another matter — specifically, where the national capital of Australia should be. In essence, this fight was between Melbourne and Sydney. The federation wouldn't exist if either of the two biggest Australian cities was the capital, so another compromise was reached.

And so Section 125 of the Constitution states that the national parliament would be located in a Commonwealth-controlled territory to be excised from New South Wales, but it had to be at least 100 miles from Sydney. This section allowed the creation of the Australian Capital Territory and the city of Canberra as the national capital.

Big States and Small States

The Melbourne versus Sydney rivalry wasn't the only political manoeuvre going on at the constitutional conventions. No less important was the division of the delegates between what were considered as the 'big colonies' in terms of population size and the strength of their economies (Victoria and New South Wales) and the 'small colonies' (Queensland, South Australia, Tasmania and Western Australia).

In addition to winning concessions on finances, including the prospect of emergency federal funding in times of dire need, the small colonies insisted on — and won — important concessions in the way the new national parliament would be set up. These concessions were intended to protect the small states when federation occurred.

The protection of the small states is a vitally important part of the federation story and the subsequent constitutional system that was formed. Its major impact on the nature of the national parliamentary system was through the introduction of the Senate.

A house for the states: The Senate

One of the most important legacies of the politics of the constitutional conventions was the idea that the national parliament had to incorporate representation for the original states.

THE SENATE'S POWERS

The only constraint on the power of the Senate in making legislation, under Section 53 of the Constitution, was to forbid the upper house to initiate or amend proposed taxation laws and *appropriation bills* (proposed laws for the allocation of government money). Apart from this, however, the Senate was a house with exactly the same powers as the House of Representatives.

The Westminster parliamentary system that the delegates were so familiar with involved a lower popular, or representative, house and an upper house. (In Chapter 4, we explore the Westminster system thoroughly.) In Britain, the upper house was the House of Lords, but Australia had no aristocracy and so a commensurate Australian Lords wasn't possible.

The constitutional conventions pondered the options for the upper house:

>> One option was to replicate the New South Wales Legislative Council (as it was back then) and have an upper house made up of people appointed by the government of the day. This was rejected, mainly because the constitutional framers were anxious to find ways to constrain the power of any future prime minister. A system of appointing people to the upper house would be eventually dominated by the prime minister, it was reasoned.

>> The other option for the upper house, which found immediate favour, was to copy an idea from the United States. The US upper house is directly elected and made up of equal representation from each of the states, with the chamber known as a Senate.

REMEMBER

The US model was agreed on. The new constitution provided for the Senate to be made up of an equal number of directly elected senators from each of the six states who would be given terms twice the duration of those elected to the House of Representatives.

You get at least five lower house seats if . . .

Protection of the small colonies (now to be small states) didn't stop at equal representation for the original states in the Senate. As part of the federation deal, the small colonies extracted another important concession in order to protect them from the dominance of New South Wales and Victoria.

ORIGINAL STATES AND NEW TERRITORIES

The Constitution mentions the original states in its preamble and in Section 3. Section 121 allows the federal parliament to create new states and give these new states the amount of representation they see fit. If the Northern Territory were to become a state, this would require an Act of the federal parliament. Because it would be a new state, it wouldn't be guaranteed five lower house seats or 12 senators. In the meantime, the federal parliament deals with the territories under the auspices of Section 122 of the Australian Constitution.

The Northern Territory was part of South Australia at the time of Australia's federation. The Commonwealth took over responsibility for the Territory from South Australia in 1911 and made its laws until 1947. At that point, the Commonwealth government passed laws for the Territory to have its own legislature. But it was not until 1978 that the Territory became self-governing, when the Commonwealth's *Northern Territory (Self-Government) Act 1978* was passed. In fact, it's this Act that serves as the Territory's constitution.

The new Constitution provided for direct elections to fill both the House of Representatives and the Senate. Whereas the Senate would have equal representation for the states, the number of seats in the House of Representatives would be allocated to the states in a somewhat proportional way, according to their population. New South Wales, with the largest population, would get the largest number of seats (originally 26 seats, today 47 seats). The least populous states, however, would be guaranteed at least 5 seats — Tasmania still has 5 seats regardless of its population. Today's territories, however, have no such constitutional protection, and so languish with 2 or 3 seats each, even though their population might entitle them to more. (The Australian Capital Territory's number of seats grew to 3 for the 2019 election, while the Northern Territory still has 2 seats.)

Changing the Constitution

One last important protection for the small states was put in place in the Constitution. Section 128 outlines the way the Constitution can be changed. The constitutional framers decided that the main mechanism for change would be a referendum conducted among the Australian electorate. However, the process could only be used if the proposed legislation was first passed in both the House of Representatives and the Senate, or by one house and with the approval of the governor-general.

TECHNICAL STUFF

To succeed, a referendum has to win a majority of the vote cast nationally. To protect the smaller states, however, a second requirement was included. A successful referendum would also have to win a majority of the vote cast in a majority (that is, four) of the states.

Australians, as a rule, don't like changing the Constitution. Some 44 referendum questions have been put to the people since 1901, of which only 8 have passed. Most of those that did win approval were minor matters such as making sure casual Senate vacancies would be filled by people from the same political parties and requiring High Court judges to retire at age 70. The more significant changes brought about by referendum include allowing the Commonwealth to make laws about pharmaceuticals and to give federal assistance to tertiary students, recognising a body called the Loan Council, which was to oversee borrowing of overseas capital (see Chapter 7), and granting Indigenous Australians full national citizenship.

State constitutions are much easier to change. These changes simply require an Act of Parliament to pass both houses to take effect.

The Australian System of Constitutional Government

The Australian Constitution and the constitutions of the states have some features in common, and for an understanding of Australia's system of parliamentary government, it's important to get to know what the written documents provide for.

Equally important to realise is that the picture provided simply by reading the constitutions is an incomplete one. An enormous part of the essence of the system of parliamentary government — the Westminster system — just doesn't appear in the written constitutions.

The governors and the governor-general

Both the federal constitution and all of the state constitutions (with the exception of the Victorian Constitution, which was altered in 2003) place a representative of the Queen at the head of government.

In the case of the states, the head of government as outlined by the state constitutions is the governor. In the case of the federal constitution, the head of government is the governor-general. As Section 2 of the Constitution outlines, the governor-general is Her Majesty's representative and exercises powers assigned by the Queen.

The Crown

The constitutions make no specific reference to any particular British king or queen, although the state of Victoria was named after Queen Victoria. Rather, the constitutions make reference to kings and queens as part of an institution. The term the Crown is often used to refer to the British monarchy and its role in constitutional practice.

The governor-general's position in the federal constitution is made all the more significant by Section 68, which states that the governor-general is the commander-in-chief of Australia's armed forces. The Constitution, therefore, backs the governor-general's executive power with military power!

State governors also hold the status of being the Queen's representative in the states, because a piece of Commonwealth legislation — the *Australia Act 1986* — says so. This Act does restrain some of the things the state governors can do, however. The Act disallows the bestowing of imperial honours, for example, and also prevents the states from going to the British Privy Council on matters of legal appeal.

The Australia Act also prevents the British parliament (and, indeed, Her Majesty) from being able to legislate on any matter relating to Australia. Although the various governors are technically Her Majesty's representatives, the Queen can't actually intervene in Australian affairs.

Reserve powers

Does the exclusion of the Crown from Australian affairs mean that governors and the governor-general are powerless anachronisms of a bygone British imperial age? Hardly!

The Australian governors (including the governor-general) actually have significant powers that can be exercised in certain circumstances. The resolution of disputes, particularly within the parliament and especially where the two houses of parliament may be in disagreement, is one such function. All of the Australian constitutions refer to the need for governors to ensure 'good government'. Governors may be required to install ministers when needs be, or dismiss ministers, or dissolve the parliament in order to call a fresh election. These powers of intervention in the name of ensuring 'good government' are known in Australia as the *reserve powers*.

The Executive in Council

The Executive in Council is another feature of the official system of government in Australia outlined in each state constitution and in the federal constitution. The aim of these constitutions was to replicate the constitutional arrangement in Britain where the Crown (whether king or queen) took counsel on affairs of state from ministers drawn from the Westminster parliament. The British body was called the Privy Council.

The Australian federal and state constitutions each outline the existence of a mechanism for the governor or governor-general to meet with ministers drawn from the parliament. The body at which this coming together of the Crown and the parliament occurs is called the *Executive in Council*. The ministers who attend the Executive in Council are given their authority to be ministers by the governor (in the states) or the governor-general, because the power to appoint members of parliament as ministers is a power officially exercised by the governor (in the case of the governor-general, this is outlined in Section 64 of the Australian Constitution).

The purpose of the Executive in Council is for ministers (now collectively known as the ministry) to inform the Crown of what the parliament has been doing. In particular, at this meeting the ministry advises the Crown of bills that have been passed by the parliament and requests that the governor or governor-general give royal assent to these bills (see the sidebar 'Royal assent').

Technically, the Executive in Council is the government. What's more, none of the constitutions (with the exception of Victoria) require the governor or governor-general to be bound by the advice that comes to them at the Executive in Council.

Ministers of the Crown

In outlining the existence of an Executive in Council, all the state and federal constitutions also provide for ministers of the Crown. The constitutions make it clear that ministers must come from the parliament. (In the federal constitution, Section 64 says this; although, oddly, it also says that the governor-general may appoint a minister, but that person must somehow find a place in the parliament within a three-month period.)

REMEMBER

The important point to note here is that the constitutions vest the governors and the governor-general with the power to appoint ministers. Technically, a literal reading of the constitutions means that it is the governor or governor-general who determines who will be in the government. (A warning at this point: The system doesn't actually work this way, as Chapter 4 explains.)

ROYAL ASSENT

TECHNICAL
STUFF

Royal assent occurs when the Crown bestows its authority on an Act of Parliament. The assigning of royal assent gives an Act legal authority and it becomes the law of the land. Acts given royal assent are published in something called the *Government Gazette* and all citizens are deemed to know the law. As they say in Latin, *ignorantia juris non excusat* — ignorance of the law is no excuse!

The parliament

Australia's federal and state constitutions provide the legal basis for the existence of parliaments. Each jurisdiction was intended to have a bicameral parliament — that is, a lower house and an upper house.

VOTE 1

Since the 1850s, all the state parliaments (and the federal parliament since Federation) have been bicameral, with one exception — Queensland. The Labor government in Queensland had tried to abolish the upper house by referendum in 1917, but a majority of Queenslanders voted no to the proposed change. The state's Legislative Council became a major election issue in 1920 and debates raged about its right to obstruct government legislation, especially as it was made up of appointed parliamentarians. In 1922 the re-elected Labor government, led by Edward Theodore, introduced a bill that proposed to abolish the upper house. The bill was supported by both houses, which meant that the Queensland upper house voted itself out of existence.

In providing for parliaments with two chambers, the written constitutions sought to replicate the parliamentary structure of Britain, although here a problem arose. Britain's upper house, the House of Lords, isn't an elected house but is appointed from among the aristocracy. What to do in Australia?

In the upper houses

In all of the states except New South Wales, the parliamentary upper houses — all called the *Legislative Council* — were given what's known as a *property franchise*, which meant that only citizens who owned a certain amount of property could nominate or vote for the upper house.

New South Wales was different in that it copied the House of Lords by having an upper house appointed by the governor (on the recommendation of the premier) whenever vacancies arose.

The federal upper house, however, was to be the states' house (refer to the section 'A house for the states: The Senate' earlier in this chapter), according to Section 7 of the Australian Constitution. And it was to be a house elected directly by the voters.

In recent times, extensive reform of the state upper houses has been undertaken. The appointment system in New South Wales was abolished in 1976 and replaced with an elected upper house. All the state upper houses eventually abolished the property franchise. Today, the four mainland state upper houses are elected using *proportional representation* — a voting system in which the number of seats won should be in proportion to the percentage of the vote won. In a proportional representative system, a candidate needs to win a quota of the vote to be elected rather than a majority of the vote. We discuss this system further in Chapter 13.

VOTE 1

Elections for Tasmania's upper house are a bit different. The Apple Isle elects 15 MPs to represent individual electorates for six-year terms. As with elections for the Commonwealth's lower house of parliament, it uses a *preferential* voting system, which means that a candidate must win a majority of the vote (50 per cent plus one vote) to win the seat. We discuss voting systems in more detail in Chapter 13.

Voting for the upper houses in the territories is unnecessary — they're unicameral and only have the lower house.

In the lower houses

All the state lower houses (*Legislative Assemblies* in all except Tasmania, where it's called the *House of Assembly*) and the House of Representatives in the national parliament are supposed to be representative, or popular, houses. This concept is important to the question of which parliamentary chamber is where government is formed. The Westminster approach is based on the idea that the lower house is the house of government. One of the big problems in the Australian approach is that the upper houses are considered to be very powerful because they can refuse *supply*, the allocation of money for government expenditure, and force early elections.

Part of the point of a bicameral parliament is to try to slow down the legislative process to allow members of parliament time to scrutinise and debate proposed legislation. Because, in the Westminster system, government is formed by the party (or coalition of parties) that wins a majority of seats in the lower house, the theory is that an upper house can act as a house of review, with a parliamentary bill needing to pass both houses before it can be referred to the Executive in Council for royal assent.

The electors

The imposition of a system of directly elected parliaments (with the exception of the New South Wales Legislative Council) is one of the key features of Australia's constitutions.

Australia has been one of the world leaders in extending the right to vote. By the time of federation, Australia had universal manhood suffrage (men 21 years of age and older — except Indigenous men in Queensland and Western Australia — could vote, regardless of whether they held property) and some colonies allowed women the vote. (See the sidebar 'The right to vote for Indigenous people' for more on this topic.)

HOW LONG IS A PARLIAMENTARY TERM?

The constitutions outline the terms each parliamentary chamber can serve. Originally, the idea of the upper house being different from the lower house was reflected in the fact that upper house members would have terms double that of lower house members. That's still the case in some states, such as New South Wales and South Australia, today.

Even more interesting is the situation in the Tasmanian upper house, which has 15 members representing one of 15 electorates. Elections there occur over a six-year cycle, with elections for three members being held in May in one year, then, in May of the following year, elections for another two members being held and so on. The result is an upper house that changes slowly over time rather than at every state election.

In the federal parliament, members of the House of Representatives get three-year terms that begin with the first sitting of parliament after an election. Senators, on the other hand, get six-year terms, commencing on 1 July in the year after they're elected. The Australian state parliaments now have four-year terms.

The last colony or state to give women the vote was Victoria in 1908. When the second federal election was held in 1903 (the first election was run under the electoral arrangements of each of the colonies), women had the right to vote for both the House of Representatives and the Senate. In 1973, the Whitlam government passed a bill that lowered the voting age for federal elections from 21 to 18.

The constitutions, then, guarantee electoral democracy. The electoral systems used to convert electoral choices into representation, however, are the responsibility of the various parliaments. Chapter 13 explains the various state and federal electoral laws as the product of parliamentary legislation.

The courts

The point of mentioning the courts, or the judiciary, in constitutions is to ensure their independence by making it clear that their existence is based on a fundamental document rather than by any particular Act of Parliament. The Australian courts are expected to operate like the British courts, including the notion of the *Separation of Powers*, which dictates that parliaments can have no influence over the courts.

THE RIGHT TO VOTE FOR INDIGENOUS PEOPLE

The history of national and state voting rights for Australia's Indigenous people is complex, and often surrounded by confusion. In fact, when the colonies began their own parliaments, from 1850, Indigenous men aged over 21 were able to vote, though in practice they weren't encouraged to enrol. Queensland and Western Australia then passed legislation, in 1885 and 1893 respectively, that specifically denied Indigenous people the right to vote. However, South Australia allowed all adults the right to vote in 1895, which in theory included Indigenous men and women.

At Federation, Section 41 of the Constitution seemed to decree that Indigenous people could vote in Commonwealth elections if they were or had been granted state voting rights. But, with the White Australia policy high on the agenda, that interpretation was challenged and, in 1902, the Commonwealth Franchise Act specifically excluded any people Indigenous to Australia, Asia, Africa or the Pacific Islands (interestingly, excluding New Zealand) from voting, except if they were on the roll before 1901.

Gradually, arguments in favour of granting voting rights to Indigenous people were aired, including the fact that Indigenous men had fought for Australia in World War II. In 1949, through the Commonwealth Electoral Act, those who had completed military service and those who already had the right to vote in the states were granted the right to vote in federal elections. Then, in 1957, the federal government declared Aboriginal people in the Northern Territory to be wards of the state and they were denied the vote.

With mounting pressure, by 1962 the Electoral Act was amended to allow Indigenous people to enrol, though it was not compulsory. Western Australia also lifted its ban and allowed Indigenous people to vote in state elections, and Queensland followed suit in 1965. Steps were also taken to provide Indigenous people with information about the electoral process and to encourage them to enrol. From that time, all Indigenous Australians had the same voting rights as non-Indigenous Australians in both state and federal elections.

It was another two years before the referendum of 1967 gave Australia's Indigenous people the right to be counted in the population census and gave the Commonwealth the right to legislate for them. In 1983, the Hawke government resolved this matter finally when its electoral reforms applied the same standards for enrolment and participation across the community regardless of race.

TECHNICAL STUFF

The Australian Constitution provides an additional reason for mentioning the courts. In Chapter III (Sections 71 to 80), it establishes the existence of a court that, in addition to its role in general law, is the judicial tribunal that hears and resolves constitutional disputes between the Commonwealth and the states. This court is the High Court of Australia. In more recent times, the Federal Court of Australia has been developed as a subordinate court of the High Court to deal with some of the less complex constitutional matters.

The High Court of Australia has seven justices. Judges are appointed to the bench by the governor-general (again, on the recommendation of the prime minister). Importantly, once a justice is appointed, she can't be removed in all but the most extreme instances of misperformance, and then only by parliamentary impeachment. The inability of governments to remove judges is seen as an important bulwark guaranteeing the political independence of the courts.

In reality then, the High Court is the keeper of the Australian Constitution. If the federal parliament passes a law that an individual, a corporation or a state thinks is outside of its constitutional authority, the aggrieved party takes the matter to the High Court. The court uses legal principles to decide if the federal government has the power to legislate. If the court rules that it doesn't have the power — that is, the federal government has acted *ultra vires* — then the law is struck down. If the court rules that the law is valid, and if the federal law conflicts with a state law, the federal law prevails.

This process whereby the High Court interprets the meaning of the Australian Constitution is known as *judicial interpretation*.

WHO CAN DO THE JOB?

The ideal person for a High Court position is usually a former state Supreme Court judge. The Supreme Court is, as its name suggests, the highest court in a state or territory, and its rulings are unable to be reviewed or overturned by another court. A lawyer with extensive constitutional legal experience may also be considered to fill a High Court position. Interestingly, Australia has a rich history of former attorneys-general being appointed to the court. Justices can hold their positions until they're required to retire at age 70.

Australian Constitutionalism: More than the Written Word

Experts sometimes use the term *constitutionalism* to describe the Australian system of government. This basically means that, to understand how the Australian system works, written constitutions have to be read and understood in the context of understanding the *Westminster system* — the technical term for the British system of parliamentary government (we cover this system in Chapter 4).

In a straightforward understanding, written constitutions provide the legal basis for the Australian system of government. The state constitutions give authority for state government, and the Australian Constitution does this for federal government, in addition to outlining the division of responsibilities between the national and state levels of government.

REMEMBER

The problem with Australia's written constitutions is that a literal reading of these constitutions gives only a part of the story as to how Australia is governed. The constitutions of Australia, including the federal constitution, are important not only for what they say about the system of government, but also for what they *don't* say about the system. The Australian Constitution is a good case in point.

The Australian system of government involves much more than simply the written rules outlined in constitutions. The Australian system, based as it is on the British system of parliamentary government, relies almost as much on the unwritten rules of constitutional behaviour, known as *conventions*. (These principles are not to be confused with the gatherings known as the constitutional conventions that led to Federation and the drafting of the Australian Constitution.)

Conventions are considered to be constitutional principles because they refer to the operation of the parliament and how the various institutions of government — the parliament, the executive, the Crown and the public service — relate to each other. They're not laws, however, for they don't rely on the courts to be enforced. Rather, they rely on the common recognition of their existence and a willingness to abide by them by those involved in the practice of parliamentary government.

The Australian system, like the British system, relies heavily on conventions, in addition to the existence of written constitutions. To understand the essence of the Australian system of parliamentary government, it's necessary to know something about the British system of parliamentary government. So read on — we take a look at the Westminster system in Chapter 4.

THE TOP JOB?

Most Australians, if asked to nominate who they think is the most important person in Australian politics, would probably nominate the prime minister. The second most important person may be the treasurer, or perhaps the leader of the opposition. Media coverage of Australian politics deals almost exclusively with prime ministers, treasurers and opposition leaders, yet none of these positions is mentioned at all in the federal constitution. Neither are premiers mentioned in state constitutions (with the exception of Victoria).

WHY NOT JUST WRITE THE RULES?

Why didn't Australia's constitutional framers write down the key features of the Westminster system? It was discussed at the constitutional conventions of the 1890s in the lead-up to Federation, but the assembled delegates reasoned that, as all Australians were members of the British Empire, they understood the intricacies of the British system of parliamentary government and, therefore, didn't need for them to be written down. It is also worth remembering that the British form of parliamentary government had been practised in Tasmania, Victoria and New South Wales since 1856. The constitutional framers knew how the system worked. The constitutional framers were more concerned about how to bring the six colonies together to form a nation, and the terms and conditions of the federal system dominate in the content of the written constitution.

IN THIS CHAPTER

» Explaining the Westminster system of parliamentary government

» Defining the convention of Responsible Government

» Exploring the adversarial nature of the Westminster system

» Looking at the role of party politics in parliamentary government

» Introducing Australia's relationship with the Westminster system

Chapter **4**

Westminster: Much More than Big Ben

Reading Australia's federal and state constitutions gives only a partial picture of how the Australian system of parliamentary government works, as we note in Chapter 3. An understanding of the British system of parliamentary government — known as the *Westminster* system — is a necessary prerequisite to understanding the Australian system.

Constitutional scholars agree that Australian constitutions have to be read against the backdrop of Westminster practice. Only then can the key ideas of Cabinet government, Collective Responsibility, Ministerial Responsibility and Responsible Government be understood and applied to the Australian approach.

This chapter is all about the Westminster system. The Westminster system of government is based on the idea that the parliament governs the nation. As such, the Westminster system is the system of parliamentary government, also referred to as *Responsible Government.*

The name Westminster derives from the Palace of Westminster — the London-based building where the British parliament sits, and made famous by, among other things, its imposing clock tower, Big Ben. The Westminster system is the British system of government, and its export to the world (including Australia) is very much the product of Britain's imperial past.

A Constitution without a (Written) Constitution

One of the key features of Britain's Westminster system is the lack of a single written legal document as the constitutional basis for the practice of parliamentary government (in major contrast, indeed, to the Australian situation). British constitutional practice revolves partly around pieces of parliamentary legislation, and partly around *conventions* — the unwritten rules of parliamentary and constitutional practice adhered to by those involved in the process.

What do conventions cover?

Many Westminster conventions deal with the way governments are formed, how long governments can survive, what's expected of ministers and, most importantly of all, the nature of the relationship between the parliament and the Crown, and between the parliament and the public service. A number of other Westminster conventions deal with the procedures and rituals of the parliament. We look at these procedures in more detail in Chapter 6.

The evolution of the Westminster system

Today, the idea of parliamentary government in Britain and Australia is closely associated with the idea of electoral democracy. Indeed, the British House of Commons and all of the Australian parliamentary chambers (state and federal) are directly elected by the voters.

Worth remembering, however, is the fact that the idea of the parliament as the main institution of government predates the idea of modern democracy. It also predates the settling of the Australian colonies, because the evolution of the parliament as the key governing institution in Britain goes back to the late 1600s.

VOTE 1

The rise of the parliament as the body that governs Britain was the product of a political struggle with another key institution of government that, up until 1649, thought it governed England. This institution was the monarchy, headed up by a king or a queen. The execution of an English king began the process by which parliament established itself as the body that would govern what would eventually become Britain.

Britain as a constitutional monarchy

From 1689, the British parliament began to exert more and more authority over the governing of the nation. However, Britain wouldn't go back to being the sort of republic that Cromwell had brought on in 1649. Instead, the parliament and the Crown found a way to work with each other. This reconciliation saw the monarchy continuing to exist (and being seen as something of a head of state) but with the power to govern passing to the parliament, making Britain a *constitutional monarchy*.

However, the power to govern was passed on to a new player who led the government in the parliament. The emerging power in British government was the position of prime minister, heading a group of parliamentarians who were given the authority to be ministers. This is the parliament-based Cabinet. The Cabinet became the body to govern Britain, with the prime minister at its head.

The Crown

The monarchy is referred to in the Westminster model as the *Crown*. The assumption is that the system that governs Britain derives its authority from the Crown. The parliament, the public service and the courts are seen as exercising their authority on behalf of the Crown, and the idea that parliamentary bills don't become law until the Crown gives them royal assent is a feature of the British system.

THE BATTLE BETWEEN CROWN AND PARLIAMENT

The willingness of the Crown to subordinate itself to the parliament is the result of a long history of power struggles between kings, queens and various parliaments for control over the government of Britain. In 1649, Charles I was deposed by Oliver Cromwell and a parliamentary-based republic was established. This collapsed with Cromwell's death, and the monarchy resumed under Charles II. The King and the parliament battled over the matter of religion (the parliament insisted that Britain would be Protestant, whereas Charles II was Catholic). The power struggle continued thereafter, but, in 1689, the parliament passed an Act instituting a Bill of Rights that established the subordination of the Crown to the parliament — and this was assented to by King William and Queen Mary. The idea of parliamentary government now had legal force.

However, even though the Crown is the core authority for the governing system, the fact that the parliament won the right to actually govern Britain resulted in the establishment of one of the most important constitutional conventions of the Westminster system. Today, it's an established constitutional principle in Westminster that the Crown only ever acts on the advice of the prime minister.

VOTE 1

In only ever acting on the advice of the prime minster, the Crown is deemed to be tied into the political choice made by the voters because the prime minister can only hold this position if he has majority support in the parliament.

The Crown's authority over the public service, the military and the courts is also severely curtailed by other conventions that are based on the notion that a *Separation of Powers* should be at work in the system. The Separation of Powers is a Westminster concept that keeps the key institutions of the courts, the military and the public service separate from the partisan politics that can occur in the legislature. The Crown, therefore, can't interfere in the operation of the public service, because the public service is the responsibility of ministers.

The courts are separate from the parliament but are also deemed to be independent of the Crown, reflected in two important features of the British legal system:

>> First is the use of juries to try cases, the idea being that citizens are tried by their peers rather than by the monarchy.

>> The second feature is that the Crown isn't above the law (that is, members of the British royal family are subject to the same law as any other citizen).

The parliament

The parliament is the core institution of government in the Westminster system because government members are drawn from the parliament, and those government members are always answerable to the parliament. (This is the very basis of the doctrine of Responsible Government, which we cover later in this chapter.) The British parliament is a *bicameral* (two-chamber) parliament, with a lower house, the House of Commons, and an upper house, the House of Lords.

The House of Commons

Originally, the *House of Commons* was made up of members elected by a small group in British society on a limited *property-based franchise* (that is, you had to own property to be able to vote). Today, Britain has a *universal franchise* — all men and women over the age of 18 years have a right to vote to elect their representatives, who will sit in the Commons. The House of Commons is, these days, referred to as the *representative house*.

LORDS AND LAWS

Originally, the House of Lords was seen as the chamber of social 'elders and betters' who would review legislation emanating from the House of Commons, whose members were originally viewed as potentially radical. The original assumption was that the Lords would constrain the radical potential of the Commons by exercising a review function. This review would take the form of debating legislation coming from the lower house, and there emerged the convention that parliamentary bills only become law if they're agreed to by both the Commons and the Lords.

In the Australian national parliament, the *House of Representatives* is the equivalent of the House of Commons. In the state parliaments, the equivalent house is the *Legislative Assembly*.

The House of Lords

The second British parliamentary house is the House of Lords — the house of the aristocracy.

The Lords wasn't, and still isn't, a directly elected house. Being able to sit in the Lords was one of the privileges associated with being an aristocrat. Today, the Lords has very many 'commoners' in it because one of the powers a British prime minister has is the ability to appoint people to the Lords.

Australian parliaments also have upper houses — the Senate in the national parliament and the Legislative Council in state governments. However, unlike the House of Lords, Australia's upper houses are directly elected.

No longer commoners and aristocrats

The idea of the British parliament being comprised of commoners and aristocrats has lost favour in these more egalitarian times in modern Britain. However, some of the key principles of this basic model persist, including that:

>> A bill can't become a law until both houses vote in favour of it.

>> The upper house continues to be seen as a house of review.

>> By convention, neither house recognises each other in internal parliamentary conversation. A member of parliament (MP) in the Commons can only refer to 'that other place', if wishing to refer to the Lords in a parliamentary speech, as, indeed, members of the Lords do when referring to members from the Commons.

>> The sovereign may not attend the House of Commons. If the sovereign comes to parliament, she's only allowed to visit the House of Lords.

>> When a new parliament is installed after an election and the sovereign addresses it for the first time, the speech that the sovereign reads from is written by the government. And it's delivered from the House of Lords. The Lords then issues an invitation to the Commons to attend the Lords to hear the speech.

Many of the features of the British parliamentary system listed here are replicated in Australia.

The executive

The executive is the government. The government may also be referred to as the Cabinet. It may also be called the ministry and perhaps even the senior ministry.

REMEMBER

In some systems of government, such as in the United States, the executive is comprised of individuals from outside the legislature. But, under the Westminster system, the government *must* come from the parliament.

One of the reasons so many terms apply to the executive is because, under the Westminster system, the government has at least three divisions. These include:

>> **The Cabinet:** This division is the collection of senior ministers who meet regularly and whose chairperson is the prime minister. This group may also be called the inner Cabinet or the senior ministry.

>> **The full ministry:** This group comprises the senior ministers (the Cabinet) and the junior ministry. Junior ministers may be those ministers who hold portfolios, or ministries, not included as part of Cabinet or, in some systems (such as in Australia, where they're now called *assistant ministers*) may be ministers who assist the senior ministers who make up the Cabinet. The full ministry meets regularly but with much less frequency than the Cabinet.

>> **Parliamentary secretaries:** These members are MPs who are junior to the junior ministers, although their status is considered to be the same as ministers and they're considered to be part of the government as well. Indeed, conventions such as Collective Responsibility and Ministerial Responsibility (see later in this chapter) also apply to parliamentary secretaries.

REMEMBER

The Westminster government technically includes all ministers and parliamentary secretaries. In practical terms, however, it's only the Cabinet that meets frequently. In real terms, then, the Cabinet is the government in a Westminster system.

Cabinet initiates policy; parliament debates policy

The Westminster model assumes something of a division of labour exists in the practice of parliamentary government. Although any MP can introduce a private member's bill (see Chapter 6), the reality is that Cabinet dominates the parliament's legislative program. The idea is that Cabinet decides on policy and, if legislation is needed, the parliament debates the policy by arguing out various aspects of the proposed legislation.

The prime minister

Under the Westminster system, the prime minister is the head of government (as the premier is in Australian state government) because Westminster convention requires the Crown to act on the advice of the prime minister as the leader of Cabinet. So, while the Queen is technically the head of state, the prime minister is the head of government.

Prime ministerial power rests in the leadership he exercises over the ministry and those in the parliament who support the ministry. In terms of the Cabinet, the power of the prime minister is based on his ability to:

>> Call Cabinet meetings and chair them

>> Set the Cabinet agenda

>> Set the means by which Cabinet makes its decisions

>> Dispense discipline among Cabinet (especially with the use of the convention of Collective Responsibility)

>> Dispense perks and privileges of office to those in the parliament who support the government, including the choice of Cabinet members, members of the full ministry and parliamentary secretaries

>> Determine who'll be in the Cabinet, and what portfolios they'll hold

The prime minister also tends to be the focus of the attention of the community whenever government or politics are discussed, particularly in the media.

VOTE 1

The real world of Australian government and politics replicates these very important features of the British system. The transferral of the British system of parliamentary government to Australia has resulted in the prime minister, rather than the governor-general, being identified by most Australians as the head of government (or, in state government, the premier being at the head of government rather than the governor).

Responsible Government

The Westminster system of parliamentary government is also referred to as the system of *Responsible Government*. This term has a couple of meanings:

>> First of all, Responsible Government refers to the way a ministry is formed in the parliament and how it stays in government in between elections. Of particular importance here is the idea that a government is understood to be responsible for as long as it enjoys the support of the parliament.

>> Second, responsibility is also understood as involving the answerability and accountability of government to its citizens, which is critical to the idea of Responsible Government.

Forming a Responsible Government

In British parliamentary practice, forming a government in the parliament is a relatively straightforward matter. A ministry is formed and installed as a government when that ministry is supported by a majority of members of parliament in the representative chamber — that is, the House of Commons.

This practice leads to another core Westminster convention. The longevity of a government is determined by its support in the popular, or lower, parliamentary house. By extension, the leader of the government (the prime minister or premier) should also come from the lower house, although it's possible for the leader to come from the upper house. Ministers can also be from either house. This convention is particularly important where the upper houses are directly elected, such as in Australia.

What this structure means in practical terms is that a ministry is formed and remains in government for as long as a majority of members vote for its legislative program when it comes before the House of Commons.

Budget and appropriation bills: Supply

Responsibility in the Westminster system can be tested by two parliamentary matters in particular. The ability of a ministry to get its supply bills through is one of these tests. *Supply* is the combination of legislation that levies taxes on the community (also known as tax bills) and legislation that authorises government to spend public money on programs (also known as appropriation bills). In order to govern, a ministry must be able to get its supply bills through the parliament. Failure to do so means that a failure of Responsible Government has occurred, and the government must tender its resignation.

In Britain, the test of responsibility is straightforward. The ministry actually only owes responsibility to the House of Commons. The House of Lords is no longer able to block supply. This situation reinforces the Westminster convention that the lower house is the house of government. It also contributes to another Westminster convention — specifically, that the upper house doesn't block budget or appropriation bills.

As Chapter 5 explains, this point is a major departure between Australian and British practice because of the fact that Australian upper houses are directly elected houses and because Australian constitutions make these upper houses quite powerful. The issue of responsibility in Australian parliamentary practice is much more complicated than in the British model.

No-confidence motions

The successful moving of a motion of *no confidence* in a government in the House of Commons is the second critical test of responsibility. These motions are moved by the opposition, and, if successful, indicate that the ministry no longer enjoys the support of a majority of MPs in the lower house. The government, then, is defeated and it should tender its resignation.

Resign! Resign!

A government that fails the tests of Responsible Government (either by losing the confidence of the lower house, or by failing to obtain supply) is expected to resign.

Resignation in such circumstances takes the form of the defeated prime minister going to see the Queen (or Crown representative in Australia) to advise of the inability to govern. The defeated prime minister is then expected to advise the Crown to seek the advice of the leader of the opposition to see if an alternative government can be formed. If the opposition can't form a government either, by convention the Crown would dissolve the parliament and call fresh elections.

In Australia, the governor-general (or the governor, in the case of a state parliament), as the Crown's representative, would perform this role.

Collective Responsibility

The Westminster system assumes that government is the result of a collective effort on behalf of those senior ministers who make up the Cabinet (sometimes known as the inner Cabinet or the senior ministry).

Cabinet meets regularly to make decisions on policy. Some of these decisions result in legislation being drawn up and debated in the parliament. Some other decisions can be made without reference to parliament. In each case, the Westminster model assumes that the power to formulate policy resides with the Cabinet.

When a Westminster Cabinet meets (with the prime minister chairing the meeting), its deliberations are held *in camera* (that is, in secret). Cabinet papers are considered to be immune from public scrutiny. Ministers are able to argue policy positions among themselves, but, when Cabinet has made a decision on policy, all members of Cabinet are bound by that decision. This convention is known as *Collective Responsibility*.

VOTE 1

In Australia, federal Cabinet documents remain confidential for 20 years, while some variation exists between the states. South Australia and Queensland, for example, recently reduced the period of confidentiality to only 10 years.

If a member of Cabinet publicly disagrees with a Cabinet decision, either in the parliament or in any other public forum, that dissenting minister must either resign or expect to be dismissed by the prime minister.

The release of Cabinet papers (say, to the media) or briefing of any person external to the Cabinet on how Cabinet deliberated on a matter also breaches Collective Responsibility, and the offending minister should resign or be sacked.

Ministerial Responsibility

Another important but very complex Westminster convention relates to members of the government and the prime minister. This convention is that of *Ministerial Responsibility*, part of the answerability process that operates in a Westminster parliament.

Being a minister is one of the things that parliamentarians aspire to. Being a senior minister (that is, being a member of Cabinet) is seen as being more important and powerful than being a junior minister. Parliamentary secretaries are seen as being less important again, but more important than being an ordinary member of parliament.

On becoming a minister, a member of parliament is given a *portfolio*, which means she's put in charge of a particular area of public policy (health, transport, education or some other specific function). The minister is given the power to make policy decisions relating to that portfolio and is put in charge of the relevant public service department. The role of these public servants is to give the minister advice on policy matters pertaining to her portfolio and to convert policy decisions into actual administration.

THE WHO'S WHO OF A MINISTRY

Clearly, the most important people in the ministry are in Cabinet, and the most important person in Cabinet is the prime minister. But who's the next most important person? It may be the deputy prime minister, who takes the reins of power in the event of the prime minister being absent or unable to discharge her duties. Some suggest that the minister in charge of finances is the next most important person, given the importance of the Budget. In Britain, this minister is called the *chancellor of the exchequer*. In Australia, this person is called the *treasurer*. The attorney-general is usually in Cabinet because of the importance of law-making and the administration of the courts. Thereafter, the ministers who make it into Cabinet reflect the policy priorities of the government.

REMEMBER

Being a minister comes with a catch. In the Westminster system, a minister who's given a portfolio is deemed to be the *responsible minister*, which means that the minister becomes answerable to the parliament not only for decisions made with regard to policy, but also for the conduct of the public service department allocated to him. A minister who's deemed to have breached Ministerial Responsibility is supposed to resign from the ministry, or should expect to be sacked by the prime minister.

The convention of Ministerial Responsibility is important to the way in which a Westminster public service is supposed to operate. In theory, the ministry is answerable to the parliament, and the parliament is answerable to the citizens by way of the electoral process.

Westminster as Adversarial Politics

The Westminster parliament is an adversarial parliament. The system recognises that there is a government and an opposition. Chapter 6 outlines what this structure means for the day-to-day operation of the parliament. Important to note at this point, however, is that the system revolves around the idea of a contest of ideas, as distinct from the search for some sort of broad consensus. In this system, the opposition is recognised as the alternative government and is expected to oppose the government.

The alternative prime minister

If the prime minister is the most readily recognisable political figure in a Westminster system, the *Leader of the Opposition* — an official position recognised by the Westminster model — is arguably the second most readily recognisable figure.

This status is partly a reflection of the political party system, because the leader of the opposition is also the leader of the main opposition party.

The leader of the opposition has the power to select and head a *shadow ministry* made up of opposition MPs who, if an election were called and the opposition were to win, would become the government, and the leader of the opposition would become the prime minister. Another rare circumstance leading to a change of government is if enough government MPs *cross the floor* (vote with the opposition) and give the opposition a majority in the house. This event means the government holds a minority of seats and, therefore, is no longer in a position to govern.

The shadow ministry

The shadow ministry copies the structure and behaviour of the ministry, including being broken up into an inner shadow Cabinet and the full shadow ministry. Shadow ministers track their counterpart ministers and have the brief of, first, seeking to highlight deficiencies in the performance of the government minister being shadowed and, second, formulating alternative policies.

Shadow ministers are also given a procedural role in the debating of legislation in the parliament. At the second reading of a bill, the responsible minister outlines the government's reasons for the legislation. The shadow minister then has the right to outline the official opposition position on the bill (which is, of course, usually one of opposing it).

VOTE 1

Working in the shadow of others is hard — just ask any shadow minister. The shadow ministry lacks a very important advantage that the government has, and that is access to the public service. The public service is a resource available to the government only. The opposition has to look elsewhere for the data, advice and other information that alternative policies may be based on.

Westminster and Party Politics

Talking about the Westminster parliamentary system without making some reference to political parties is impossible. The evolution of the Westminster system predates the rise of modern parties. The advent of the disciplined political party has fitted in well with the Westminster system, however.

In Britain and in Australia, the vast majority of parliamentarians are members of political parties. Westminster governments are, therefore, usually governments drawn from a political party or a coalition of parties. Although they're assumed to represent the districts that elected them, Westminster MPs tend to also be party representatives. They sit together in the parliament and vote as a party block whenever a vote is taken in the parliament. Here it's possible to further define how government is formed in a modern Westminster system. Government is formed by the party or coalition of parties who have a majority of seats in the lower house.

From that definition, it's also now possible to further define who'll be the prime minister and who'll be in the ministry. The prime minister will be the leader of the political party that has the majority of seats in the lower house. The ministry will be made up of the leadership team of the party with the majority. In the meantime, the leader of the political party that doesn't have the lower house majority will be the leader of the opposition, and the shadow ministry will be the leadership team of the minority party.

The partisan basis of the government and opposition has implications for elections, too. In Westminster systems, voters don't elect a prime minister directly, the way, say, US voters get to vote for their president. Instead, Westminster electors vote for candidates in their local districts, nearly all of whom are party candidates. The best the voter can do is cast a vote for the party that is led by someone who the voter wants to be prime minister. (The exception, of course, is those voters who live in the prospective prime minister's own electorate.)

Tyranny of the executive?

Critics of the Westminster system point to the rise of disciplined political parties and their domination of the parliament as evidence of the way the Cabinet, and especially the prime minister, dominates the system. This view that Cabinet decides on policy and then has policy rubber-stamped by a compliant parliament is sometimes described as the *tyranny of the executive*. Some go on to suggest that modern party politics has rendered the backbench MP redundant.

The other side of this argument is that the advent of disciplined party politics has brought great certainty and stability to the system. Governments know they can govern because they know that the MPs who support the ministry are tied to it by party discipline.

Winner takes all?

The Westminster parliamentary system is sometimes described as a *winner-takes-all* system. What this means is that the party or parties that win a majority of seats in the lower house and can form a government enjoy all the privileges and advantages of the parliamentary system. In Chapter 6, we show that any opportunities that oppositions have to participate in the process are, at their most basic, privileges extended to the opposition by the government. By having a majority in a parliamentary chamber, the government can dictate the way that chamber operates.

WHAT THE PARTY GIVES, IT CAN TAKE AWAY

Because in the Westminster system the political party, rather than the voters, select who'll be prime minister by virtue of its need to elect a leader from among its number, it's also possible for the political party to withdraw that privilege simply by voting for a new party leader. This became a feature of Australian politics in recent years. In 2010 the Labor caucus elected Julia Gillard to replace Kevin Rudd as party leader. In doing so, Gillard became prime minister, without voters being involved. In 2013, the Labor caucus decided to reinstate Rudd to the leadership and, in so doing, ended Gillard's prime ministership. In 2015, the Liberal parliamentarians decided to remove Tony Abbott as party leader in favour of Malcolm Turnbull who, in turn, was replaced by Scott Morrison in 2018. If this sounds exhausting, spare a thought for those who have to continually update resources about Australian prime ministers!

The opposition leader's fate is also in the hands of the party. If enough members of the opposition party feel that their leader isn't performing effectively, they can elect a new leader. Party leaders, then, serve as long as their party supports them.

No doubt the winner-takes-all ethos underpins Westminsterism, resulting in a powerful Cabinet and prime minister. This can be demonstrated by pointing to the way so many commentators have noted that being leader of the opposition is the most thankless and difficult task in Westminster politics. With so little to do other than constantly oppose what the government is doing, oppositions can find their time in the parliament very frustrating.

Westminster and Australia

So many features of the British model of parliamentary government are replicated in Australia. Government in Australia is of the Westminster variety, with bicameral parliaments, ministries drawn from the parliaments, a prime minister in national politics and premiers in state politics. Collective Responsibility and Ministerial Responsibility both apply in Australian government. So, too, does the notion that government in Australia is Responsible Government.

Why Australia's system of government is based on the British model is no mystery. The transferral of the British system of parliamentary government to Australia occurred with the creation of the Australian colonies and was part of a general transferral of other British institutions, including the British monarchy and the British legal system. The process officially commenced with Britain passing what's known as the Australian Colonies Self Government Act in 1850 (formally the *Act for the Better Government of Her Majesty's Australian Colonies 1850*). From 1850, it would take another five years before the colonies of New South Wales, Victoria and Tasmania obtained constitutions that provided for full parliamentary systems.

Still, the application of the British system had to be modified to accommodate the Australian environment. We outline the Australian variations of the Westminster system in Chapter 5.

Chapter **5**

Washminster: The Australian Hybrid

The Australian system of government is primarily a Westminster type, with some important points of difference from the British model. The system of national government in Australia is sometimes called the *Washminster system*, reflecting that the system is basically like the British system (Westminster) but modified to accommodate the federal system in a way that borrows heavily from the United States of America (Washington).

Among political pundits, debate often rages as to whether or not this amalgamation of systems works well. On one hand, the national system of government has been working functionally for over 100 years. Yet a constitutional problem that became a full-blown political crisis in 1975 cast some doubt over how well a Westminster model can be incorporated into a federal system.

In this chapter, you get to look at how Australia's system of government and its parliamentary conventions have evolved, by examining some of its key positions and institutions, in particular the potential for conflict between the Senate and the House of Representatives. And we give you a blow-by-blow analysis of how the constitutional crisis of 1975 unfolded and what few changes it brought about.

British or American?

The transfer of British ideas about government into Australia is easily explained by Australia's establishment as a British colony. The American impact on Australia, however, is a little more difficult to account for.

Like Australia, some parts of North America were part of the British Empire. Unlike Australia, however, the British colonies in America rebelled against Britain and sought to establish a self-governing republic with a constitution that, among other things, outlined the idea of individual liberty. This rebellion was the War of Independence against the British (1775–1783).

From this point, the new American republic was a source of interest to much of the world, including the Australian colonies (after they were established from 1788 on), where similar liberal ideas about individual liberty were embraced by some. In 1849, a gold rush occurred in California. In 1851, Edward Hargreaves, a New South Wales man who went to California to prospect for gold, came back to Australia and officially discovered gold near Bathurst. The Australian gold rushes began, and many free men came to Australia to look for gold via California. The American–Australian cultural exchange was established.

Australia's constitutional framers were very aware of the American approach to federalism, mainly because of the popularity of published works on the subject by the French writer Alexis de Tocqueville (who published *Democracy in America* in 1835) and the British writer James Bryce (who wrote *The American Commonwealth* in 1888). Bryce's work was particularly influential, partly because of its timing and partly because at least one very influential Australian seeking to achieve Federation, Alfred Deakin, had personally met Bryce in London in the 1890s. The framers were also aware of the British North America Act of 1867. This was the Canadian constitution, and it was constantly referred to during the Australian constitutional conventions in the 1890s.

American federalism: A model for Australia

The Australian Federation Movement was at its most active in the 1890s. By that stage, all of the Australian colonies had their own constitutions and were already practising Westminster-style Responsible Government (refer to Chapter 4 for more on this and other Westminster conventions). The controversy that had to be addressed by Australia's constitutional framers was not about what model of government should be used. As loyal members of the British Empire, this matter was never in doubt. The system that would be used would be the Westminster system.

Rather than worrying about Responsible Government, the real issue before the constitutional framers was how to get the six independent colonies to agree to come together and form a national government. At this point, the models of federal government became the main source of interest.

Thanks to Bryce and to Deakin, the American federal model was the most influential in debates about how the Australian system of federal government would be structured.

A Senate, a court and a written constitution: The American legacy

The American model was very important to the development of the federalist dimension of the Australian Constitution. The American approach was based on previously independent states coming together and giving the new national government specific powers. The idea of the autonomy of the American states remained enshrined in the American model, however. National government in America didn't mean the end of the American states. The creation of the Senate was critical to all this. Canada had a Senate, but it was appointed. What the Australian framers liked was the American idea of an elected Senate representing the states. The Australian constitutional framers took this principle from the American model and sought to enshrine it in the Australian document.

The American features of the Australian federation include:

» An outline of the specific powers the federal government (called the *Commonwealth*) could exercise

» A court that, like the American Supreme Court, would oversee the Constitution and deal with any disputes between the national government and the states over the exercise of governmental power (the High Court in Australia)

» The creation of an elected parliamentary chamber, the Senate, clearly written up in the Australian Constitution as the house representing the federating states made up of elected (not appointed) senators

» Equal representation of the states in the Senate, regardless of their population size

Limits to Americanisation: Responsible Government

Australian enthusiasm for the American approach to government had serious limitations. Colonial Australians may have been impressed by American federalism, but they had absolutely no sympathy for American republicanism! There would be no war of independence between Australia and Britain. On the contrary, Australian colonial politicians saw themselves as being part of the British Empire and appeared to go out of their way to confirm their loyalty to Britain by being as polite to the British sovereign as possible.

The rejection of American republicanism entailed a rejection of the American political system. The American presidency wouldn't be copied in the Australian system. To do so may have been construed as a slight against the British Crown and the British system. The adoption of Responsible Government, on the other hand, was a confirmation of the Australian commitment to the British way of governing. Rather than a president, Australia would have a prime minister — a point so obvious to Australia's constitutional framers that they saw no need to write it down in the Australian Constitution.

Responsible Government the Australian Way

The term *Washminster*, to describe the national system of government, is sometimes used with a hint of derision. Some aspects of the way state governments are organised also highlight a few strains and stresses in common with the federal system. These stresses relate particularly to the role of the governor in the system and the power of the Legislative Council (in those states that have one) and, significantly, are similar to some of the contradictory themes present in the federal system. Perhaps the Australian way of governing is indeed a locally developed hybrid and not just a mishmash of British and American systems!

The Australian approach to Responsible Government is clearly based on the Westminster model, as we explain in Chapter 4. The fact that written constitutions underpin the system for both the federal and state governments does modify some of the Westminster conventions that apply, however. In the case of the federal system, the imposition of the federal element also makes some very major modifications to the system.

The Australian modifications to Westminster practice are particularly important to the role of governors (especially the governor-general), the role and status of the Executive in Council, and the role of the upper houses (especially the Australian Senate).

Executive in Council or Cabinet?

The written constitutions for the state systems and for the federal system outline the existence of Executive Councils, and expressly mention the role of the sovereign's representative within those bodies. The Executive in Council is basically a meeting of the Crown representative with government ministers to note and ratify government business, as we explain in Chapter 3. A literal reading of the constitutions suggests Executive Councils are the official institutions of Australian government.

VOTE 1

Despite the written constitutions, the practical reality is that the Cabinet, and not the Executive in Council, governs the states and the Commonwealth because the conventions of Westminster practice, rather than the written word of the constitutions, prevail in the practical day-to-day governing of Australia. The Executive in Council is, therefore, something of a formal body that ratifies decisions made by Cabinet.

The governor-general or the prime minister?

Again, the written Australian Constitution makes no reference to the prime minister, but says plenty about the governor-general. Yet the practical reality in Australian government is that the prime minister is the head of government. In other words, the Westminster convention that the Crown only acts on the advice of the prime minister (or, in the states, that the governor only acts on the advice of the premier) applies in Australia.

The only exception to this rule is in those rare occasions of constitutional crisis usually brought on by some problem for government in its day-to-day dealing with the parliament. In the event that the Cabinet can't govern but the prime minister won't relinquish executive power, a case for the intervention of the Crown's representative (an exercising of reserve powers, as we note in Chapter 3) may arise.

What about the states?

These days, the prospect of reserve powers being exercised is more of an issue for the federal system than for the states. Changes to many of the state constitutions have significantly reduced the likelihood of a dispute between lower and upper houses resulting in the government having supply denied (effectively starving the government of funds and forcing an election). Queensland no longer has an upper house; Victoria, South Australia and New South Wales have fixed parliamentary terms, denying the upper house the legal right to force early elections, and the upper houses of Western Australia and Tasmania have electoral arrangements that make it unlikely that a major political party could force the blocking of supply.

House of Representatives or the Senate?

The potential for the two houses of the federal parliament (as opposed to state parliaments) to clash is very real, and the power of the Australian Senate to force early elections remains enshrined in the Constitution. In fact, the Australian Constitution explicitly outlines a role for the governor-general in resolving deadlocks between the two houses.

REMEMBER

The issue of relations between the house of the people (the House of Representatives) and the house of the states (the Senate) is critical to the operation of the Australian parliament and, by extension, to the way in which a prime minister and a Cabinet seek to govern. The matter is also somewhat complex, partly because of the way the Australian Constitution is written and partly because of the evolution of some important Australian conventions about how the national parliament should operate.

Before considering the complexities of Australia's bicameral system, though, you must first recognise some basic assumptions.

The Reps: The house of government

The first core assumption is that the House of Representatives is the house that determines who forms national government. The government is formed by the party or parties that have a majority of seats in the House of Representatives. 'The Reps' is also the house where the prime minister and leader of the opposition are. In all but the most extreme circumstances, a government's responsibility is owed to the House of Representatives.

The Senate: Still the states' house?

The second important thing to note is that, although the Australian Senate is seen as the states' house in a literal reading of the Constitution, the reality is that the Senate replicates the party politics of the House of Representatives. Senators rarely, if ever, vote as state representatives. Rather, they vote as party representatives — a fact observable in the chamber by the way Australian senators sit and vote together with their party colleagues in the day-to-day operation of the upper house.

In fact, as early as 1910 it had become clear that people elected to the Senate were really party representatives. Occasionally, casual vacancies occurred in the Senate in between elections. The Constitution said that, in such circumstances, the governor of the state from which the vacating senator came would nominate a replacement. The convention that evolved, operating until about 1975, was that the premier of the state would advise the governor to nominate someone from the same political party as the vacating senator. This convention was justified on the grounds that it maintained the party political choice made by the electors at the previous election.

In lieu of this notion that the Senate is the house of the federating states, the Senate now tends to see itself as the house of review. In this way, the function of the modern Senate is closer to the function of Britain's House of Lords than to the American Senate.

Making laws

Although the House of Representatives is recognised as the house where government is formed, it's not in any way superior to the Senate. Indeed, Section 53 of the Australian Constitution actually says that the two houses have 'co-equal powers' in all matters except the introduction of taxation bills and legislation authorising government spending (supply — refer to Chapter 3). The Constitution says such bills must originate in the House of Representatives and must not be amended by the Senate. The Constitution says nothing about blocking or rejecting supply, however.

On the basis of Section 53, it's understood in Australian parliamentary government that bills must pass through both the House of Representatives and the Senate before they can be presented to the Executive in Council for royal assent (refer to Chapter 3). In all matters other than taxation bills and government spending legislation, the Senate has the right to suggest amendments to bills coming from the House of Representatives. When presented with bills that have been amended by the Senate, the Representatives then has to decide if it accepts those amendments.

Since 1949, two very different electoral systems have been used to elect members to the House of Representatives and to the Senate. In the House of Representatives, the candidate who wins the majority of votes wins the seat. But winning in the Senate relies on candidates securing a certain proportion of the statewide vote in order to win a seat. See Chapter 13 for more on these voting systems. Proportional representation in the Senate has made it difficult for the major parties to win the sort of majorities they can win in the lower house. The system has also allowed minor parties to win seats in the Senate.

What this means is that the political party that has the majority in the lower house and can form a government doesn't usually have a majority in the Senate. The usual situation, then, is for the opposition parties to have the numbers in the upper house. Viewed as a contest between the political parties, the capacity for disputes between the lower and upper houses over legislation becomes very clear.

Deadlocks

The delegates who wrote the Australian Constitution actually intended the Senate to have the power to frustrate the legislative program of the lower house (that is, of the government and its prime minister). This intention is very clear because a section was inserted in the Constitution designed to resolve disputes between the houses over legislation. This section of the Constitution is known as the *deadlocks provision*.

The keys to resolving deadlocks

Section 57 is the deadlocks provision of the Constitution. It's a long and very complicated section, and its operation over the years has also been the subject of another evolving Australian convention of parliamentary practice.

REMEMBER

In a nutshell, Section 57 allows for an election of the Australian parliament in its entirety to be called on the basis of the defeat of government legislation in the Senate.

TECHNICAL STUFF

Section 57 outlines the procedure for dealing with deadlocks; if a bill is sent to the Senate, and the Senate makes amendments to the bill that the Representatives (that is, the government) does not agree with, the bill is considered to have been defeated for the first time. A period of at least three months must elapse and then the House of Representatives can try again with the original bill. If the Senate amends this bill in ways unacceptable to the Representatives again, the bill is deemed to have been defeated for a second time. Here the section gets a bit tricky. The Constitution says that if the second defeat occurs, the governor-general may dissolve both the House of Representatives and all of the Senate (in a normal election situation only half of the Senate would be up for election). This occurrence is called a *double dissolution*.

Section 57 as a prime ministerial power

An important Australian parliamentary convention has evolved regarding the circumstances in which Section 57 is invoked. Usually, the power to invoke Section 57 rests with the prime minister. Again, this stipulation is a reflection of the importance of the Westminster convention that the Crown acts on the advice of the prime minister. The usual practice in Australia is that the governor-general doesn't invoke Section 57 until advised to do so by the prime minister.

When the prime minister asks the governor-general to invoke Section 57, the defeated legislation is nominated in the legal writs issued to allow for the double-dissolution election to take place. The importance of nominating the legislation becomes a little clearer when the matter of a *joint sitting* of the parliament, a sitting of both houses in the one chamber, arises (read on for more on joint sittings).

Stockpiling defeated legislation

A prime minister isn't required to advise the governor-general of the need for a Section 57 election as soon as a bill is defeated. The timing of the request, by convention, is usually up to the prime minister. Some prime ministers have allowed very many bills to be defeated by the Senate with the intention of nominating all of them in the election writs so they can be dealt with in a subsequent joint sitting of both houses. This practice is called *stockpiling*. Prime ministers may also stockpile defeated bills so that one or all can be conveniently used to call for a snap election for political reasons — such as exploiting a fall in the standing of the opposition in the opinion polls.

The joint sitting

Although it has only ever been used once since 1901 (in 1974), Section 57 also allows for the calling of a joint sitting of the Australian parliament. If the government is returned at a double-dissolution election, the bill (or bills) that had been defeated and was nominated in the election writs as the reason for the election may be dealt with in a joint sitting of the parliament. The members of the House of Representatives and the Senate then sit as one chamber and debate and vote on the bill (or bills) in one sitting.

Because of the nexus provision (see the sidebar 'Double up!'), the House of Representatives has twice the number of members of the Senate. The use of preferential voting for the lower house (see Chapter 13) means that the governing party has many more seats than the opposition parties, and the assumption is that the government will eventually get its legislation through.

Clash of the Houses: The 1975 Constitutional Crisis

For most of Australia's political history, conflicts between the House of Representatives and the Senate have tended to be confined primarily to disputes over bills. In 1975, however, a major conflict between the two houses occurred over the fate of the supply bill coming from the lower house at the behest of the then prime minister, E. G. (Gough) Whitlam, who headed an Australian Labor Party government.

Anxious to force an early election, the leader of the Liberal–Country coalition opposition, Malcolm Fraser, used his party's majority in the Senate to threaten the Whitlam government's supply bill. The intensity of this political manoeuvre and the way in which it pitted one parliamentary chamber against another was so significant that this incident has been referred to ever since as the *1975 constitutional crisis*.

The politics of the crisis

The political dimension of the 1975 crisis had much to do with the intense rivalry between Labor and the coalition parties in the policy debate. The Labor Party was in government because it had a majority in the House of Representatives, and Gough Whitlam was prime minister because he was the Labor leader.

REMEMBER

One of Whitlam's big problems was that his party didn't have a majority in the Senate. As a result, his government's extensive legislative program was constantly being rejected in the Senate. The situation worsened when a Labor senator from Queensland died in 1975, and the non-Labor Queensland premier nominated an anti-Whitlam replacement (thereby breaking the previous convention of replacing vacating senators with candidates from the same party). This outcome altered the balance of the Senate by giving the Liberal–Country coalition an absolute majority in the upper house.

Citing a range of alleged policy failures by the Whitlam government, opposition leader Malcolm Fraser told the House of Representatives (which was debating the 1975 Budget at the time) that the parties he led wouldn't consider the Budget in the Senate unless Whitlam advised the governor-general of the need for fresh elections. Whitlam, mindful of his government's lack of popularity at that moment, refused to acquiesce to the demand.

The crisis: The deferral of supply

The 1975 Budget passed the House of Representatives, where the Labor government had a majority, but, as Malcolm Fraser had threatened, the Senate refused to consider the bill until Gough Whitlam resigned. Whitlam refused to resign, and the Budget was caught between the two parliamentary chambers.

This stalemate lasted for months, during which time a debate about the Australian Constitution raged. Whitlam and his supporters argued that, as Australia was a Westminster system, the prime minister had a right to govern, given the majority he commanded in the House of Representatives. Fraser argued that, because Australia was a federation, a government had to be able to get its Budget through the House of Representatives and the Senate. He argued that failure to do so constituted a failure of Responsible Government.

Beyond Canberra, electors began to worry about the implications of the supply bill failing to get through the parliament. Such a failure would mean that the Commonwealth wouldn't be able to honour its financial commitments. Those people who depended on the federal government for their income and livelihood were particularly concerned. Political commentators in the media reasoned that this looked like a potential failure of good government and argued that the governor-general would probably have to intervene.

The governor-general: The reserve powers exercised

Sir John Kerr was the governor-general at the time of the crisis. As the stalemate between the two houses continued, Kerr began to indicate his awareness of the role he may need to play by seeking advice from a range of sources as to what he might do.

This search for advice was controversial in itself. Consistent with his defence of the Westminster argument, Gough Whitlam declared that the governor-general could only take advice from the prime minister. The problem for Whitlam was that the governor-general had legal advice that he was free to take advice from other sources, including the law officers for the Commonwealth, the Chief Justice of the High Court and even the opposition leader himself.

As the crisis dragged on into November, Kerr decided the time had come for him to exercise his reserve powers and resolve the impasse. On 11 November, he summoned both Whitlam and Fraser to Yarralumla, the suburb in which Government House (the governor-general's residence) is located.

On meeting Whitlam, Kerr asked him if he was in a position to advise on the need to call fresh elections and to have the Budget passed in the Senate. Whitlam refused the invitation to resign and said he could not, as yet, pass the Budget. Kerr then handed a letter to Whitlam advising him that the governor-general had withdrawn Whitlam's authority to be prime minister forthwith and that other members of the ministry had also been dismissed. Whitlam was now the opposition leader. Back at Parliament House, Whitlam famously addressed supporters and journalists from the steps (see Figure 5-1).

FIGURE 5-1:
Gough Whitlam speaks on the steps of Parliament House, Canberra, after his dismissal by Governor-General Sir John Kerr in November 1975.

On meeting Fraser, Kerr again asked if the Budget could be passed and fresh elections called, were Fraser to be installed as prime minister. Fraser said that he could answer yes to both questions. Kerr then handed him a letter authorising Fraser to be a *caretaker* prime minister to allow for the passage of the Budget and the furnishing of advice that Section 57 of the Constitution would be invoked.

The governor-general's actions: The controversies

Sir John Kerr's actions shocked and stunned the Australian community, whose understanding of the governmental process had until now been based on the Westminster notion that the prime minister was the powerful person, given that he had won the last federal election. Critics of Kerr were infuriated at the idea that the Queen's representative appeared to have usurped the role of the electoral process. Defenders of Kerr's actions pointed out, however, that the written word of the Australian Constitution allowed the governor-general to act unilaterally and to install ministers, and that the need for the governor-general to ensure good government was also in the Constitution.

Labor supporters were furious, and there was a rush to get back to the parliament to tackle Malcolm Fraser in the House of Representatives. The lower house moved a motion of no confidence in Fraser, but the exercise was futile. The Senate had already passed the Budget, Fraser had already asked that Section 57 be invoked, and the parliament had already been doubly dissolved ahead of elections to be held in December 1975.

The meaning of the 1975 crisis

The 1975 constitutional crisis was a bitter and controversial moment in Australian politics and government. Stripped of its politics, however, the crisis was really about the Australian Constitution and some of the problems with it. First and foremost was the problem associated with trying to have a constitutional approach based partly on the written word (the Constitution) and partly on unwritten conventions (the Westminster system).

REMEMBER

The crisis also showed the problem of having co-equal parliamentary chambers with no clear sign as to which of them is the definitive chamber of government. In Britain, this problem doesn't arise because the House of Commons is the elected house. In Australia, however, both houses are directly elected and both have constitutional recognition of their importance. Those people who'd previously forgotten just how powerful the Australian Senate could be were given a red-hot reminder in 1975.

VOTE 1

WHERE WAS THE QUEEN DURING THE CRISIS?

When the Speaker of the House of Representatives tried to contact Queen Elizabeth II to inform her of the no-confidence motion against Malcolm Fraser (after Whitlam had been dismissed by Kerr), he was politely told that the governor-general was Her Majesty's representative in Australia and all such constitutional matters should be referred to him. In December 1975, the Liberal–Country coalition under Fraser's leadership won a landslide election victory.

In the years since, however, more has come to light about the Crown's involvement before and during the crisis. As part of his seeking advice from other sources in the lead-up to the dismissal, Kerr wrote to Buckingham Palace many times — and the Palace responded, through Sir Martin Charteris, Private Secretary to the Queen. Only released in 2020, the letters are now available via the National Archives of Australia.

You can check out these letters between Kerr and Buckingham Palace online at the National Archives of Australia website — www.naa.gov.au/explore-collection/kerr-palace-letters. The resource provides access to over 200 letters that were written during, and after, the Whitlam government's time in office.

Also to consider was the matter of the role of the Crown. Some people were incredulous that a representative of the monarchy had intervened in the affairs of a democratic system, and some others pointed out that Kerr appeared to have exercised powers far in excess of those exercised by the Queen he was supposed to be representing. The counter argument was made by those who simply referred to the written word of the Australian Constitution. Read literally, the governor-general did indeed have the power to intervene in the dispute in the way that he did.

Kerr's argument: Parliamentary Responsibility

Sir John Kerr was to become a target of abuse, especially among Labor supporters who felt he had acted in a partisan manner. Amid the wide-ranging criticism he sustained as a result of the 1975 crisis, Kerr's reasoning as to why he acted the way he did tended to be overlooked.

In addition to arguing that he had an obligation to exercise the powers he believed the Constitution bestowed on him, Kerr provided an interesting insight into how he saw the application of the idea of Responsible Government in Australia. Kerr's published reasons agreed that Australia was a Westminster system, but, he pointed out, it was a Westminster system applied to a federal system with the Senate being the house of the states. He further argued that this rationale meant that Responsible Government in Australia embraced the idea of popular will (the House of Representatives) and the will of the federated states (the Senate). So was born Kerr's doctrine of *Parliamentary Responsibility*.

The test, he noted in the best Westminster tradition, was the fate of supply. In the Australian situation, a Responsible Government had to get its Budget through both the House of Representatives *and* the Senate. As Kerr put it, a government that can't secure supply in these circumstances must either advise the Crown of its intention to resign, or it must expect to be dismissed.

After the crisis

As contentious as the 1975 crisis was, little of the Australian constitutional arrangements that allowed the crisis to occur have changed. In fact, the only real change was a successful referendum in 1977 that altered the casual Senate vacancy-filling provision (Section 15). The previous convention that had been broken in 1975 was restored, this time as a constitutional provision that a vacating senator must be replaced by someone from the same party — the only reference, incidentally, to the idea of a political party in all of the document.

Other attempts at reform have failed. In 1988, a referendum to institute fixed parliamentary terms (thereby denying the power of the Senate to force early elections) was defeated. In 1999, a referendum to replace the position of governor-general with a head of state and to convert Australia from a constitutional monarchy to a republic also failed. (Refer to Chapter 2 for more on the push for a republic.)

The contradictory principles contained in Australia's constitutional practice that were exposed by the 1975 crisis are still very much in place.

VOTE 1

IN THIS CHAPTER

» **Exploring the history of the physical structure of the parliament**

» **Meeting the important people in the parliament**

» **Understanding the operation and rituals of a Westminster parliament**

» **Creating and implementing laws through parliamentary process**

» **Exploring methods of debate and discussion**

Chapter **6**

Parliament: The House on the Hill

Parliament House in Canberra is the iconic building where the operation of Australian politics in its parliamentary form is undertaken. It's a massive building that dominates the Canberra skyline, but is clearly not just a functional building where the parliamentary politics of governing Australia goes on. It is also a recognisable symbol of the idea of parliamentary government.

The national parliament on Capital Hill in Canberra isn't the only important parliament house in Australia. Because Australia is a federation, each of the state parliaments is just as significant as the national house, and the two territories also have their Legislative Assemblies.

In this chapter, we look at the physical configuration of Australian parliaments and how the various roles within the parliamentary structure interact. We examine how parliaments vote and how they debate legislation, as well as the various mechanisms in place to promote (and, in some cases, hinder) discussion of policies and other issues.

Housing the Houses of Parliament

The fact that the Australian system of government is primarily of the Westminster type is most readily identifiable in the way each of the Australian parliaments is structured and how it works. A British visitor to Australia, familiar with the operation of the parliament in London's Westminster, would immediately feel at home in any of the Australian parliaments.

Although smaller in size (the British House of Commons has over 600 members while Australia's House of Representatives has 151 MPs), the Australian parliaments mostly use the same livery of green upholstery for the lower house and red for the upper house (the Western Australian lower house has blue carpeting). Australian parliaments also use the same presiding officers and basically the same procedures and rituals. And, most importantly of all, the parliaments are the place where the prime minister, or premier, and the Cabinet are found.

An American visiting Australia's national parliament would be familiar with a Senate, but would find the operation of the Australian parliament to be completely different from the way the US Congress is structured.

The new house

In 1988, on the bicentenary of the arrival of the First Fleet in New South Wales, Queen Elizabeth II officially opened the newly completed national parliament of Australia at Capital Hill in Canberra, shown in Figure 6-1. The modern parliamentary building — known at the time as New Parliament House — had always been planned to be built at its present location. A major parliament building was part of the design for Canberra put together by Walter and Marion Burley Griffin, the American-based architects commissioned to plan Canberra in 1913 after the site had been selected in 1908. The modern parliament building was commenced in 1978 after Italian architect Romaldo Giurgola's design was selected.

First impressions of the building? Well, it certainly is big. All members of the House of Representatives and the Senate have their own offices. The offices cluster around the two parliamentary chambers. In between the chambers is Queen's Hall. At the back of the new parliament building are the executive offices — that is, the offices of the prime minister and the ministers. Check out Figure 6-2 for a plan.

VOTE 1

The new parliament building has its own eating facilities, a gymnasium and a pool, and even a meditation room. Most of the parliament is closed off to the public, and the prime ministerial office even has its own vehicle access so that the media and the public can be avoided if the PM wishes. When parliament is sitting, the place is full of MPs, their political staff, a massive media entourage, service and facility staff, and security staff. In other words, the parliament becomes a city within a city and a place definitely worth visiting when in Canberra.

FIGURE 6-1:
New Parliament
House officially
opened its doors
in 1988.

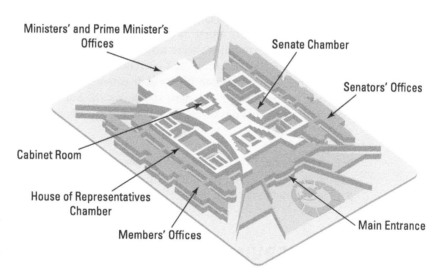

Ministers' and Prime Minister's
Offices

Senate Chamber

Senators' Offices

Cabinet Room

FIGURE 6-2:
Floor plan of
Australia's
Parliament
House.

House of Representatives
Chamber

Members' Offices

Main Entrance

The old house

The proper name of what is now called Old Parliament House was the Provisional Parliament House, shown in Figure 6-3. It's a rather more understated building than the new Parliament House, constructed as a temporary parliament until the completion of a permanent building. Today it sits just a little down the hill from its replacement. The Provisional Parliament House was opened in 1927 — long before work on the new parliament building began. To generations of Australians, it looked as if the provisional building would be the permanent home of national government.

FIGURE 6-3:
Old Parliament House now serves as the Museum of Australian Democracy.

VOTE 1

Old Parliament House was characterised by a lack of space. Until the 1950s, female MPs didn't have toilets either. MPs often had to share offices and, even up until the 1970s, the female toilets were insufficient. The main entry was up the steps and into King's Hall, meaning that everyone — politicians, the media, members of the public — all mingled in the Hall where the Senate and Representatives chambers opened onto. By modern standards, the building was a security nightmare, but, in the old days, the place had a very democratic feel, as MPs and the public came into close contact.

Before Provisional Parliament House was opened, the national parliament was located in the Victorian parliament in Spring Street, Melbourne. (The Victorian parliament had to decamp to the Melbourne Town Hall during this time.)

STILL SERVING THE COUNTRY

The depth of sympathy for the old building was very noticeable on the completion of the new parliament building. Under the original plan, Provisional Parliament House was to be demolished, so that New Parliament House would dominate Capital Hill. This plan was abandoned, however, and the old parliament building survives today as the Museum of Australian Democracy.

Westminster parliaments: An overview

The Westminster system is an adversarial system, as we explain in Chapter 4, and Westminster parliaments are adversarial parliaments. This key point is the first one you need to grasp, for it influences the way the parliamentary chambers are set up.

REMEMBER

In Australian parliaments, both the upper and lower houses have an adversarial configuration. On one side of the chamber — always to the right of the presiding officer — sits the government. To the left of the presiding officer sits the opposition. Members of parliament sit according to whether they support the government or the opposition. Whenever a vote is taken on the floor of the parliamentary chamber, the presiding officer asks those who intend to vote aye to move to the right and those who intend to vote no to move to the left.

The Westminster parliament is intended as a place of debate. Here are a few of the things that most of the parliament's time is spent on:

>> **Debating:** Usually the debates are over pieces of proposed legislation that, if passed, become law.

>> **Asking and responding to questions:** A specific session of parliament is set aside for backbenchers and the opposition to ask questions of the government, about general issues or specifics on legislation or policy (see the section 'Question Time' later in this chapter).

>> **Representing constituents:** Members of parliament can make representations on behalf of their constituents on particular local matters, asking questions of relevant ministers.

>> **Accepting petitions from citizens:** Petitions come in many forms, but are mostly from interest groups or other representative organisations such as community groups.

>> **Voting:** When all is said and done, the parliament votes on proposed legislation.

COLOUR MY (PARLIAMENTARY) WORLD

The Australian parliaments almost universally recreate the British parliament at Westminster. The House of Representatives, like the House of Commons, is furnished in green, while the Senate, like the House of Lords, is in red. The shades of green and red used in the Australian parliamentary chambers were chosen to represent the tones apparent in Australian nature. In almost all the state parliaments, the Legislative Assemblies are in green, and the Legislative Councils are furnished in red. Only Western Australia goes against this tradition, and uses blue in its Legislative Assembly instead of green.

Never the twain shall meet?

In Britain, the Commons and the Lords are also adversaries whose antipathies date back to the 1600s at least. The English Civil War in 1649 was a triumph of the House of Commons over the House of Lords (the House of Lords was abolished for some fifty years thereafter). The Lords and the Crown were considered to have been in league with each other, and upon the restoration of both institutions it was made very clear that the Commons was now the dominant house. For this reason, the British Queen or King can't and doesn't ever attend the House of Commons when required at parliament. In modern times, the sovereign is only ever required at Westminster to deliver the Queen's Speech at the beginning of every new parliament (this speech is written, of course, by the government). The Queen can only deliver this speech at the House of Lords.

The antipathy between the Commons and the Lords is reinforced in parliamentary ritual. MPs from one house don't normally mention the other house directly, preferring instead to refer euphemistically to 'that other place'. Believe it or not, this notion of the common house refusing to acknowledge the aristocratic house applies in Australia, even though our upper houses are directly elected and Australia has no aristocracy. Even the Senate gets caught up in this ritual, with senators refusing to refer directly to the Representatives in their speeches. And the governor-general delivers the Australian equivalent of the Queen's Speech at the beginning of a new Australian parliament only in the Senate, with the House of Representatives invited (not commanded) to attend and listen.

Who's Who? Putting People in Their Place

You would be forgiven for thinking that the most important person in the parliament is the prime minister; however, technically, when it comes to the actual running of the parliamentary chambers, the most important person is actually the presiding officer.

Beyond that position, both houses of parliament have numerous positions for both the government and the opposition, all with clearly defined roles, parts to play and rituals to observe.

The Speaker

The presiding officer of the lower house is the Speaker. The Speaker is responsible for the running of the house and works with the leaders of the government and the opposition to work out the running order of debates, the order that questions are asked and other such procedural matters. The lower houses have rulebooks for their operation called the *Standing Orders*, and the Speaker ensures that the Standing Orders are applied and adhered to by other members of the house.

Keeping order and dispensing discipline in the context of the operation of the chamber are some of the most important functions of the Speaker. Most people know the Speaker as the person who sits in a grand chair at the head of the lower house constantly muttering (or, if needed, shouting) 'Order! Order!' in a bid to bring unruly parliamentarians to heel. In more extreme circumstances, the Speaker may name unruly MPs and have them expelled from the house for a period of time.

The Speaker has an officer of the parliament to assist in disciplinary tasks called the *Sergeant at Arms*. The Sergeant at Arms carries the *mace* (the big ceremonial baton that sits in the house to signify that the Speaker is in the chair) and, when an MP is expelled from the services of the house, the Sergeant at Arms escorts the member out.

Sometimes the Speaker wears ceremonial dress when in the chair, comprising a black gown and a wig not unlike those worn by barristers and judges. In Australia, the modern practice has been to not wear the wig. Labor Speakers have also jettisoned the gown.

In Britain, the Speaker is meant to be an independent umpire in managing the conduct of the Commons. The British MP who becomes Speaker is guaranteed of contesting his electoral seat without opposition. In other words, the Speaker is expected to be independent of party politics. In Australia, however, the Speaker remains part of the party system and is usually elected by the party with the majority of seats (that is, the government). The impartiality of Australian Speakers is, therefore, always subject to doubt.

THE DANGERS OF BEING SPEAKER

The Speaker's job was, in the late 1600s, a dangerous one. In those times, the Speaker communicated between the parliament and the Crown. On occasions, a Speaker would return from meeting with the sovereign to inform the Commons that its legislation had been rejected by the Crown. The Commons would show its displeasure by executing the Speaker. As a result, the Speaker employed a disciplinarian, the Sergeant at Arms, to defend him against unruly members, as well as to ensure that the Speaker's discipline of members was carried out. The Sergeant at Arms carried a mace to use as a weapon. Both the Sergeant at Arms and the Mace have survived in to the modern era. Today, a curious Westminster ritual can occur to pay homage to the threat to Speakers past. When an MP is elected to be Speaker, she's expected to remain in her seat until she's 'dragged' to the chair by fellow MPs in a show of reluctance.

The President

The presiding officer of the Australian Senate (and the state Legislative Councils) is called the *President*. The President performs exactly the same functions in the Senate as the Speaker performs in the lower house. The President also has an enforcer — in this instance, the upper house aide to the President is called the *Usher of the Black Rod*. The black rod is the upper house equivalent of the mace (see the preceding section, 'The Speaker', for more information).

Frontbenchers and backbenchers

In the House of Representatives, the Speaker sits at the head of the chamber. To the left sits the opposition, and to the right, the government. The government (that is, all of the ministers and parliamentary secretaries) sit at the very front row of benches, with the Cabinet occupying positions closest to the Speaker and the parliamentary secretaries sitting way out towards the middle runway of the house. Figure 6-4 maps out who sits where in the House of Representatives.

Because ministers occupy the front row of the seating, they're often referred to as *frontbenchers*. This term is important because it demarcates the government from those MPs who aren't in the government but who support the government by voting for it in the house. These non-government MPs who support the government are known as *backbenchers*.

The opposition has the same configuration. The shadow ministers sit in the front row of the bank of benches to the Speaker's left, and behind them sit the opposition backbenchers.

VOTE 1

The Australian parliamentary configuration differs from the House of Commons in one interesting way. In the House of Commons, the Prime Minister and Leader of the Opposition sit with their colleagues on the frontbench. In Australia, however, the Prime Minister and the Leader of the Opposition (as officially recognised roles) each have a chair at the central table. The Australian state parliaments have a similar arrangement for the premiers.

The crossbenchers

The *crossbenchers* refers to those MPs who don't belong to one or other of the major political parties that fill the government and opposition ranks. These MPs — members of the Australian Greens, for example — literally sit in between the phalanx of major party MPs, clustered behind the government or the official opposition. *Independent* MPs (that is, those MPs who have no party affiliation) also make up the crossbench.

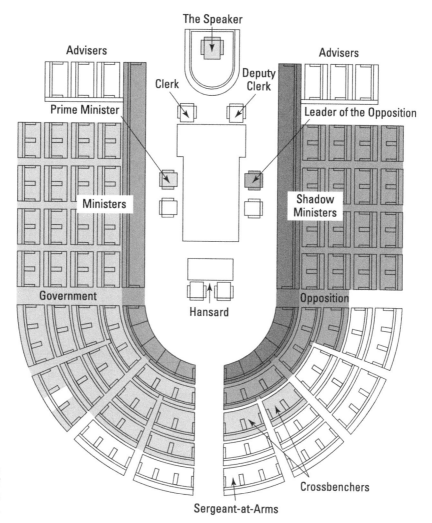

FIGURE 6-4:
The House of
Representatives
seating plan.

In the Senate?

Exactly the same configurations apply in the Senate, shown in Figure 6-5 (and in the state Legislative Councils, except in Tasmania where most councillors are actually independents), as can be found in the House of Representatives. Senators sit in party blocks to the left or right of the President, depending on which major party is in government in the lower house. So, the party that has a majority of seats in the lower house sits to the right of the President, even though that party may not have a majority in the Senate.

Because the usual practice is for some ministers to be senators, the Senate also has a frontbench of ministers and a shadow ministry on the opposite frontbench.

As with the lower house, a chair sits at the central table for the Leader of the Government in the Senate (an officially recognised position) and the Leader of the Opposition in the Senate (also officially recognised). Both leaders are selected by their respective parties and are charged with leading their parties in the Senate.

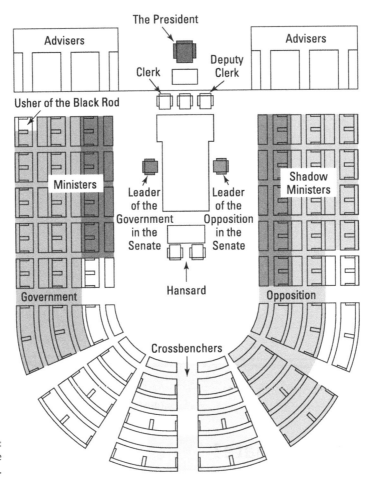

FIGURE 6-5:
The Senate
seating plan.

VOTE 1

The use of proportional representation as the electoral system for the Senate (and all the mainland state Legislative Councils) means that many more crossbenchers (independents and members of minor parties) are in the upper house than the lower house. This weighting can make for interesting and difficult times for governments as they may need to negotiate (and make deals concerning policy) with independents and minor party senators to try to get their parliamentary bills through the upper house.

The Whips

The term *Whip* comes from fox hunting in England, referring to the person who was responsible for 'whipping' the hunting dogs (not literally) into a pack to chase the fox. In parliament, the term refers to a number of MPs who play a very important role in assisting the organisation of the affairs of each of the houses.

Both houses have a manager of business for both the government and the opposition, whose job it is to set the order that bills will be considered and what the business of the parliament will be each day. The Manager of Government Business (usually a senior minister but not the prime minister) is particularly important, because this person outlines the government's legislative program for the house.

The Whips (in Australia, the government and opposition each have a Whip and a Deputy Whip) assist these managers. The Whip is a member of the main political party in government, with a counterpart in the main party of opposition, who organises backbench MPs on things such as voting and attendance in parliament. Whips also assist ministers in organising the asking of questions at Question Time (see the next section).

Question Time

Question Time is crucial to Westminster parliaments. It's the session when backbench MPs may ask questions of ministers, and the opposition may ask questions of the government. When backbenchers are asking the questions, it's usually MPs from the party in government. They usually ask friendly questions known as *Dorothy Dixers* of their party colleagues, who happen to be ministers or even the prime minister. Opposition questions usually come from the leader or from shadow ministers. Question Time is important for the opposition, and it can try to use this time to embarrass the government or pressure a minister over matters of policy. Question Time is also keenly observed and reported by the media.

Pairing

No, pairing doesn't refer to a Westminster parliament's ability to act as a match-making service. Rather, pairing is one of the most brilliant examples of the importance of the Whips and of the assumption of a certain degree of fairness in the operation of a parliamentary chamber.

WHIP IT!

The Whips are at their most noticeable on those occasions when an actual vote is taken on the floor of the parliamentary chamber. In such a situation, after asking MPs to go to the left or the right of the chair, depending on whether they are voting aye or no, the Speaker appoints the Whips to tally the result. The Whips are a sign of the way modern Westminster parliamentary practice has now become inextricably linked with the party system.

The Whips are there to ensure that party-aligned parliamentarians vote as a block. The government Whip is there to ensure that backbench support for the ministry is solid. The use of party discipline has assisted the Whip significantly in undertaking this role. Government and opposition Whips also may find occasions where they have to consult each other to ensure the smooth operation of their respective chambers.

Pairing occurs when the government and opposition Whips get together to deal with unforeseen absences from the chamber — a matter that could be really important if, for example, the government's majority was very narrow when voting on a bill takes place. If an MP from the governing party were absent for personal or professional reasons, the government Whip asks the opposition Whip to ensure that an opposition party MP is also absent from voting. Unfortunately for the opposition, pairing is only relevant for government MPs (not the other way round). This practice is based on the assumption that the composition of the house was determined by the election, and that the sense of majority given to the government by the voters should be preserved in the functioning of the house.

Voting in the Parliament

Electors vote for candidates to represent them in parliament. The elected representatives are usually bonded together by political parties. Most MPs sit either as backbenchers supporting the government or backbenchers supporting the official opposition. A few may sit on the crossbenches.

When in their respective parliamentary chambers, the business of the parliament revolves around MPs being asked to cast their vote on a range of issues. Voting may be on a bill or a procedure. In any case, the way voting is conducted in a Westminster parliament is interesting and can be a little perplexing, especially to those not used to the ways of the British system and who expect to see a record of every vote taken by MPs.

Casual observers of voting in the parliament are often perplexed at the way the Speaker in the lower house often says, 'The question is that the motion be agreed to — those in favour say aye; those against say no. I think the ayes have it.' And scarcely a vote appears to be cast. Moreover, sometimes hardly any MPs are in the chamber when the vote is taken or, indeed, many more opposition MPs than government MPs are present when the Speaker goes through this ritual.

What the Speaker does here is simply consider that the motion will be resolved in the way the government wants it to be resolved. The rigid party discipline that dominates the parliament (refer to Chapter 4) means the Speaker knows that the government will get a majority if a formal vote is taken.

Ring the bells! The division

The opposition MPs have the right to call for a division. A *division* is a formal vote. If a division is called, the Speaker instructs the clerk of the house to 'ring the bells'. A bell then rings throughout the parliament to indicate to all MPs that their presence is required in their particular chamber to participate in a formal vote. After a period, the doors are locked, and the Whips tally the votes. The result is usually the same every time — the government wins the vote, unless large numbers of government MPs cross the floor (in which case, the government is in crisis).

VOTE 1

The time allowed for MPs to get to the chamber was increased in 1988 from three minutes to four minutes because the new Parliament House is so much bigger than the old one, and MPs found it took longer to get to their respective chambers when divisions were called. But the size of parliament still means that senators have to be fleet of foot to get into the Senate before the doors are locked.

Crossing the floor

When the bells ring for a division and a formal vote is taken in either the House of Representatives or the Senate, MPs normally vote as a party block — a situation that's reinforced by the Whips, whose job it is to make sure that MPs vote as their party and their leader wish them to vote. Occasionally, however, an MP defies the party and the wishes of the Whips, and votes with the other side. When this happens, an MP has to physically cross from one side of the chamber to the other to register this vote, known as *crossing the floor*. This occurrence is rare in the highly disciplined world of party politics, but it can happen. An MP who crosses the floor usually does so on a matter of personal principle.

Conscience voting

Nearly all parliamentary votes are subject to the overarching discipline of the Whips, who, of course, act on behalf of their party. Occasionally, the government decides that an issue may be voted on in the parliament without it directing how it wants its MPs to vote via the Whips. Such votes are known as *conscience votes*, because MPs are allowed to vote on an issue according to the way they personally feel about the matter, rather than being told how to vote by the Whips.

Government rules, OK?

The situation in the Australian parliament replicates the British tendency towards executive tyranny. But because of the difficulty parties have in being able to win majorities in both the lower house and the upper house, the possibility of the government in Australia not being able to get everything its own way when dealing with the parliament is very real. In this contest, Australia's upper houses — and especially the Australian Senate — have a very big reputation for frustrating the will of the executive. We look at how the government dominates the operation of parliament in Chapter 4.

Making Laws in the Parliament

One of the key functions undertaken by the parliament is to make laws. A law begins its existence as a bill that's debated in parliament and, if passed by both houses, makes it into our legal system by way of an Act of Parliament.

Proposed legislation that comes before the parliament for debate and for ratification (or perhaps rejection) is called a *bill*. A bill doesn't become law until it has passed the parliament and has obtained royal assent, as we outline in Chapter 3.

The life of a bill begins in Cabinet, where the government decides on a policy and then asks the public service to draft the necessary legislation that would need to come into effect to enable the policy to be realised in the public realm. The draft legislation that results becomes the bill.

The bill is introduced to the parliament by the responsible minister (refer to Chapter 4 for more on the convention of Ministerial Responsibility). The first time a bill is dealt with in the parliament is known as the *first reading*, and usually takes the form of the Clerk of the House (an official position designed to assist the presiding officer) reading the title of the bill. Ministers can come from either the upper or lower house, so the first reading takes place in the chamber in which the relevant minister resides.

After the first reading, comes — yes, you guessed it — the *second reading*. Here the responsible minister outlines the reasons the government is pursuing its policies and, indeed, why the bill is being introduced. The shadow minister from the opposition then makes a speech outlining the opposition's views on the bill. The debate is then adjourned.

The next stage of the bill is the *committee* stage. Here the Speaker or President vacates the chair, and another MP, designated as Chairperson of Committees, takes over the running of the house. The bill is then debated and voted on, clause by clause. At this point, the parliamentary chamber (usually in the form of the opposition) can move amendments to the bill.

After the bill has gone through committee, it's subject to a *third reading*, which usually involves the Speaker or President resuming the chair and being informed by the Chairperson of Committees that the bill has gone through the committee stage.

The bill then goes to the next parliamentary chamber to go through exactly the same process.

Amended bills

If the second chamber, either the upper or lower house, depending on where the originating minister sits, amends the bill at its committee stage, the amended bill returns to the first chamber. The first chamber then has to decide if it accepts the amendments. If the first chamber agrees, the bill is agreed to and then goes through to the Executive in Council for royal assent. The bill then becomes law through an Act of Parliament.

TECHNICAL STUFF

Things get complicated if amendments aren't accepted. The failure of the first chamber to accept the second chamber's amendments means that the bill is defeated. What happens next depends on the rulebook specific to that parliament (refer to Chapter 5). In the case of the Australian state parliaments, all sorts of complicated mechanisms exist where the leaders of government and opposition in both houses meet in what's usually called a *Joint House Management Committee* to try to work out some compromises and get the bill through.

In the federal parliament, as Chapter 5 outlines, Section 57 of the Constitution can come into play if a bill is defeated twice over a three-month period.

Legislating: The Representatives versus the Senate

In the federal parliament, for all practical purposes, the House of Representatives is usually where bills begin their life, and the Senate becomes the second chamber doing the reviewing. Governments like to start the legislative process in the lower house because they know they command majority support there.

The problem that can arise when the responsible minister is from the Senate is overcome by the practice of having ministers in the lower house who represent the responsible minister. The opposition can try to move amendments at the committee stage in the lower house, but this is a futile exercise. The government, controlling the numbers in the lower house, will simply vote these amendments down. In fact, the government can use its numbers to hasten the debate by imposing *gags* to stop an opposition member from making a speech and applying the *guillotine* to the parliamentary debate by imposing stringent timeframes to deny time to the opposition (see the sidebar 'Of gags and guillotines').

The government's ability to impose gags or guillotines in the Senate depends on the numbers, and the usual situation in Australian politics is that the government doesn't have a majority in the upper house. So, the opposition has much more scope to have their amendments (moved at the committee stage in the Senate) taken much more seriously.

TECHNICAL STUFF

OF GAGS AND GUILLOTINES

Not just items used to dispense with the aristocracy in the French Revolution, gags and guillotines are also procedures available to the government in a Westminster parliamentary chamber to control the way it operates and help the government get its bills through the parliament quickly.

A *gag* occurs when the government moves to stop a speech being made by the opposition. The Manager of Government Business (usually a frontbencher) moves that 'the member for [wherever] no longer be heard' and the government-supporting backbenchers vote accordingly.

A *guillotine* is used when the government sets stringent timeframes for the passage of a bill. This usually involves denying time to the opposition to make speeches or move amendments during the committee stage.

Facing a majority of opposition numbers in the Senate, Australian governments can do one of two things. They can either try to negotiate with some or all of the opposition and trade off support for some opposition amendments in exchange for passage of the bill through the upper house, or the government can refuse to deal with the opposition and leave the matter to Section 57 of the Constitution (refer to Chapter 5).

The People's Forum or a Rubber Stamp?

In an era of politics when the major political parties are so dominant, some political pundits debate the very role of parliament. Critics worry that disciplined party politics is undermining the idea of the parliament as a forum. They argue that the 'tyranny of the executive' (refer to Chapter 4) is a reflection of the dominance of the parties and the way they stop MPs from being representatives of the regions they've been elected from. They also point out that, if both houses of parliament end up being controlled by the same party, parliament simply becomes a 'rubber stamp' for the executive.

The counterargument to this rationale rests on two points. First, the parliament is dominated by the political parties because that's the way the voters choose to elect their representatives, whether anyone likes it or not. Second, parliamentarians themselves still see their role more in the Westminster tradition of a forum for debate and discussion rather than simply as a place to approve Cabinet's legislative program. The tendency for Australian voters to deny the party of government in the lower house a majority in the upper house means that, at the end of the day, parliament still has a meaningful role to play in the day-to-day political debate.

To be a member of parliament is still important, with scope for an individual MP to have an impact on the political debate.

Adjournments and grievances

The parliamentary process allows time for backbench MPs to discuss matters. *Grievance debates* allow MPs to raise issues of concern, and *adjournment debates* are an opportunity for an MP to make a quick speech on any matter she wishes to address.

Newly elected MPs are also accorded a special time to make their first parliamentary speeches (these used to be called *maiden speeches*, but this term has fallen out of favour because of its rather sexist overtones). By convention, first speeches are listened to with great respect and it's not the done thing for MPs to heckle or interject.

A privileged position

MPs also enjoy a number of protections as a result of being in the parliament. The rules of engagement in a parliamentary chamber — known as the *Standing Orders* — outline a list of behaviours that are considered unparliamentary and so aren't permitted. (It's up to the presiding officers of the chambers to apply the Standing Orders.)

One legal protection given to MPs is that of *parliamentary privilege*, which means that MPs' utterances and speeches made in the parliament are protected from defamation and libel laws. This protection is supposed to allow for a full and frank exchange of views in the parliament. It's thought to derive from an original intention to allow commoners to attack the Crown, the aristocracy and/or the church, back in the time when the parliament and the Crown were involved in their power struggle over which institution would govern Britain (refer to Chapter 4).

The rise of standing committees

The emergence of parliamentary standing committees has been another interesting development of mechanisms designed to give backbench MPs a more meaningful role to play in governing. Borrowing from the American congressional practice, *standing committees* are committees of backbench MPs brought together to inquire into specific policy matters.

One of the powers the Westminster parliament has is to call people to give evidence before it (just like the courts). The technical term for parliament to secure a witness is known as a *subpoena*. Refusing to answer a parliamentary subpoena is a contempt of parliament that can be punishable by imprisonment.

Using this power as its basis, standing committees are formed and hold inquiries by subpoenaing witnesses to give evidence. This process usually involves calling up public servants, although here a problem arises in that a backbencher seeking information from a public servant contradicts the Westminster principle that public servants should be answerable only to the responsible minister (refer to Chapter 4 for more on the convention of Ministerial Responsibility).

VOTE 1

The power of parliamentary committees was illustrated in 2009, when it was revealed that Godwin Grech, a public servant in the treasury, had fabricated an email from the prime minister's office regarding the OzCar scheme. It was later revealed that Grech had acted in a partisan way to support the then leader of the opposition, Malcolm Turnbull.

TIP

You can check out the work of the committees of the Australian parliament on the parliament's website at www.aph.gov.au/Parliamentary_Business/Committees.

What about Hung Parliaments?

Hung parliaments are rare in the Australian parliament, because the voting system and single-member electorates are geared towards manufacturing a majority for either of the major parties.

Hung parliaments tend to occur in state parliaments more often than the federal parliament, mainly because the state lower houses have fewer seats than the House of Representatives. Hung parliaments are most likely in Tasmania, because its lower house has only 25 seats and the use of proportional representation as its voting system always results in close outcomes.

When hung parliaments do occur, the question of who will form a government becomes very difficult and can only be determined after negotiations between the parties and any independents who may have won a lower house seat at the last election.

REMEMBER

A parliament is considered to be 'hung' if no party or coalition or combination of parties has won enough seats to enable it to muster enough members to have a majority in the lower house. (The lower house is the House of Representatives in the federal parliament, or the Legislative Assembly in state parliaments.) In this case, if some MPs in the lower house aren't usually supporters of one or other of the major parties (they may be independents or be from a minor party), they're considered to be holding the balance of power, in that they eventually decide which party can form government. (See Chapter 8 for an overview of the party system in Australia.)

The other way in which a hung parliament can occur is when both major parties have an equal number of seats (no minor parties, no independents, no cross-benchers). This last happened in 1961.

At the time of writing, the House of Representatives has 151 lower house seats, so, in order to win government, a party must have the support of at least 76 members of the House of Representatives. These MPs must be prepared to vote for the government in the event of a motion of *no confidence* and/or to vote for it when it brings down its annual Budget. A government that loses a confidence motion is obliged to inform the governor-general of this event and the prime minister would tender her resignation. Likewise, if a government could not get the House of Representatives to pass its Budget bills, the government is obliged to resign.

How common are hung parliaments?

Australia's political history suggests that predicting a hung parliament is like predicting a draw in a grand final. They are extremely rare. However, they do occur.

VOTE 1

The general election in 1940 resulted in a hung parliament. This election occurred just as World War II began. In this election, the coalition of the United Australia Party (UAP) and Country Party, led by Robert Menzies, was supported by two independents, which gave the coalition a majority over the Labor Party. (For more on the UAP, see Chapter 10.) Later, these two independents crossed the floor, voting with the opposition, to throw their support behind the Labor Party. The UAP government had to resign and, in its place, Labor's John Curtin was able to advise the governor-general that his party now had majority support in the House of Representatives and that he should be sworn in as prime minister. (For more on the history of the Labor Party, see Chapter 9.)

THE 2010 MINORITY FEDERAL GOVERNMENT

For the first time since 1961, the 2010 federal election ended in an almost equal number of seats for Labor and the Coalition. And, for the first time since 1940, the question of which major party would be able to govern was in the hands of independent MPs.

With a handful of independents and a Green holding the balance of power in the House of Representatives after the 2010 election, both the caretaker prime minister and the opposition leader entered into dialogue with the crossbench MPs. After about two weeks of negotiations, Prime Minister Julia Gillard was able to announce that she could form a minority government with the support of the Greens and three of the four independents in the lower house.

To be able to declare the ability to form government, the Labor prime minister had to agree to a range of policy outcomes for the constituents of the independent MPs, as well as agreeing to undertake reform of the way the House of Representatives does its work.

In the 1961 federal election, both Labor and the coalition won 37 seats each. Two of Labor's seats, however, were from the Northern Territory and the ACT and, in those days, those MPs had limited voting rights in the lower house. Menzies was thus able to claim a two-seat majority and become the prime minister.

The most recent example of a hung parliament occurred in 2010 — see the nearby sidebar for more information.

REMEMBER

Hung parliaments have been more common in the smaller lower houses of the states. Since the 1990s, hung parliaments (and, as a consequence, minority governments) have occurred in Victoria, South Australia and New South Wales, and in Tasmania and the ACT, where proportional representation (such as is used for the federal upper house, the Senate) is used to elect the lower house. For more on the difference between proportional representation and preferential voting, see Chapter 13.

Who governs while the crossbenchers are making up their minds?

Government doesn't stop just because a hung parliament has eventuated. When an election is called, the prime minister (or premier, in the case of the states) and the ministry stay in place in what is known as *caretaker mode*, ensuring government continues but in a minimal form, undertaking no new policy decisions, initiatives or appointments (see Chapter 14). This ministry normally stays in place until an election is held and the outcome is clear enough to allow the caretaker prime minister to tell the governor-general she is able to form a new government (this can happen as soon as the day after the election). In the case of a hung parliament, however, caretaker mode is maintained until the newly elected House of Representatives can meet and then decide who it supports as the next government.

Each Australian state and the national system have constitutional rules for the calling together of the lower house after an election. In the main, these constitutions require the lower house to meet not later than 30 days after the return of the election writs (that is, at the official completion of the electoral process). The caretaker government stays in place until the lower house meets.

In the event of a hung parliament, the caretaker prime minister or premier stays in place until an agreement between the parties and the crossbenchers is reached as to which major party will form government and what sort of government it will be (that is, minority or coalition — see the 'Minority or coalition?' section, later in this chapter, for an explanation of the difference).

The role of the governor

The fact that the positions of governor and governor-general are outlined in the respective state and federal constitutions gives a sense in which the representatives of the Crown may be involved in the matter of resolving a deadlocked parliament. Under the conventions of Westminster practice, the Crown can only act on the advice of the prime minister, provided the prime minister is assured of having the majority support of the lower house.

VOTES OF 'NO CONFIDENCE'

A vote of no confidence occurs when an MP (usually from the opposition and usually the opposition leader) moves that the business of the lower house be suspended to allow a vote on a question of confidence in the government. An opposition wouldn't normally do this unless it was sure of winning the resulting vote. If the vote is taken and a majority of members in the lower house vote for the motion, the government is deemed to have been defeated and the prime minister (or premier) is obliged to resign and advise the governor-general (or governor) to call on the opposition leader to see if he can form a government.

If the caretaker prime minister were to lose the support of the lower house, the advice that should be tended to the Crown is that the governor or governor-general should call the opposition leader to see if he can form a government.

The key Westminster principles (refer to Chapters 4 and 5) that apply are

>> The matter of whom shall form a government is determined by the lower house.

>> The advice furnished to the Crown (that is, the governor-general or, in state politics, the governor) shall come from the prime minister (or premier), but should be good advice in that the next principle is observed.

>> All possible options for forming a government derived from the last election should be tested before a new election is called.

>> If the lower house cannot clearly resolve the question of the formation of a government, the advice that can be furnished to the Crown (the governor-general or the governor) should be that of calling fresh elections.

Minority or coalition?

Basically, a hung parliament where crossbenchers hold the balance of power can be resolved in one of two ways.

The formation of a coalition government is one possibility. In this situation, the *coalition* is understood to result from a political bargaining process, where the crossbenchers exchange promises of support for access to executive power, usually in the form of a position in the ministry. A government that has ministers from a minor party or incorporates an independent from the crossbench is thus considered to be a coalition government.

The formation of a *minority* government is the other alternative. In this instance, crossbench MPs may promise to support a government by voting for it in the lower house without actually demanding access to a ministerial position. Political deals may be done to achieve this support, but these tend to come in the form of letters of agreement about future policy commitments or even charters of political and/or policy behaviour. The key point of difference from a coalition government is that a minority government does not have members of the crossbench in the ministry.

COALITIONS AND MINORITIES: THE TASMANIAN EXPERIENCE

VOTE 1

A number of minority governments have been formed in state politics due to hung parliaments. Tasmania, with its proportionally elected lower house, has had the most extensive experience of minority and coalition governments as a result of hung parliaments. In 1989, five *green independent* MPs (independents with an environmental platform) were elected to the lower house, where they held the balance of power in a hung parliament. In the time between the election and the convening of the House of Assembly (this is technically what it is called in Tasmania), the green independents signed an accord with the ALP that allowed it to form a minority government. This agreement saw the defeat of the caretaker Liberal premier, Robin Gray.

In the 2010 Tasmanian election, the Australian Greens, by then a minor party, again won five seats and the balance of power. This time, the Greens negotiated a coalition agreement with the Labor Party. Unlike in 1989, the Greens this time demanded — and got — ministerial positions in the government. Tasmania then had a Labor–Green coalition government. (See Chapter 12 for more on the Greens.)

Stable or volatile?

The knife-edge margins associated with hung parliaments hint at the possibility of volatility. The example of the 1940 situation in the House of Representatives (refer to the section 'How common are hung parliaments?') showed how changes in the alignment of the crossbenchers can lead to changes in government without the need for an election to occur. The Tasmanian minority governments that happened in the 1990s didn't go their full term, yet the minority government of Victoria between 1999 and 2002 did nearly serve a full term and was never prone to dissolution or instability.

Most parliamentarians prefer to go as close to full term as they can in order to minimise the prospect of an early election that may result in very different outcomes or, in the case of the crossbench MPs, may result in them losing their seats. Hung parliaments, therefore, have the potential to be volatile, but they can be quite stable as well.

IN THIS CHAPTER

» **Dividing responsibilities between the Commonwealth and the states**

» **Exploring federal–state financial relations**

» **Examining both cooperative and adversarial federal–state relations**

» **Understanding the task of policy-making**

» **Weighing up the size of the public sector**

Chapter **7**

Governing the Great Southern Land

The point of politics is to be able to wield executive power, or at least influence the wielding of executive power. To wield executive power is to govern. The government of Australia involves more than just simply forming majorities in parliaments. The whole point of government is to be able to convert policy decisions into actual programs.

In Chapter 3, we examine the Australian Constitution in its role as the rulebook for the operation of the national parliament. In this chapter, we again examine the Constitution, this time because of its status as the legal document that outlines the division of governmental powers between the federal, or Commonwealth, government, and the states and territories. And we analyse the nature of the relationship between the federal and state governments, in terms of financial issues as well as the level of cooperation between them, and the role of the courts in settling disputes.

This chapter also delves into the roles that various bodies and positions, such as statutory authorities, departmental secretaries and ministerial advisers, play in creating public policy and putting it into action.

The Constitution and the Division of the Powers of Government

The Australian Constitution is the foundation legal document that outlines the division of governmental responsibilities between the two levels of government in Australia — the federal government (often referred to as the Commonwealth) and the states and territories. Local government exists in Australia, but, legally, it does so as a power of the state governments. Some state constitutions make reference to local government, but the general rule is that local government is subordinate to the state parliaments.

As a result of the negotiations that went on between the colonies in the lead-up to Federation, the system of national government was given a rather narrow set of specific responsibilities that the national parliament could legislate about. These powers are outlined in the Constitution. The Australian Constitution also outlines some shared powers. Beyond that, all other matters of government were meant to be left to the states.

REMEMBER

That the original intention of the constitutional framers was to have the Australian states retain the largest share of governmental responsibilities is very clear. Indeed, the states were intended to be the most important level of government. Also very clearly, this situation has changed quite a bit in more recent times.

Section 51

Section 51 of the Australian Constitution is arguably one of the more important in the document, because it outlines the powers given to the new national parliament by the federating colonies. The responsibilities originally outlined in this section partly reflect the reasons Australia's colonies were willing to federate. Many of the responsibilities outlined in Section 51 relate to matters of national security and external affairs, with some additional powers to manage matters such as currency and marriage. The Commonwealth parliament was given powers over corporations, but only foreign corporations. Likewise, the Commonwealth was given power to regulate imports and exports — mainly for financially strategic reasons.

The division of governing responsibility in Australia throws up three categories of powers — exclusive, concurrent and residual — as we briefly outline in Chapter 3.

Exclusive powers

These are powers that were given to the national parliament in order that policy be made in particular areas by the national government alone. The exclusive powers are mainly to do with defence, national security, the regulation of foreign people and foreign corporations, and the management of currencies and marriage.

Concurrent powers

These powers are shared between the Commonwealth and the states. Constitutionally, concurrent powers cover three areas, each of which has its own set of complications. These include industrial relations (complicated by the Howard government's Work Choices laws), the levying of income taxes (complicated by the 1942 changes to taxation arrangements — this topic is discussed a little later on in this chapter) and Aboriginal affairs (thanks to the 1967 referendum changes to Section 51, which we touch on in Chapter 2).

TECHNICAL STUFF

In matters of concurrency, Section 109 states that, where a state and a Commonwealth law conflict, the Commonwealth law will prevail. However, Section 109 only comes into effect if the Commonwealth has the power to make the law that's in conflict with the states. The task of determining the constitutional authority of Commonwealth laws falls to the High Court (see the section 'Uncooperative Federalism', later in this chapter, for more on settling disputes of this nature).

Residual powers

Any area of responsibility that isn't an exclusive power, or isn't subject to concurrency, is considered to be the concern of the states. The residual powers are actually quite substantial areas of policy responsibility. Technically, state governments have the power to make policy on health, education, transport, the criminal code, locally based corporations, local government, land use and land planning, and so on.

REMEMBER

Each state government has a long history of dealing with these matters, including the establishment and operation of public service departments and agencies that have been planning for and delivering services since the 1850s. In other words, the states have huge administrative capacity derived from their areas of policy responsibility. State government, then, is actually very important to the government of the country.

Federal–State Relations

The question of how the two levels of government relate to each other is vital to the day-to-day functioning of government in Australia. Federal–state relations are important in two matters in particular — how services are delivered and how Australia's public finances are managed.

The matter of federal–state relations is further complicated by the increasing tendency on the part of the Commonwealth to involve itself in a wider range of areas, including those responsibilities, such as health and education, that are supposed to be residual — the responsibility of the states.

The rise of the Commonwealth as a major player in policy-making is due to various reasons. Most importantly, federal power over policy tended to advance during moments of crisis. Three crises in particular — World War I, the Great Depression and World War II — saw the Commonwealth emerge as the important level of government that could coordinate the states. The use of emergency power in World War II was particularly important, because it saw a major piece of legislation passed — the Income Tax Act — that helped recast Australian federal–state financial relations in the modern period.

Adopting (and challenging) the Uniform Tax system

As part of its coordination of the war effort, John Curtin's Labor government decided that it would be necessary for the Commonwealth to take control of the levying of two important taxes — income tax and company tax — and introduce what became known as the Uniform Tax system. To do this, the government passed the *Income Tax Act 1942*, which increased Commonwealth income tax rates to raise more revenue. The legislation also included provision of reimbursement grants to the states — as long as they ceased to levy their own income taxes (previously, the states had levied such taxes).

The states weren't happy with this arrangement and, at the end of World War II, challenged the law in the High Court in 1947, in what became known as the First Uniform Tax case. The High Court found that the Commonwealth did have the power to levy income tax as a wartime measure. Then, in 1952, the two big states (New South Wales and Victoria) had another go at the law in the High Court — known, you guessed it, as the Second Uniform Tax case. This time the court argued that the Commonwealth had the power to levy income tax, but so too did the states — indeed, levying of income tax is a concurrent power.

TAXING TIMES

Thanks to the Income Tax Act and its consequences, Australians now pay their income tax and company tax to a Commonwealth taxation authority — the Australian Taxation Office (ATO), headed by the Chief Commissioner of Taxation. The ATO is part of the treasurer's portfolio and is charged with the collection of revenue to fund government services. You can even complete your tax returns on the ATO's website at www.ato.gov.au.

Trying to simplify the often complex structure of the Australian taxation system has been tackled numerous times throughout the nation's history. In 2008, the Future Tax System Review Panel was established to examine state and Commonwealth taxes. Informally known as the Henry Tax Review, it was intended to guide tax system reforms over the next 10 to 20 years.

Unfortunately, the review findings were handed in during the aftermath of the global financial crisis, and few of its recommendations have been adopted. One major item that was implemented by the Rudd Government was the creation of a resources Super Profit Tax. The proposal was highly controversial, and has been suggested as a key reason Rudd lost the prime ministership in 2010.

To check out a summary of the Henry Tax Review and its final report, go to treasury.gov.au/review/the-australias-future-tax-system-review/final-report.

VOTE 1

Since this ruling, the states have had the power to levy their own income taxes. The reason this hasn't occurred is political. Few state politicians would want to go to an election promising to levy an income tax in addition to federal taxes. For its part, the Commonwealth has refused to give up either income tax or company tax powers.

Controlling the purse strings

The matter of levying taxes and handing out large amounts of money constitutes the tricky world of federal–state financial relations. The subtext to this issue is an argument about which level of government is the more important, with one allegation being that the level of government that controls the purse strings is the dominant authority.

On this basis, the Commonwealth emerges as the more powerful level of government, notwithstanding the extensive residual powers in the hands of the states. The Commonwealth's power manifests itself in a number of ways — control of taxes and the manner in which those taxes flow back to the states, dominance in the setting of national economic policy, and a perceived imbalance between federal economic power and state responsibility.

THE GRANTS COMMISSION

A federal body exists to advise the Commonwealth on how much money should be allocated to each state and territory. This body is called the *Grants Commission*. Originally set up in the 1930s to advise the federal government on what emergency funds needed to be allocated to claimant states during the Great Depression, the body these days looks at the delivery of government services to all states. Its enabling legislation requires it to advise the Commonwealth on ways to allocate funds to the states to ensure that all Australians enjoy the same level of government services regardless of where they live. This policy means that the Commission often recommends that Queensland, Western Australia, South Australia, Tasmania and the Northern Territory get much higher per capita rates of federal funding than New South Wales and Victoria — a situation that always angers the premiers of the 'big states'.

What the Commonwealth takes it can also give away

One power the Commonwealth government has is control over the flow of money from income and company tax. The Commonwealth has a practical monopoly over these two major sources of revenue. The tax revenue flows to the Commonwealth via the ATO, and then the Commonwealth gives a large amount back to the states. Between 1947 and 2000 (when a new tax, the goods and services tax, or GST, was introduced), money was given back to the states as General Purpose Grants to be used by the states to fund their state-based programs and operations. Since 2000, these allocations have been called *General Purpose Financial Assistance to the States*.

Section 96: Specific Purpose Grants

Another source of Commonwealth power lies in Section 96 of the Australian Constitution. This section states that the Commonwealth can make financial grants to any of the states on 'such terms and conditions as the Parliament sees fit'. Originally intended as a source of emergency funding, after the Income Tax Act of 1942, Section 96 became the basis on which the federal government was able to involve itself in the state's residual responsibilities. These days, the Commonwealth has such financial power (thanks to the revenue it obtains from taxation) that it's in a position to make large annual allocations of funds to specific programs under Section 96. These allocations are known as *Specific Purpose Grants*.

Coordinating national economic policy

In 1927, a referendum was passed by the Australian public that altered Section 105 of the Constitution. A new section (105A) was inserted so the Commonwealth could take control of state debts, and future agreements about borrowing overseas capital for government purposes in Australia would have to be agreed to by both the Commonwealth and the states under the auspices of the Loan Council.

Originally, Loan Council decisions were made via a vote (each state had one vote; the Commonwealth had two votes). The Commonwealth's dominance of the council occurred with the advent of the Income Tax Act arrangements. The Commonwealth had the power to dictate terms if it wanted to, but an interesting political development occurred that circumvented the need for crude power politics. As it turned out, Western Australia, Tasmania, South Australia and Queensland found the new financial arrangements to their liking, because the Commonwealth was effectively using revenue raised in the most populous states (Victoria and New South Wales) to cross-subsidise the other states. So the Commonwealth could usually count on the support of the four other states.

VOTE 1

As a consequence of the combined weight of the smaller states, New South Wales and Victoria vote together in a futile bid to alter federal–state financial relations and try to at least mitigate their subsidisation of especially Western Australia and Queensland. This feature remains a part of the politics of federal–state financial relations to this day.

These arrangements have helped reinforce the dominance of the Commonwealth. The federal government sets the parameters of national economic policy. The states more or less have to follow the directions set by Canberra, or they put in jeopardy the funds that can be allocated to them by the Commonwealth.

Vertical fiscal imbalance

In the 1980s, the states began to complain that the money given to them by the Commonwealth was failing to meet the demands placed on state budgets by such expensive services as education, health and social welfare. The states began to talk about *vertical fiscal imbalance*, which means that the Commonwealth has financial power, but the states have the vast bulk of responsibility for providing services. To the states, this represented an imbalance in the federal arrangement.

NEW TAX, OLD ARRANGEMENTS: THE GST

In 2000, the goods and services tax was introduced to Australia. As part of the new tax system, an agreement was struck between the Commonwealth and the states whereby all revenue raised by the GST would be allocated to the states. This allocation of revenue replaces the old arrangements for the General Purpose Grant in name only, for the dynamics of allocating funds to the states remains the same. The GST revenue is handed back to the states according to a formula put together by the Grants Commission, so the old features of cross-subsidisation that have been a feature of federal–state relations since 1942 continue.

SOLVING THE IMBALANCE: GAMBLING

One of the ways the states have increased their own revenue flow is through the liberalisation of gambling. In particular, states such as Victoria and South Australia, previously known for their opposition to poker machines and casinos, finally allowed licensed venues to install electronic gaming machines and issued licences for casinos. The financial returns have been stunning for the states, but community concern about the social impact of gambling has sparked much debate in state politics.

The problems of vertical fiscal imbalance have been mitigated in more recent times by two developments. One of these was the onset of the GST and its promise of a flow of revenue to the states. The second was an increase in efforts by the states to raise their own revenue. The Commonwealth may have income tax power, but the states retained the right to certain indirect taxes such as stamp duties. During the 1990s, the states successfully found ways to raise their own revenue from indirect taxes.

Cooperative Federalism

The grounds for disputes to arise between the two levels of government, especially over funds, are numerous. On occasion, also, the states have objected to federal laws and programs, and have taken their objections to the High Court for resolution. However, an important cooperative side to Australian federalism exists. The Commonwealth may have financial power, but the states have greater administrative capacity. For all the financial considerations, the fact remains that Canberra can't govern without the assistance of the states.

With a system of policy-making fragmented by federalism, Australian governments need to find ways to work with each other. The Commonwealth has some areas where it can impose its policy from the centre (immigration, defence, some aspects of economic policy and so on). However, a great deal of Australian governance involves the Commonwealth and the states coming together and agreeing to work cooperatively on matters. Three forums in particular have been important for cooperative federal–state relations.

From COAG to National Cabinet

The *Council of Australian Governments (COAG)* was the highest level of intergovernmental activity between 1992 and 2020. The council met a number of times a year as the state premiers, territory chief ministers and the prime minister got together to finalise agreements on matters such as health policy, education policy, economic policy and environmental policy. In its last few years, COAG was involved in attempts at finding new ways to deal with old problems such as the degradation of the Murray–Darling river system.

COAG replaced the old premiers' conferences. These gatherings used to be a summoning of the premiers and state treasurers to Canberra, where the prime minister would tell them what money they would be getting and (via the Loan Council) how much money they could borrow. These events always ended in acrimony.

In May 2020, COAG was replaced by the *National Cabinet*, which was primarily geared towards coordinating the national approach to the COVID-19 pandemic. The National Cabinet maintained many of the roles of COAG, especially in being the forum for the premiers, chief ministers and prime minister to discuss key national policy issues requiring joint governmental attention.

TIP

You can keep an eye on reforms to intergovernmental relations by checking out the Department of the Prime Minister and Cabinet's website — go to pmc.gov.au/domestic-policy/effective-commonwealth-state-relations.

Ministerial councils

These days, each portfolio area has a minister in each of the states and territories, and a federal minister responsible for policy-making — a total of nine ministers in each portfolio area! In a bid to try to coordinate a national approach to policy, regular meetings of ministers for a portfolio area are held, interspersed with meetings of public service departments from each jurisdiction. These meetings are called *ministerial councils* and they discuss issues relevant to the portfolio area.

REMEMBER

One of the features of ministerial councils is that they sometimes result in all ministers agreeing to common legislation. They then all go back to their respective parliaments and pass identical bills, allowing the federal system to come up with a single uniform legal approach.

Intergovernmental agreements

Sometimes ministers and staff of ministerial departments of the Commonwealth and the states and/or territories meet with each other to discuss the coordination of regulations. These meetings and their subsequent outcomes are known as *intergovernmental agreements*. Some of these agreements have had a profound impact on economic policy, where the federal government has sought to get the states to agree to nationwide micro-economic reform. The National Competition Policy, which saw the Commonwealth offering to reward those states that agreed to privatise and nationally integrate aspects of the states' economic infrastructure, is one such important example.

Uncooperative Federalism

Of course, great scope for conflict exists in Australian federal–state relations. Some of this friction can be staged or feigned. Old premiers' conferences used to be like this, with premiers flying back from Canberra decrying the evils of federal government. Some premiers (usually from Western Australia and Tasmania) even threatened to secede from the Commonwealth!

Serious disputes, however, tend to be of the legal kind. In intergovernmental relations, disputes usually arise with regard to the legal authority of the federal government to legislate in areas that the states claim as their responsibility. When such disputes arise, they usually end up in the courts.

The High Court of Australia

The High Court is the keeper of the federal constitution. If the federal parliament passes a law that an individual or a state thinks is outside of the constitutional authority of the federal parliament, the aggrieved party takes the matter to the High Court. The court uses legal principles to decide if the federal government does, indeed, have the power to legislate. If the court rules that it doesn't have the power — that is, the federal government has acted *ultra vires* — then the law is struck down. If the court rules that the law is valid, and if the federal law conflicts with a state law, the federal law prevails. This process, whereby the High Court interprets the meaning of the Australian Constitution, is known as *judicial interpretation*.

The Federal Court

The sheer volume of legal work that the High Court has had to deal with has led to the creation of a subordinate federal court to share some of the load. The Federal Court does a lot of work in areas such as industrial law and federal administrative law, as well as dealing with some minor constitutional matters. These days it's sometimes used to review cases to consider whether they should proceed to the High Court.

Policy-making Australian Style

Government goes on in three realms. National government occurs in Canberra, state governance goes on in each of the states (including the self-governing territories) and local government goes on in the town halls and shire offices across the land (but subordinate, of course, to the states).

A key challenge for governments is how to best coordinate their approach to making policy. What may start out as a clear goal for government can quickly unravel if it's unable to translate its vision into a workable policy.

REMEMBER

National and state governance is *parliamentary governance* — that is, Responsible Government as per the Westminster model. The process revolves around Cabinet making a decision and parliament enacting the necessary legislation.

Public policy

Governance these days involves the creation of *public policy*. This means that government makes a decision on policy and seeks to have its decisions converted to actual programs. Public policy can be created in a variety of ways, including:

» **Laws:** The parliament passes a bill that becomes an Act of Parliament and the citizens are expected to abide by it.

» **Policy programs:** The government allocates money to a program or a service.

» **Regulations:** A government authority makes regulations on behalf of the parliament that, once again, citizens are expected to abide by.

» **Intergovernmental agreements:** The federal government and the state governments agree to a common policy action.

Cabinet government the Australian way

Australian government is based on the Westminster system, so Cabinet is the key policy-making body, and the prime minister (or, in the states and territories, the premier or chief minister) is the leader of Cabinet.

Ministers of the Crown hold portfolio responsibility for their departments. *Portfolio responsibility* means that a minister is responsible for a department that can be made up of a large number of public servants. To assist in channelling advice to a minister, and in communicating decisions back to the department, each ministerial department is headed by a senior public servant whose job it is to liaise with the minister. Prior to 1987, these departmental heads were known as *permanent departmental secretaries* because, as the wording implies, these departmental heads held their positions permanently.

In 1987, however, changes were made to the way Cabinets are structured in Australia. These reforms also changed the way the top level of the public service is structured. The reforms were undertaken by the federal government and were soon copied by all of the states.

Super Cabinets

Before 1987, Cabinet involved between 12 and 16 senior ministers holding portfolios considered to be of such importance as to warrant being at the centre of government. Under this system, about half of the government's ministerial departments were represented in Cabinet, with the other half languishing as portfolios held by junior ministers.

The 1987 reforms saw the 32 ministerial departments that had previously existed amalgamated into 16 super departments. Each department now has a senior minister, which means that every ministerial department is now represented in Cabinet. Each of the 16 departments had their internal structure broken up into two or three sub-departments, which have an assistant minister in charge. The assistant minister is the equivalent of the junior minister under the old system and is answerable to the senior minister.

Departmental secretaries

Under the Westminster model, the public service exists to give the government the administrative power to govern, advise and convert government decisions into actual administration.

The next most important person in a ministerial department after the minister is the *departmental secretary* — the person who gives departmental advice to the minister and who conveys the political directives back to the department. Under the 1987 reforms, departmental secretaries became part of what is now called the *senior executive service* (SES). The SES is a pool of senior people from which the government can draw to appoint departmental secretaries for fixed terms. So, today's departmental heads don't have the permanent tenure in charge of a department that was once enjoyed by their predecessors.

Creating policy

Policy-making occurs as a result of a variety of possible inputs. One of the most important drivers of policy-making is the government itself. In Australian politics, the political parties contest elections with policy platforms that they intend to pursue if they're elected to government. Australian governments usually come to the policy-making process with an agenda of policies they'd like to enact.

RAZOR GANGS

For many years now, federal and state governments have been trying to reduce government expenditure. To do this, prime ministers and premiers have set up a Cabinet committee to review expenditure proposals. The committee, indeed, is often called the *Expenditure Review Committee* (ERC) and is usually made up of the treasurer, the finance minister, the prime minister (or premier) and perhaps one or two other senior ministers. The ERC looks at proposed expenditure and then reports back to Cabinet. The public rarely hears the ERC referred to by its proper name. The media prefers to call ERCs *razor gangs*, mainly because the ERC's brief is to find expenditure savings. So, you can say that, when it comes to decisions on government expenditure, ERCs are on the cutting edge.

Other sources also exist, however. Interest groups are important players in the debate, especially where they have an agenda and try to pressure governments into addressing their concerns and meeting their demands. A great deal of community demand for policy outcomes is conveyed to government by interest group politics. These groups often represent sectional interests, particularly in strategically important fields such as economics and development. Governments anxious to ensure they can secure economic prosperity are always open to the input of powerful economic interests.

If a government seeks to make policy, it can do so in a variety of ways. One method is to include decisions and programs in the annual Budget. The Budget is a crucial piece of legislation, and its fate in the parliament is one of the determinants of whether or not the government is meeting its requirements under the Westminster convention of Responsible Government.

REMEMBER

In policy-making terms, the Budget is arguably the most important bill, because it allocates funds to a wide range of programs. These days, the Budget is handed down in May, but in the months leading up to the treasurer giving the Budget speech in parliament, intense lobbying from interest groups and from ministers and ministerial departments takes place to try to influence Cabinet's decisions on financial allocations.

TECHNICAL STUFF

In simplest terms, Cabinet meets to decide on policy. However, as part of the process, Cabinet is furnished with advice from the relevant ministerial departments via the responsible minister (this advice comes from the public service via the departmental secretary). When a decision is made, the responsible minister requests that his department drafts the necessary legislation and provides Cabinet with any other information and documentation it requires. Remember, all of this goes on *in camera* (behind closed doors). Cabinet documents are secret documents, and cabinet deliberations are secret too. Under the convention of Collective Responsibility, all ministers are bound by the decision and no minister is allowed to reveal to a third party how Cabinet came to its decision.

When the enabling legislation (if required) is passed, the public servants in the relevant or responsible ministerial departments ensure that the government's policy is applied practically (referred to by the experts as *public administration*).

Ministerial advisers

In Westminster theory, the public service should be the sole source of advice to Cabinet and the ministry. In reality, however, an auxiliary group has emerged that does similar work to that of the public service but does so as part of the minister's political team rather than as a part of the public service. This emergent group are known as *ministerial advisers* and aren't part of the public service. Rather, they're an extension of the minister's political office.

In the past, ministers have brought in policy experts from outside of the public service as advisers, presumably to tap into expertise in places other than the bureaucracy (ministers may draw on academic expertise, perhaps, or expertise from the private sector). In more recent times, journalists, public relations people, former interest group leaders and party functionaries have found their way into the ministerial advisory role.

Statutory authorities

Ministerial departments aren't the only important components of the Australian public sector. The creation of *statutory authorities* in national and state government administrations to carry some of the burden of providing government services and applying government rules and regulations has been common practice.

Statutory authorities are different from ministerial departments, which are part of the public service and are subject to ministerial direction. Statutory authorities are public corporations, but, when their enabling legislation has been passed and they're set up, they're not subject to direct ministerial intervention. Rather, the authority is run by a board of directors, and the only answerability to parliament is via an annual report. In other words, statutory authorities are given a certain degree of autonomy from government so they can get on with whatever it is the government set them up to do in the first place.

In a bygone era, statutory authorities were a major presence in Australia because they provided important economic services such as health, education, transport, energy and telecommunications. In the 1980s and 1990s, Australian governments began to privatise many of these authorities.

The more common form of statutory authority today undertakes regulation and overview of private sector service provision, or coordinates complicated matters such as national superannuation, national broadcasting and electoral service delivery. One of the main reasons authorities are created is to try to relieve the government of the onerous task of regulation. This is why authorities are given regulatory powers, so they can apply regulations that have the same status as laws. This allows the public sector to have a framework of laws (by-laws, actually) and regulations that don't have to go through the parliament in order to be applied.

Big Government or Small Government?

Australia has always had a very large public sector, especially when some of the big statutory authorities are taken into account. From the 1980s, this situation had been a cause of concern among some economists who felt that a large public sector was crowding out the private sector. Meanwhile, some other commentators argued that the country couldn't afford the expense of large numbers of public servants.

As a result, over the 1980s and 1990s, state and federal governments — both coalition and Labor — began to find ways of reducing the public sector. This tended to take the form mainly of privatising former statutory authorities such as the Commonwealth Bank, Telstra and Qantas. Governments also sought to reduce the total number of public servants, but found this to be a difficult task. Although total public sector employment in Australia has fallen quite dramatically over the last 20 years, public servant numbers dipped for a while, but have slowly risen. Elected government sees a real need for its public service, particularly in the complex world of furnishing advice and converting political decisions into government programs.

Party time!

Understand the Australian party system and the origins of the major parties.

Get your head around the many minor parties that have bobbed up in a system dominated by the big parties.

Explore the 'party machine' and alternatives to party politics such as interest groups and social movements.

Chapter **8**

Parties, Parliament and Politics

Political parties are central to politics and all political systems. Liberal democracies, such as Australia, are usually characterised as multi-party systems. However, as briefly outlined in Chapter 1, Australia's political system is actually dominated by two major parties — as well as including a smattering of minor parties. In this chapter, we take a preliminary look at these major and minor parties, which are examined in depth in Chapters 9 to 12.

This chapter also shows how party politics dominates Australian politics. Nearly everyone who votes in an Australian federal or state election votes for a party candidate and, therefore, votes for the policy platforms of that candidate's party. Party politics is the prism through which Australians view politics.

Political parties spend a lot of their time and energy putting these policy platforms together, which requires enormous organisation and funds. Here, we delve into the machinations of what makes a political party tick. We also have a look at alternatives to party politics, through the influence of promotional interest groups and social movements.

What Is a Party?

Classical political science defines *political parties* as organisations of citizens who come together in order to select candidates to contest elections in a bid to win executive power. In other words, parties are the organisations through which citizens participate in elections in order to win government, which usually means having a majority of seats in the lower house.

This definition certainly works when referring to the two major parties — the Australian Labor Party (also known as the ALP or Labor) and the Liberal Party of Australia (the Liberals) — and perhaps even the National Party of Australia (sometimes referred to as the NPA, but more usually as the Nationals or even the Nats). The Liberals and the Nationals are generally viewed as partners in Australian politics. This partnership is often referred to as the *coalition*.

All three parties are the main players in the electoral contest for government, be this in national politics or in the battle for government in the states. The exception here is Tasmania, where the proportional representation system allows smaller parties such as the Greens to win lower house seats and, if a smaller party holds the balance of power, it can have a say in which major party forms government.

REMEMBER

Minor parties or independents are said to hold the *balance of power* when neither major party holds a majority of seats in a parliamentary chamber and must, therefore, rely on the support of the crossbenchers to pass (or in the case of being in opposition, block) particular legislation. In essence, those holding the balance of power have the deciding vote. This situation sometimes occurs in the House of Representatives, but is more usual in the Australian Senate, thanks to its voting system, which enhances the chances of minor parties and independents winning seats. This topic is discussed more in Chapter 13. The failure of either Labor or the coalition to have a majority in the lower house results in what is commonly known as a *hung parliament*. (Refer to Chapter 6 for more on hung parliaments.)

Many other political parties — referred to in Australian politics as *minor parties* — contest elections for reasons other than trying to win government. Some contest elections to advance policy agendas. Some run to try to spoil the chances of other parties — maybe even the major parties. Some minor parties are actually interest groups in disguise. These parties give voters an array of choice at election time and reinforce the idea that Australia is a multi-party democracy.

TECHNICAL STUFF

Parties in liberal democracies can also be thought of as *extra-institutional actors* — that is, they are associations that are independent of the official structures of the system. This point can be illustrated by referring to Australia's federal and state constitutions. Until the change to Section 15 in 1977, the Australian Constitution made no mention of political parties at all. Reference to political parties is also absent from the state constitutions, which is partly a reflection of the idea that political parties are the creation of the citizens.

Majors and Minors

Differentiating the major parties from the minor parties is the place to start in understanding the party system. A party is a *major* party because it wins enough seats in an election to make it a serious contender in forming a government. A party is considered to be *minor* when it receives a very small percentage of the vote and — perhaps even more importantly — when it fails to win seats in the parliament or wins a very small number of seats.

Oddities of the Australian majors

Clearly, the ALP and the Liberals are the two major political parties in Australia. Between them, they rarely poll less than 75 per cent of the vote cast in elections, and they generally win 90 per cent to 100 per cent of the seats in the parliament.

REMEMBER

Most importantly of all, the ALP and the Liberals are the two parties that basically share government — when either party has a lower house majority, that's the party in government. No other parties, with the exception of the Nationals, are in the position to determine government (the Greens in Tasmanian state elections are another exception).

The National Party: A major minor?

Political analysts have trouble categorising the National Party. At one level, it's a minor party because it only ever wins a small share of the national or state vote. This vote, however, is concentrated in certain parts of regional Australia, which means that the party is able to win lower house seats.

Winning lower house seats gives a minor party the opportunity to influence which major party forms government. In a political practice known as *coalition politics*, a minor party can do a deal to support a major party to form a government and, as part of the deal, secure ministerial positions for the minor party.

VOTE 1

In Australia, coalition politics is complicated a little by the historical tendency for the Liberals and the Nationals to combine in a bid to form governments in order to keep Labor out of office. In federal politics, the Liberal Party has rarely been able to win enough lower house seats to govern in its own right. The result is that, in Australia, a coalition usually only involves the Liberals and the Nationals.

The Country Liberal Party

More complications arise in the party system, thanks to Australia's federal structure. The Northern Territory has no Liberal Party or National Party. Instead, it has a purely Northern Territorian party called the Country Liberal Party (the CLP). The CLP runs against Labor in Territory and federal elections. When elected to the federal parliament, however, CLP MPs always attend Liberal Party (not National Party) meetings. In other words, the CLP is the Northern Territory version of the Liberal Party.

Queensland is different! The Liberal National Party

In 2008, the Queensland Liberal and National Parties decided to merge and create a new party — the Liberal National Party (LNP). Candidates for state and federal elections are now endorsed as LNP candidates. Even though, technically, they're in the same state party, National-designated members meet with their fellow Nationals from other states, and Liberals sit with fellow Liberals.

Issues for the Australian minors

Minor parties are all those parties that exist that aren't the ALP, the Liberal Party or the National Party (excluding the CLP and LNP as well). The number of minor parties that contest elections can vary from election to election. A minor party also has no guarantee that it will survive beyond one or two elections, although a handful of minor parties have proven to be resilient over the years.

Minor parties are affected by a number of features of Australian politics (and especially the electoral system). Most Australian states and the national system use preferential voting (a form of majority voting — see Chapter 13). This method of casting and counting votes actually disadvantages minor parties because, in order to win a seat, a candidate has to win a majority of the vote. Minor parties rarely poll more than 10 per cent of the vote — nowhere near enough to win a seat.

TECHNICAL STUFF

The situation is a little bit different in upper house elections that use proportional representation (including the Senate and the upper houses of New South Wales, South Australia, Victoria and Western Australia). Proportional systems lower the vote needed to win a seat. In the case of the Senate, a candidate needs to win about 14.5 per cent of the vote to win a seat, still a high threshold to achieve, but a lot lower than the preferential system, and one of the reasons so many minor parties contest Senate elections rather than House of Representatives elections.

Leaders and resources

In addition to electoral disadvantage, the minor parties also have to contend with other barriers. Because the two major parties dominate the vote and because nearly all the parliamentary seats are carved up between Labor, the Liberals and the

Nationals, minor parties tend to get very little attention from political commentators in the media. (Chapter 15 looks at the influence of the media in politics.)

One way a minor party can get around this problem is to have charismatic leaders who are able to attract attention to themselves and to their parties. Leadership then becomes very important to minor parties.

VOTE 1

The minor parties also struggle to obtain resources to run campaigns. Even in the era of public funding for election campaigns, parties don't start receiving assistance until they poll in excess of 4 per cent. The vast majority of minor parties hardly ever poll more than 1 per cent. In addition to not receiving funds, candidates who fail to poll more than 4 per cent also lose the deposit they're required to pay to the Australian Electoral Commission (AEC) as part of their nomination (see Chapter 13).

Why do they run?

Why, indeed, do minor parties run in elections? Some run in order to draw attention to a policy matter. Sometimes a minor party is actually an interest group that puts up candidates in the hope of exerting some pressure on the policy debate. Some run simply because they can. And some run because they think they can actually win a seat and make the transition from being a minor party to becoming a minor parliamentary party.

Minor parties in the parliament

Hundreds of minor parties have contested elections in Australia, but only a small number have ever been so successful as to actually win a seat in the federal parliament. (The success rate of minor parties in the state parliaments has not been that much better.)

REMEMBER

Minor parties didn't start winning seats in the national parliament until after 1948, the year proportional representation was introduced to the Senate. Even then, it wasn't until the mid-1950s that a minor party — the Democratic Labor Party (DLP) — finally broke the drought for minor parties and won some Senate seats. Since the mid-1950s, the minor parties that won seats in the Senate include:

>> The Australian Democrats

>> The Australian Greens

>> Family First

>> Liberal Democrats

>> The Liberal Movement

>> Motoring Enthusiast Party

>> The Nuclear Disarmament Party

>> Palmer United Party

>> Pauline Hanson's One Nation

>> The Valentine Peace Group

>> The West Australian Greens

We examine a selection of these parties in Chapter 12. Some of these parties have also managed to win seats in state parliaments.

Few of these parties have survived long term, although the Australian Democrats were successful in winning seats between 1977 and 2001. The volatility of these minor parties stands in stark contrast to the endurance of the major parties.

Minor parties have also found winning seats in the lower house very difficult. The Australian Greens succeeded in 2010 when its candidate, Adam Bandt, won the seat of Melbourne. In 2013, Clive Palmer won the Queensland seat of Fairfax, while in 2016 Rebekha Sharkie won the South Australian seat of Mayo representing the Nick Xenophon Team, which changed its name to Centre Alliance.

Beyond the Parliament: Party Organisation

A political party has more to it than just the members who sit in the parliament. Behind the parliamentary wing of a party is an organisation. The organisation of a party is critically important because of the role it plays in the following key functions:

>> Selecting candidates for election (the technical term for this function in Australia is *preselection*). The federal Labor party now has a mechanism that allows party members to participate in the selection of the parliamentary leader.

>> Raising money to fund election campaigns.

>> Coordinating party workers to do the campaigning (handing out how-to-vote cards, putting leaflets in letterboxes, organising and attending public meetings, and so on).

>> Debating party approaches to policy (in Australia, party approaches to policy are called *policy platforms* or just *platforms*).

Each party arranges its organisational affairs in its own way, which is one of the considerations that differentiates parties from each other. The party organisation is really important, however, because it's the organisation that takes care of running election campaigns, as well as preselecting candidates.

Mass membership, mass parties

All sorts of political parties and all sorts of party types exist in Australia. The major political parties, and a number of the minor parties that have been able to win parliamentary representation, tend to be understood as *mass parties*. That is, they're political parties that allow ordinary citizens to join them as members in ways not dissimilar to any community association, such as a football club or a community group. These parties, therefore, have a mass membership.

The way the mass membership influences the affairs of a political party varies from one party to another, and is important to the role parties play in democratic systems. One of the critical roles played by political parties has been to act as an important link between the citizenry and the formal institutions of government. Many argue that citizens have the opportunity to directly influence government policy by being involved in political parties.

VOTE 1

WHY JOIN A PARTY?

Political parties in Australia are, technically, incorporated not-for-profit associations. Anyone can join a party, provided they agree to conform to the party's rules of association. People tend to join parties as a way of expressing their support for what the party stands for.

In the old days, political parties offered people a place to socialise (more than one Australian prime minister met his future spouse at a party dance). But, these days, parties are grappling with a decline in membership. Some argue that factionalism has pushed out ordinary members. Others argue that parties have become too reliant on professionals (such as opinion pollsters and media consultants), also resulting in the marginalisation of ordinary members.

Evidence suggests that the people who join parties now do so because they want to do more than support the party's ideals. Rather, these people aspire to a political career themselves.

The party machine

Political journalists often refer to party organisation as the *party machine*, a short-hand reference to the administration of the political parties. The party machine involves those people who hold senior positions in the parties, are responsible for administering the day-to-day affairs of the party and help to liaise between the party membership and the party's parliamentary wing.

The party machine may undertake other vital tasks, such as conducting opinion polls and market research on behalf of the parliamentary wing to ascertain the public's reaction to party policies.

VOTE 1

The machine also works hard at one of the key tasks of the administration — specifically, liaising with the business community to try to secure donations of money to help the party fund its operations. This function is important to the major parties in particular, although some minor parties may be in a position to obtain donations from companies. Raising finances to fund the operation of a party and election campaigns is one of the most important functions undertaken by the party organisation.

Raising money

Major parties need to raise enough money to pay for important infrastructure such as buildings and offices, and to create and maintain online sites and resources. The major parties also have secretariats made up of people paid to do important work ranging from undertaking polling and working on social media, through to answering constituent enquiries on the telephone or by email. These things all cost money, and the party administration must raise the money to pay for them.

REMEMBER

The major parties also need to raise money to pay for election campaigns. At least in this endeavour, the major parties in Australia now enjoy a taxpayer subsidy for election expenditure. This subsidy isn't enough on its own, however. The party organisation still needs to raise large amounts of money to pay for things such as online and television advertising.

THE MACHINE MEN AND WOMEN

No, mentioning machine men and women doesn't concern robots making a meaningful contribution to political parties — not yet anyway. The term is used by journalists to refer to key people who work within the party organisation. As with any association, a party has an executive committee that runs its affairs, including the important party executive positions of president, secretary and treasurer.

Usually, the machine people hold positions such as party president or party secretary (in the Liberal Party, party secretaries are called party *directors*). Party treasurers may also figure as important machine people, again because of the work needed in gathering financial resources. These days, increasing interest is focused on the people within parties who help organise subgroups or factions.

The thing to remember about machine people is that they're not readily identifiable — and certainly not to the same extent that the parliamentary leaders of a political party can be identified. The work that machine people do tends to be a bit obscure as well. Yet machine men and women are powerful, especially when it comes to conducting internal party business.

Minor parties also have infrastructure demands, although they're unlikely to have offices as extensive as the major parties. The minor parties also get a much smaller share of the taxpayer subsidy for election campaigns, if they get any assistance at all, making the fundraising activities of the organisation particularly important.

The media spends a lot of time drawing attention to how corporations make donations to parties. As important as these donations may be for the major parties, the vast bulk of the money raised by parties to fund their operations is drawn from membership fees. The ALP has an interesting approach to this practice. Trade unions are able to affiliate with the ALP provided they pay an affiliation fee, which is a major source of revenue for the party.

The Liberal and National Parties don't allow external interest groups to affiliate with them. Membership is restricted to individuals, and to become a member of the party an individual pays a membership fee.

Despite the hint of sinister undertones to the payment of money to parties, especially by corporations, the party fundraiser is still a critical form of raising revenue, beyond membership. Fundraisers may take all sorts of forms, from the very basic (a raffle for members) through to the elaborate (gala dinners where people pay to eat high-quality food and be in the presence of party luminaries, especially ministers and party leaders).

MONEY AND CORRUPTION

The issue of fundraising and donations is very contentious. Many suspect that donations are made as a means of securing influence over decision-makers. Politicians usually deny this claim and point out that it's the party organisation, rather than the parliamentary wing, that undertakes fundraising activity. In this way, the party organisation acts as a firewall between donors and the party wing — at least in theory. Concern about donations and elections, meanwhile, provides the basis for *disclosure laws*.

All parties must now tell the Australian Electoral Commission whenever they get donations for election campaigns, how much the amount was and who donated it. The issue of political donations is a theme regularly examined by governments.

To keep up to date on political parties and financial disclosure, search 'Financial disclosure' on the AEC's website at www.aec.gov.au.

Raising candidates

Another core function performed by the party organisation is to identify potential candidates to contest elections. Party candidates usually start out as party members, but it's not an iron law. Sometimes candidates are drafted from outside the party membership, although becoming a member of the party on being endorsed is expected. Party organisations are also becoming increasingly sensitive to the call for greater diversity in the choice of candidates.

The need to achieve a gender balance has arguably become one of the more pressing matters for party organisations, although pressure is also increasing for the parties to select more First Australians as well. If nothing else, these debates remind us how important party selections are in determining who gets to sit in parliament.

The procedures for how candidates are selected are subtly different for each of the parties, which we explain in Chapters 9 to 12. The same underlying principle exists, however, that the party draws on its membership to provide a pool of people to be candidates and then determines which of these people will win party endorsement.

In national elections, parties need to be mindful of Section 44 of the Australian Constitution. This section lists the prohibitions for candidates, and includes those serving prison terms, those who are undischarged bankrupts, those who are in 'receipt of profits from the Crown' and — most controversially — those who might 'owe an allegiance to' or stand to gain from being aligned to a 'foreign power'. After the passage of the *Australia Act 1986*, a definition of what constitutes an Australian citizen now exists in law and can be applied to Section 44 (i). Since 1987, a number of parliamentarians have been thrown out by the High Court for being in breach of Section 44 (i) — either because they held foreign citizenship and they didn't know it or because their parents had been born in a country other than Australia. No such prohibition exists in any of the state constitutions.

Preselection

The process where parties select their candidate for each election contest is called *preselection*, or *party endorsement*.

In some instances, the preselection decision made by a party determines which individual will sit in the parliament, particularly where the major parties preselect candidates for those electorates that are very safe for one or other of the parties. In such instances, the voters in the safe electorate ratify the choice made by the major political party. The same thing can be said for preselections for parliamentary chambers using proportional representation such as the federal Senate or state Legislative Councils. Mathematically, the candidates selected in the top two or three positions on a party ticket will win an upper house seat.

REMEMBER

The essential point to grasp here is that preselection is a keenly contested competitive pastime. In the safe seats, the preselection battle determines who gets elected to parliament, so these seats are contested very robustly indeed. Because of the strength of party voting in Australia, winning a preselection contest is arguably the usual or essential first step on the way to securing a parliamentary career.

Factions

Political scientists sometimes define *factions* as organisational sub-units, but a better description would be that factions can operate like little parties within a bigger party. Parties tend to involve the organisation of large numbers of people, often with differences of opinion over things such as what the party policy should be, what the party ideology should be or even something as basic as who should lead the party. So members of a party tend to meet in smaller like-minded groups to try to resolve some of these questions.

One of the key purposes of factionalism is to use collective action to try to achieve political outcomes within the organisation. A group that wants to impose a certain ideology on the whole party becomes an ideological faction. A group that wants to have the deputy leader replace the leader is a leadership faction, and so on.

HOW TO VOTE? IT'S ON THE CARDS

Political parties hand out how-to-vote cards at polling booths on election days (except for during Tasmanian state elections). These cards show voters how to order candidates on their ballot paper if they want to vote for the party's candidate and follow the party's preferences. Of course, voters may decide not to follow any how-to-vote card and instead number candidates in any order they wish.

A *party ticket* is political jargon for the way parties list the order of their candidates on how-to-vote cards. A party ticket is simply the list of party candidates ranked from most preferred to least preferred. The ticket is then published as the party how-to-vote card so voters can identify the party-endorsed candidates and what order all candidates should be ranked.

REMEMBER

Every party has factions. Factionalism is a feature of politics, whether people like it or not. (And some commentators don't like it, seeing factionalism as either a form of political corruption or as irrational political behaviour.) The nature of factionalism can and does vary widely between parties, however, as we show in Chapters 9 to 11.

Alternatives or Wellsprings: Interest Groups and Social Movements

Parties are not the only means by which citizens try to affect politics. Certain forms of interest group politics also utilise membership and organisation as a means to give individuals the opportunity to try to influence policy debates and interact with governments. (Refer to Chapter 1 for more on the various types of interest group.) In recent times, the rise of new social movements in Australian politics has aroused some interest, especially because some of these movements appear to have resulted in the formation of new minor parties.

Promotional interest groups

Some interest groups are closed to general public membership, but others rely heavily on membership in order to affect the political process. The groups that offer the greatest prospect of an alternative to party politics are the *promotional interest groups*. These groups are formed to bring people together to pool their resources in an attempt to achieve their agendas.

Promotional groups usually organise in pursuit of specific policy objectives, often by influencing public opinion. The appeal of this approach to politics is that it allows people to get involved in politics by addressing specific issues. The process relies heavily on the ease with which people in a liberal democracy can form associations and seek to have an impact on the political debate.

Social movements

Social movements are rather more difficult phenomena to track; however, commentators now assume these movements are involved in some forms of politics. These are broad-based phenomena, where people can choose to get very active on specific issues or perhaps do as little as simply agreeing with (or 'liking') the views and outlooks of the movement, and signing the occasional online petition. This form of politics is usually associated with things such as environmental politics, Indigenous rights politics and women's liberation politics. This approach is often noted as a more activist-oriented form of politics that appeals to young people especially, because of the way it offers them the opportunity to get active in pursuit of matters of high principle.

A great deal of interest in social movements is also generated because of their link with emerging minor parties in the Australian system. The rise of the Greens, a party linked with the environmental movement, is the most obvious example. See Chapter 12 for more on the Greens and other minor parties.

IN THIS CHAPTER

» Tracing the origins of the Labor Party

» Explaining the party's structure

» Exploring Labor's internal politics and factions

» Examining policy objectives

» Checking out the historical splits in the party

» Reviewing Labor's record in national government

» Looking at Labor in the states and in the future

Chapter **9**

The Australian Labor Party

The Australian Labor Party (the ALP or, even more popularly, Labor) is the oldest political party in the country. The ALP was being formed at about the time Henry Parkes and some of his friends were thinking about reorganising Australia as a federation. Indeed, with its origins dating back to the early 1870s and the formation of Australia's first trade unions, the ALP is the oldest trade union–based political party in the world.

In this chapter, we explore those origins and examine some of the important phases of the party's internal organisation, objectives, splits and factions, right up to the Labor governments of the modern era, from those of Gough Whitlam to Kevin Rudd and Australia's first female prime minister, Julia Gillard.

VOTE 1

FROM LABOUR TO LABOR

In 1912, the Australian Labour Party decided to change the spelling of its name. Initially, the party used the British spelling of *labour*, but the 1912 decision adopted the American spelling, *labor*. It is believed that this change was made in a show of solidarity with the American trade union movement, which had recently decided to establish a pan-American organisation. Since 1912, then, the ALP has been the Australian Labor Party.

REMEMBER

Establishing what Labor stands for has created enduring controversies. Some see the Labor Party as a socialist party. Others disagree, describing it instead as a social democratic party. Some accuse the Labor Party of being a mouthpiece for the union movement, yet plenty of unions don't belong to the ALP and plenty of union leaders get angry at Labor governments, particularly over industry policy and industrial relations laws.

The Unions Create a Party

No single moment defines when the ALP was formed. Rather, the creation of the party was the product of evolution, kicked along by the formation of trade unions in the 1870s. Unionism was particularly strong in rural Australia due to the spread of mining jobs and the large rural workforce that was scattered across the land, tending stock, shearing sheep and cutting sugarcane. Historians have found evidence of Labour Caucuses having been formed in the New South Wales colonial parliament in the 1870s. (Yep, the ALP started off as the Australian *Labour* Party — see the nearby sidebar — but for simplicity's sake we stick with the later spelling from here on.) Occasionally, trade union–backed candidates also ran for election in New South Wales and Victoria at that time.

The strikes of 1891

After a period of prosperity in the 1880s, the Australian colonies were hit by a serious economic recession in 1890. In 1891, the combined unions coordinated what was effectively a national strike in defence of pay and conditions. This strike was defeated across all the colonies. In the aftermath of this experience, the unions decided to create a political party with the express intention of contesting elections to win government and use the policy-making powers of government to pursue the union movement's agenda. The Australian Labor Party had begun, with the Queensland and New South Wales branches of the party being the first to be formed, followed soon after by the various other colonies.

By the time of the first federal election in 1901, the ALP had branches in every state and put up Labor-endorsed candidates. On election to the new national parliament, those Labor-endorsed candidates who were successful met as a caucus (see the sidebar 'The Caucus'). This meeting was a sign that disciplined party politics had arrived in the national parliament. The ALP was there at the very first meeting of the new federal parliament and has been one of the two major political parties that have dominated the Australian party system ever since.

The connection between Labor and the trade union movement is very important. The ALP was the world's first legal trade union–based social democratic party (but not the first union-based party — that honour belongs to Germany's Social Democratic Party). When federal Labor leader John Christian Watson stitched together a minority ministry in the House of Representatives in 1904, he gave the world its first union-based political party government, earning the ALP a place in Australian and world political history. (See Chapter 16 for more on Watson's contribution to Australian politics.)

The union movement's delegates?

From the moment the Labor Party was created and began sending endorsed candidates to the parliament who were prepared to caucus, Labor was (and continues to be) seen as the parliamentary delegation of the union movement. Part of the reason for this view derived from the way the party was structured.

The newly formed Labor Party gave trade unions the opportunity to affiliate with it. Affiliating unions were required to pay a fee to the party, which, in fact, became an important source of revenue, giving the party the financial ability to run election campaigns. In exchange for this fee, affiliating unions were entitled to send delegates to the party's internal policy-making forums. These forums met regularly to decide on official party policy. Labor parliamentarians were then expected to convert Labor policy into actual national policy if enough Labor MPs were elected to form a government.

Root and branch representation

The notion that the ALP is simply the parliamentary wing of the affiliated trade unions isn't a complete picture of the party by any means, not even back in the old days when the party was in its infancy. In addition to the affiliated unions, Labor membership was (and still is) always open to individuals. Right from the very beginning of the party, membership of the ALP was open to anyone who could pay a membership fee and participate in the party's internal affairs through the Labor branches.

THE CAUCUS

Labor Party rules recognise a body called the *Caucus*. The Caucus is the entire parliamentary wing of the Labor Party to be found in each jurisdiction's parliament (that is, all the federal Labor MPs are in the Federal Caucus, all the Labor MPs who are in the Victorian state parliament are in the Victorian Caucus, and so on). Party rules require the Caucus to meet ahead of formal parliamentary sessions. At Caucus meetings, the parliamentary wing of the Labor Party collectively decides on how it will vote in the parliament. In making these decisions, the Caucus is expected to follow official party policy. When Caucus makes collective decisions, all members of the Caucus are bound by the decisions. Any Labor MP who votes against Caucus is expelled from the party.

UNION AFFILIATION AND THE ALP

Not every trade union in Australia is in the ALP. Unions can choose to affiliate with the Labor Party, but a number of unions over the years have preferred to stay outside of the party. Famously, a number of unions affiliated with Labor's great rival — the Communist Party of Australia (CPA). When the Communist Party disbanded in 1986, some unions rejoined the ALP.

Similarly, some unions left the ALP in the 1950s to join the Democratic Labor Party (DLP). When a union affiliates with the ALP, the affiliation allows the executive of the affiliating union to choose who its delegates to Labor forums will be.

Individuals who belong to an affiliated union are *not* automatically members of the Labor Party. To join the party as an individual, a person has to go through the local branches. Union representatives elected as delegates to Labor conferences must be party members, however.

The idea that a party should have a large organisation where delegates would have the power to debate official party policy, and reinforce compliance of its parliamentary wing, was very new back in 1901. This decision was the beginning of what is often referred to as *disciplined party politics*. The party's rules were quite clear. The power to make party policy rested with the organisation and the parliamentary wing was expected to follow party policy. The expectation of the compliance of Labor MPs was reinforced by the fact that, right from the outset, the Labor Party expected its members to sign a pledge of loyalty to the party (see the sidebar 'The pledge').

THE PLEDGE

Ordinary members of the ALP are expected to sign an oath of loyalty to the party, pledging to uphold its rules and — most importantly of all — to never run as candidates against endorsed Labor candidates in any election. For those Labor members who become parliamentarians, the pledge also requires a promise to never break Caucus (in other words, to never vote against a collectively held position within Caucus).

Individual membership continues to be important to the party to this very day. Individuals can join the Labor Party at the local level. The party is actually six state and two territory branches of the party, which, in turn, are made up of all the local suburban branches of the party.

The party's broader organisation seeks to give representation to both the affiliated unions and branch membership, the latter organised through Federal Electoral Assemblies (FEAs). Through the FEAs, the local branches of the Labor Party are clustered together according to the federal electoral division they're in, and from this cluster a number of delegates are elected to attend the various party forums that exist. The number of positions that members can be elected to within the organisation is divided roughly in half between the affiliated unions and the branch membership, though each state and territory branch of the ALP has slightly different rules on the exact number.

The Party Organisation

Each of the six state and two territory branches of the Labor Party elect delegates to the national organisation. These delegates attend state and national conferences held as major forums at the centre of the Labor Party's organisation. The parliamentary leaders of the party also attend as delegates. In each of the states, this forum is called *State Conference*, and the national forum is called, you guessed it, *National Conference*. Overall, it's important enough to the party to simply be called *Conference*.

The supreme organ: Conference

The structure of Conference has changed a bit over the years, although the intended functions have remained the same ever since 1901. In short, Conference is the policy-making organ of the Labor Party. State Conference outlines the policy platform of each state branch, and National Conference formulates the national policy platform. Under the party's rules, the decisions made at Conference are supposed to be binding on the parliamentary party, the Caucus. In summary, the Labor Party's membership decides policy via its delegates and expects the Caucus to enact that policy when Labor is in government. Check out Figure 9-1 for an overview.

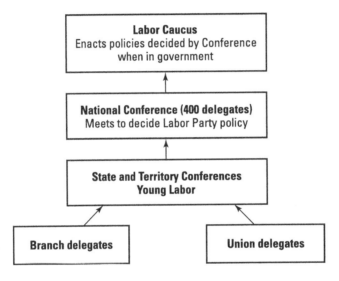

Conference also has the authority to discipline members, including parliamentarians, and can expel people from the party, if it votes to do so. It can even expel members of parliament from the party (although an MP who suffers this fate doesn't lose her parliamentary seat — she simply ceases to be a member of the Labor Caucus).

The party structure entails a strong sense of hierarchy. Although the party has state and territory branches, the national organisation of the party has the power to discipline the state and territory branches. The national organisation also has the power to intervene in the affairs of the state and territory branches (see the sidebar, 'Federal intervention'). In other words, National Conference is the supreme policy-making organ of the Labor organisation in its entirety.

State and National Executive

Conferences are convened regularly, but not often. The states hold an annual Conference. The National Conference, however, is now held every three years (called *Triennial National Conference*). Obviously, another body is needed to run the party's administrative and organisational affairs in between the meetings of Conference. This body is the *Executive* (the State Executive in the states and the National Executive in the case of the national organisation). Members of the Executive are elected at Conference.

TECHNICAL STUFF

The Executive meets frequently during the year and is charged with all of the disciplinary powers of Conference. It's made up of the following representatives:

» The party president (in the case of National Executive, now three rotating party presidents)

» The party secretary (who's also responsible for running election campaigns during election years)

» The party treasurer

» A number of other delegates

One thing the Executive can't do is change policy agreed to at Conference. In the event of the need to address the policy platform ahead of a regularly scheduled Conference, Executive can convene a Special Conference. These Special Conferences are called to deal only with the matter that caused the Conference to be convened in the first place.

FEDERAL INTERVENTION

Those rare moments when the national organisation seeks to deal with the state and territory branches of the ALP is known as *federal intervention*. The national organisation can direct the state branches on matters such as how the party is structured and who may or may not be expelled from the party.

The national intervention powers also include the ability to say who will win Labor pre-selection at the local level — a crucial power that allows the national branch to override the state branches on one of the key functions performed by the party organisation.

From 36 faceless men to 400 delegates

The annual State Conference of each state and territory branch of the Labor Party is made up of delegates from the affiliated unions, the FEAs and the state parliamentary leadership of the party. Apart from dealing with state matters and making policies oriented towards state politics, the State Conference also elects delegates to National Conference.

Before 1967, the six state Labor branches (territory branches didn't exist back then) each elected six delegates to attend National Conference. In those days, party rules didn't allow Labor parliamentarians to be represented at any of the conferences. So National Conference tended to be made up of the State Executive of the six state branches (mathematical note: 6 times 6 is 36).

VOTE 1

In 1967, the National Executive called a Special Conference to work out Labor policy on an American request to build surveillance facilities in Australian territory. The 36 delegates attended a meeting at the Kingston Hotel in Canberra. The parliamentary leaders — Arthur Calwell and his deputy Gough Whitlam — were also summoned but were forbidden to participate in the meeting. Calwell and Whitlam had to wait in the lobby to be informed of Conference's decision. A famous political journalist of the time, Alan Reid, saw the Labor leaders sitting around waiting for Conference to decide. Arranging for a photographer to come to the hotel to capture the moment, Reid penned the phrase *36 faceless men* to describe Conference. This label hurt Labor's reputation with the public, and later Whitlam — who would replace Calwell as leader — reformed Conference to have the parliamentary leaders included as part of National Conference. The state branches followed soon after.

The model introduced by Whitlam stayed in place until 1981, when the then federal parliamentary Labor leader, Bill Hayden, succeeded in having the party reform Conference yet again. This time, Conference was expanded to 99 delegates, with the state and territory branches sending delegations in proportion to their size (New South Wales had the most delegates, the Australian Capital Territory and the Northern Territory the least). The leader and deputy leader of the Senate joined the leader and deputy leader of the House of Representatives as part of the federal leadership delegation at Conference. The parliamentary leadership of all the state and territory branches were included, as well as representatives from Young Labor.

The last Labor leader to modify National Conference was Mark Latham. Just before the 2004 election, Latham secured an agreement with the party organisation to increase Conference to 400 delegates and for it to meet every three years (previously, it had been meeting every second year). Latham also persuaded the party to increase the size of the National Executive and to have three rotating party presidents instead of one. Table 9-1 outlines the various incarnations of the Labor Conference structure.

TABLE 9-1   Evolution of the ALP's National Conference Structure

	Number of Delegates			
	pre-1967	1967	1981	post-2004
ACT	n/a	n/a	2	7
New South Wales	6	6	24	111
Northern Territory	n/a	n/a	2	7
Queensland	6	6	15	71
South Australia	6	6	11	35
Tasmania	6	6	9	23
Victoria	6	6	20	87
Western Australia	6	6	11	43
Federal leaders	n/a	2	4	4
Young Labor	n/a	n/a	1	3
Federal presidents	n/a	n/a	n/a	3
Caucus delegation	n/a	n/a	n/a	6
Total	**36**	**38**	**99**	**400**

A youth wing: Young Labor

The major political parties all have youth wings to their organisations. These wings are part of the political parties' function of socialising the next generation of political activists, some of whom will go on to be parliamentarians and community leaders. The ALP has a Young Labor organisation open to people aged from their mid-teens all the way through to their mid-20s.

A BLOKES' PARTY? WOMEN IN THE ALP

With its connections to what was, for some time (and in some quarters still is), the very masculine world of trade union politics, the Labor Party used to be seen as something of a blokes' party. Few women were part of the Caucus until the 1980s, when the number of female Labor MPs began to rise (indeed, a number of women were also elected as leaders of some of the affiliated unions).

(continued)

(continued)

Within the Labor Party, a group called Emily's List operates. This group of female Labor members (drawn mainly from the party's Socialist Left faction) works tirelessly to get more ALP women preselected to winnable seats. This campaign has had some success. The ALP has committed itself to gender equality and now has rules regarding the pre-selection of requisite numbers of women to 'winnable seats'. The party also introduced targets for the percentage of women in the federal Labor Caucus. (The first target set was 35 per cent. This was raised to 40 per cent in 2002 and, following the 2015 ALP National Conference, was lifted to 45 per cent by 2020 and 50 per cent by 2025.) This in turn has resulted in an increase in ALP female representation in the federal parliament to 47 percent after the 2019 election.

By the 1990s, women were leading some of the state parties (Carmen Lawrence in Western Australia and Joan Kirner in Victoria, both of whom also served as premiers). In 2009, Queensland Labor leader Anna Bligh was the first Labor woman to win an election as the leader of a state branch of the party.

The most significant moment for Labor women, and Australia's female politicians as a whole, came in 2010, when Julia Gillard successfully challenged Kevin Rudd's leadership to become Australia's first female prime minister.

The Labor Organisation: Internal Politics

Labor's organisation is a major arena for internal politics. Major struggles go on within the party for control over its various organs — Conference, the Executive and all the subcommittees that are formed, especially in the state branches. Each of the state branches of the Labor Party has a subcommittee that deals with pre-selections. Positions on this committee are particularly keenly contested because of its importance in determining which aspiring Labor person becomes the officially endorsed candidate to whom all Labor members have pledged their loyalty!

Meanwhile, power struggles for control over Conference are important because of the power Conference has over the party's policy platform. The battle for control over the Executive is important because of its administrative role.

The importance of factions

With so many committees, conferences and executives to struggle over, not to mention the battle to determine who will become a Labor-endorsed candidate at the next election, power struggles within the ALP go on constantly. Because the party is so disciplined and because the idea of *collective politics* (that is, seeking to achieve political ends through unified, disciplined action) is so important to the party's ethos, factional politics have been readily applied to the party's operation.

As we note in Chapter 8, factions may be thought of as small parties operating within the larger party organisation. This description is particularly apt for the Labor Party where, at various times, the party factions have indeed operated like political parties in their own right. Factions have had their own caucus, their own membership lists, their own disciplinary standards and, in the case of one faction in the 1980s, even their own newspaper.

REMEMBER

Labor factionalism has evolved over the years, and is always in a state of flux. A faint echo of ideology has always existed in Labor factionalism, with the party's left wing usually associated with socialist ideas, while its right wing has tended to be more avowedly social democratic. Some other important factional divides have taken place over the years, however.

Organisational Labor versus parliamentary Labor

The distinction between the party's organisation and its parliamentary wing has been one important source of factionalism, particularly back in the old days of the '36 faceless men' arrangement at Conference. The notion that the parliamentary Labor Party is bound by the policy platform written by Conference has been a source of contention. This issue has usually resulted in tensions between the party organisation and the parliamentary leader, especially when Labor has been in government. In such circumstances, the parliamentary leader, as premier or prime minister, has tended to see the party platform as a guide to policy-making rather than as a definitive blueprint.

After his election as prime minister in 1983, then federal parliamentary leader Bob Hawke established a precedent when his Cabinet ministers sought to have party policy changed according to their wishes before enacting policies in government. Hawke became a constant user of the Special Conference to change the party platform to suit the policy objectives of his government.

Affiliated unions versus the parliamentary party

Sometimes major disagreements arise between the delegates elected to Conference from the affiliated unions and the parliamentary wing of the party (and especially the parliamentary leader). On certain issues of particular importance to the unions, such as industrial relations and maybe even economic policy, union delegates may seek to put pressure on the Caucus and the leadership via Conference.

BRINGING DOWN LABOR PREMIERS

In 2008, the premier of New South Wales, Morris Iemma, was forced to resign because he no longer enjoyed sufficient support within his own party. In particular, he couldn't gain support for his proposal to privatise the New South Wales power industry. However, Iemma was not the first Labor premier to be 'rolled' by the party organisation over policy.

Back in 1982, Tasmanian Premier Doug Lowe tried to preserve the Franklin River from being dammed for a hydro-electric scheme. The Tasmanian unions supported the dam and used a State Conference to have the dam included as party policy. Lowe's refusal to acquiesce to the organisation's demand resulted in his resignation from the party. Labor then lost the next state election.

In an even more celebrated dispute in 1954, the Queensland Labor secretary threatened Queensland Premier Vince Gair that his preselection would be withdrawn if he didn't toe the party line. Gair resigned and formed the Queensland Labor Party, which later became the Democratic Labor Party.

Again, these attempts inevitably create arguments between the party organisation and the parliamentary leader. Usually the leader prevails, on the grounds that Labor needs to be able to appeal to an electorate that may be put off by shows of union strength, and this tack tends to do the trick. Union delegates often rationalise that they'd rather have Labor in government than be ideologically pure in opposition. However, sometimes these disputes are irreconcilable and cause a Labor parliamentary party a lot of trouble.

Left versus right

Today's factional politics tends to transcend the divisions between the affiliated unions and the parliamentary wing. These days the vast majority of Labor members in a position of importance in the party — be it in the organisation or the parliamentary wing — belong to basically two (possibly three if the Queensland factional system comes into play) broad factional groups.

The consolidation of the factional system coincided with the move to a 99-delegate conference in 1981 (refer to the section 'From 36 faceless men to 400 delegates', earlier in this chapter). Within a year, two broad factions appeared that have been the mainstay of internal politics in the party ever since.

The Socialist Left

The Socialist Left is the party's main left-wing faction. During the 1980s, the faction was quite solid, with its power based primarily in Victoria. In more recent times, however, the faction has lost some of its rigid unity and some subgroups can now be identified within it. Of these subgroups, only one — the Pledge Left in Victoria — evolved into being a faction in its own right. When it comes to organising preselections and the share of frontbench positions in the parliamentary Labor Party, the Socialist Left does tend to act as a block.

The right-wing factions

The party has three main right-wing factions. The Victorian right faction is Labor Unity, and the New South Wales right faction is the Centre Unity. In all the other state branches, the faction is simply known as the Right. The situation in Queensland is complicated a little by the fact that one affiliated union — the Australian Workers' Union (or AWU) — is so powerful that it operates in state party matters as a separate faction in its own right.

Everyone who's anyone is in a faction

Only an estimated 20 per cent of Labor members are in the two major factions. This fact doesn't diminish their importance, however, for the people who are organised into factions tend to be the really important members of the party — that is, the members of the Executive, the delegates who attend Conference, the members who get preselected, the Labor members who become MPs and, indeed, all the way up through the Labor frontbench to even involve the parliamentary leader.

WHO CHOOSES THE LABOR LEADER?

Up until 2013, the ALP Caucus chose the Labor leader. But the party changed its rules following the instability that led to Julia Gillard replacing the then Prime Minister Kevin Rudd as leader in 2010, and Rudd then replacing Gillard just three years later (still during a Labor government). When Rudd returned to the party leadership role, he advocated for a new way of choosing the leader that included ordinary members in the process.

Now, the Labor leader is selected by ballot of Caucus and grass-roots members with a weighting of 50 per cent each.

Removing a serving Labor prime minister has also been made more difficult. Now, 75 per cent of Caucus members must support a change, while at least 60 per cent of Caucus members need to support a change of leader when the party is in opposition.

The factional system also includes the affiliated unions. Some unions are from the Socialist Left, such as the CFMMEU (the Construction, Forestry, Maritime, Mining and Energy Union), and some are Labour Unity or Centre Unity unions, such as the AWU and the SDA (Shop, Distributive and Allied Employees' Association). The delegates from these affiliated unions who attend Conference in fact belong to the factions.

Although a few exceptions exist, nearly everything that happens in the internal operation of the Labor Party involves the factional system.

Labor and Policy: What Labor Stands For

Is the Labor Party the party of Australia's workers or is it a pragmatic middle-class party, or perhaps a combination of the two? The party's historical link with the union movement has led many to consider its traditions to be inextricably linked with the working class. Yet, the party also appeals to a middle-class constituency, especially those interested in social reform. And this phenomenon isn't recent. As early as 1923, author Vere Gordon Childe published a book on Labor's first 30 years of existence in which he observed the importance of middle-class intellectuals to the party's life, both in the branches and in the parliament.

REMEMBER

What this duality of the party's core constituency means is that trying to sort out exactly what the Labor Party stands for is actually a very difficult job. It's possible to identify all sorts of ideologies and philosophies at work. The task becomes even more difficult when assessing Labor's record in government.

The Socialist Objective

Reflections on what Labor stands for have always been influenced by the historical fact that, back in 1921, the party voted to include a Socialist Objective in the policy platform.

The *Socialist Objective* was a statement committing the Labor Party to nationalising important parts of the nation's economy — especially banking, insurance and transport. Indeed, the Objective stated that Labor would commit itself to 'the socialisation of industry, production, distribution and exchange'.

Interest in a strong and favourable position on socialism had been well asserted in the immediate aftermath of World War I. The huge social dislocation caused by the war had affected politics across the globe, and increased agitation by unions and worker organisations for better conditions and pay had been one of the consequences. The situation was made all the more volatile by the fact that a communist state was being consolidated in Russia. Many in working-class and union politics thought the time had come for a stronger stand against capitalism.

Ben Chifley and bank nationalisation

The only federal Labor government to have seriously attempted socialisation of a sector of the economy consistent with the Socialist Objective was that headed by Prime Minister Ben Chifley. In 1947, as part of his government's postwar reconstruction plans, the Chifley government passed legislation in the national parliament converting the private ownership of the country's banks to government ownership.

REMEMBER

The Chifley government had succeeded the wartime government headed by John Curtin. (Curtin had died in office and Chifley took over as Labor leader and prime minister.) During the war, government had effectively taken over the running of the Australian economy. The Chifley government argued that it was simply carrying on the wartime management of the economy into postwar reconstruction and that its intention was to free up capital to help other private businesses get established.

THE BLACKBURN DECLARATION

The increasing interest in socialism in the Labor Party found expression in the Socialist Objective, but it must be remembered that even at the time opinion about socialism was divided within the party. The adoption of the Socialist Objective passed at the 1921 Conference on a vote of 22 to 10.

At the same Conference, however, moderates succeeded in having a clause inserted immediately after the Objective that said that nationalisation of industries important to the economy, such as banking and transport, would only occur 'to the extent necessary to prevent exploitation'.

Known as the *Blackburn Declaration* (named after the delegate who moved it), it must be understood as a serious qualification of the party's preparedness to pursue socialisation. The Declaration was passed 15 to 13.

CHIFLEY AND THE UNIONS

So, you think the Labor Party is merely a cipher of the unions? Then consider this: In 1948 and 1949, Australia's coalmining unions went on strike across the country. This strike was a major challenge to the government's reconstruction plans, and Prime Minister Chifley decided to reassert his authority by using the Australian army to mine and transport coal. Of course, that action looks like an act of treachery committed by one arm of the labour movement against the other. However, the unions involved in the strike were not affiliated with the Labor Party. Rather, these unions belonged to the Communist Party of Australia. A massive rivalry was developing between the ALP and CPA that would erupt into a major split in the Labor Party in 1955 (see the next section, 'The Splits').

The bank nationalisation plan was a political disaster, however. The banks were furious at what the government had done, and the anger extended down to bank employees as well. And both the banks and their workers were sent into the arms of a newly formed anti-Labor political party, the Liberal Party, at the 1949 election (see Chapter 10). But, before then, the banks took Chifley's legislation to the High Court of Australia, which ruled it contravened Section 92 of the Australian Constitution. The Act was invalidated.

Chifley was the only Labor prime minister to try to nationalise anything. Previous Labor prime ministers had overseen the creation of government-run corporations to provide goods and services, including banking (the Fisher Labor government established the Commonwealth Savings Bank in 1912), but these corporations were usually intended either to provide a service that private enterprise wasn't willing to provide, or to have a state-owned company provide competition in an otherwise monopolised industry. This thinking was also behind a number of state Labor governments setting up public corporations to provide services such as transport and electricity. As a result, Labor is also traditionally seen as the political party that supports the idea of public enterprise as distinct from private enterprise.

Labor was to pay a high price for its attempt to nationalise the banks. The move lost the ALP support in the following ways:

>> The party lost the support of bank employees.

>> It alienated the business community.

>> The perception was the ALP had done something illegal when the Act was disallowed by the High Court.

>> It frightened large sections of the Australian electorate.

In 1949, Labor lost the national election to the Liberal Party and was in opposition federally for another 23 years. And, in 1955, with this controversy still reverberating, the party experienced a cataclysmic split.

The Splits

While much interest is focused on Labor's split in 1955, the party had already experienced two other major splits in its history. The first was in 1916, when the party tore itself apart over then Labor Prime Minister William (Billy) Hughes's proposal to introduce conscription as part of Australia's effort for the Great War, which grated with many Labor people of Irish Catholic descent.

Then, in 1931, the rancour over the Great Depression that underpinned the division of opinion between James Scullin and Jack Lang over what to do about the Niemeyer scheme (see the section 'Labor and the Great Depression: 1931') saw the federal Labor government collapse again. The party organisation divided into one group that supported Scullin and another group supporting Lang Labor.

VOTE 1

These Labor splits were devastating. They rendered the Labor Party unelectable in the eyes of the general public and so confined the party to periods of opposition. Interestingly, these splits helped form new anti-Labor parties — the Nationalists in the case of the 1916 split and the United Australia Party in the case of the 1931 split (see Chapter 10 for more on the UAP).

But these splits were nothing compared with the split of 1955. (See the section 'Many tensions, one big split' a little later in this chapter if you want to cut straight to the chase; otherwise, simply read on.)

Labor and conscription: 1916

Billy Hughes's plan to introduce conscription in 1916 divided the party in two ways. One group of left-wing Labor MPs were highly critical of the Great War on the grounds, they argued, that it was a class war. The left argued that conscription was against socialist principles. The other group that opposed the idea was the party's very many Irish Catholics. At that time, most of Australia's unionised workers were of Irish Catholic descent. Inevitably, Irish Catholicism figured prominently in the ancestry of the Labor Party at this time, too.

Hughes's proposal on conscription was unfortunately timed for this group, coming as it did immediately after the Easter Uprising in Dublin (in April 1916) that had been brutally put down by the British. A number of local agitators, including young Catholic Archbishop of Melbourne Dr Daniel Mannix, campaigned against Hughes as part of their protest against the British approach to Irish nationalism. It was the first, but not the last, major incursion into internal Labor politics that Mannix made.

Labor and the Great Depression: 1931

At the time Labor was debating its Socialist Objective policy platform in 1921, it was in federal opposition. The party wasn't to be returned to government until 1929, amid the economic emergency of the Great Depression. The Labor government of 1929 to 1931 was beset by internal division over policy, especially when Prime Minister James Scullin proposed to cut government expenditure as recommended by the Bank of England's Otto Niemeyer. (Niemeyer argued Australia had to make sure it first paid its interest liabilities to its international creditors — hardly socialism and certainly not consistent with the Labor platform.)

VOTE 1

Part of Scullin's problem was that the Labor government of New South Wales, headed by Premier Jack Lang, had taken a very different approach to the Depression. Lang proposed to increase his government's debt in order to finance public works projects aimed at getting the unemployed back to work. He also pioneered the idea of state government help for the jobless in the form of unemployment assistance (also known as *the dole*).

The volatile politics of the time were such that neither Scullin nor Lang was to stay in government. (One lost an election; the other was sacked by the state governor who ruled that Lang's plan to defer paying interest to overseas creditors until after the Depression was illegal.)

Two important things need to be understood about the Labor approach to policy at this time. First, the Scullin approach showed how parliamentary leaders of the Labor Party could ignore the party platform when seeking to govern. Second, Lang's legacy was to associate the Labor Party with the rise of the provision of government assistance to those in economic trouble. This philosophy, of course, is the beginning of the idea of the *welfare state* in Australian policy, which Labor tends to be closely associated with.

Lead-up to the 1955 split: The Industrial Groupers

Labor in the immediate post–World War II period looked to be in great shape. At that time, it was the anti-Labor parties that were hopelessly divided, and Labor held government nationally as well as in New South Wales, Queensland, Tasmania and Victoria. Then, along came the 1947 bank nationalisation plan and the 1949 coal strike.

The bank nationalisation plan alienated the voters, but it was the coal strike that planted the seeds of internal disaster for Labor. Returning to opposition federally after the 1949 election, the Labor organisation turned its attention to the union movement. A plan was hatched for Labor to win back control of unions affiliated with the Communist Party. To carry out this plan, a group of Labor people — known as the *Industrial Groups*, or *Groupers* — set about trying to win election to the executives of the communist-controlled unions. In some instances, the Groupers were successful.

Initially, the Industrial Groupers had the support of the parliamentary Labor Party. However, with every success in winning back a previously communist-controlled union, the Industrial Groupers increased their influence within the party organisation. The tactics used to win back unions were suddenly starting to be applied in the party's local branches.

Having won control of unions, the Groupers were now setting about winning control of the local branches using the tactic of accusing their adversaries of being communist sympathisers. The prevailing world political environment, dominated as it was by the suspicions of communism as part of the Cold War, added to the tensions.

By 1954, the momentum of the Groupers was such that it alarmed sections of the parliamentary Labor Party, with many Labor MPs fearing they'd be next on the Grouper hit-list. The federal leader, Herbert Vere (Doc) Evatt, sought to rein the Groupers in. At the National Conference held in Hobart in 1954, Evatt sought to have the Groupers disbanded. Those in the Labor Party with Grouper alignment refused Evatt, and the party literally split as the Groupers decamped to hold a separate Conference on the other side of town.

Many tensions, one big split

The 1954 battle at the National Conference in Hobart became the lightning rod for tensions brewing in other state branches of the Labor Party. In Queensland, for example, tensions had been growing between the party secretary, Jack Edgerton, and Premier Vince Gair. Having been threatened by Edgerton, Gair split from the ALP to create the Queensland Labor Party. Gair's split coincided with the 1954 arguments, so, in effect, the Labor Party was already split, even before Evatt tried to expel the Groupers.

DOC EVATT AND COMMUNISM

Herbert Vere Evatt (also known as 'the Doc' because he held a PhD, as well as being an eminent constitutional lawyer and Queen's Counsel) was a major figure in Australian history. He is sometimes known as the first President of the General Assembly of the United Nations, from 1948 to 1949.

Evatt was also a giant in the Labor Party — although, as a lawyer, his entry to the party was from the branches rather than from the unions. He was very much an intellectual with a strong commitment to social justice. In the fraught times of the Cold War, however, this stand got Evatt into trouble.

Evatt was by no means a communist. (How could he be? He was in the ALP, after all.) And he supported the Groupers when they tried to win unions back from the CPA. However, in 1951, Liberal Prime Minister R. G. (Bob) Menzies (see Chapter 10) passed laws to make the Communist Party illegal. The CPA challenged this move in the High Court, and Evatt provided his services as the party's legal advocate. Evatt and the CPA won this case.

Menzies then held a referendum to alter the Constitution to make the Communist Party illegal. Evatt successfully led the campaign against this move as well, allowing scope for his opponents to accuse him of being a communist sympathiser. Evatt was also caught up in the Petrov Affair (see the nearby sidebar).

The situation in Victoria, however, was very different and much more sectarian, mainly because of the involvement of Archbishop Mannix — the very same Mannix who'd involved himself in the 1916 arguments over conscription (flick back to 'Labor and conscription: 1916'). Mannix had been concerned about the rise of communism as well. Given the link between Irish Catholicism and Labor politics, he had more than a passing interest in the struggle against the Communist Party going on in the unions.

The Victorian Catholic Church formed its own organisation to work against communism among the church's constituency, the National Civic Council (NCC), headed by a lay official in the church named Bartholomew (Bob) Santamaria. Like the Groupers, the NCC was out and about, trying to subvert the communists. Unlike the Groupers, however, the NCC had no affiliation with the Labor Party at all (in fact, the NCC was suspected of recruiting on behalf of the Liberal Party). Still, the link between being a worker, being in a union and being Catholic was very strong in Victoria, and Labor people may well have been associated with the NCC. The NCC's secrecy made it difficult to know who was in it, a reflection of the way Santamaria himself tended to operate.

By 1955, Labor's split was so comprehensive it had led to the creation of a new political party — the Democratic Labor Party. Vince Gair and the Queensland Labor Party also joined the DLP. The ALP lost branch members, unions and parliamentarians to the DLP. The DLP became a bitter enemy of the ALP. It accused the ALP of communist sympathies, it ran candidates against Labor candidates and, when DLP members were elected to parliament, they voted with the Liberal Party. This divide went on in Australian politics until 1974, when the last DLP senator associated with the 1950s split was finally defeated in the double-dissolution election of that year.

The 1955 split also saw the collapse of a Labor government in Queensland and in Victoria. In retaliation, the ALP declared that, in addition to the Communist Party, the DLP and Santamaria's NCC were to be *proscribed organisations* — if you were a Labor member and belonged to any of these bodies, you'd be expelled.

Staying solid: New South Wales

The split did not affect New South Wales Labor to anywhere near the same extent as in Queensland and Victoria. The New South Wales Catholic Archbishop, Dr Norman Thomas Gilmour, refused to become involved in internal Labor politics, and the New South Wales branch did not split. Consequently, Labor continued to win government in state elections in the state until the 1960s.

THE PETROV AFFAIR

Paranoia about the Soviet Union and international communism was at its height in the mid-1950s, and Australia was not immune.

On 3 April 1954, three years after the Menzies government had tried to make the Australian Communist Party illegal and right in the midst of Labor's split, Vladimir Petrov was a secretary at the Soviet embassy in Canberra. In what became known as the Petrov Affair, Petrov defected and sought political asylum in Australia. His wife, Evdokia, was dramatically snaffled from the hands of KGB agents while she was in Darwin on her way back to Moscow. The Petrovs were both later granted asylum.

Robert Menzies' Liberal–Country government convened a royal commission into communist activities in Australia after the Prime Minister hinted that Labor members might have been involved in spying for the communists! (Members of Opposition Leader Dr Evatt's staff were named in the Petrov documents.) Dr Evatt acted as counsel for Labor people dragged before the commission. In a snap election called by Menzies in 1955, Evatt then led a divided Labor Party to one of its heavier defeats.

The split: Ancient history or relevant?

The split devastated Labor and probably contributed to the long periods of electoral failure for Labor in federal elections as well as in Queensland and Victoria.

The tensions associated with the split started easing in 1974, when the DLP lost its last senator. It wasn't until 1984, however, that the split was reconciled. At a Conference held in Melbourne, four unions that had split in 1955 were re-admitted to the party, including the massive Shop, Distributive and Allied Employees' Association (the SDA, which covers workers in the retail sector) that today is one of the powerbroking unions in the ALP organisation.

REMEMBER

The faint echoes of the split live on in today's ALP via the factional system. For a long time, the New South Wales branch of the party had been the home base of the Right faction, mainly because the party didn't split in 1955. The Victorian branch, on the other hand, was the power base of the Socialist Left, precisely because the Catholic Right had decamped to the DLP. By the same token, the return of the four unions altered the factional balance in Victoria, with Labor Unity now the strongest faction.

Modernising Labor: From Whitlam to Rudd and Gillard

Between 1949 and 1972, Labor experienced a long period in federal opposition. Then, in 1972, under the leadership of Edward Gough (known by Gough) Whitlam, Labor was finally returned to government amid great excitement associated with its election slogan: It's Time.

Within three years, the Whitlam government was gone, mired in a welter of controversy over its policies, the way it behaved, its use of a joint sitting and then, to top it all off, being dismissed by the governor-general amid the constitutional crisis of 1975 (refer to Chapter 5). One thing that can be agreed on is that the Whitlam government marked the beginning of the emergence of what can be thought of as modern Labor.

But Labor continued to evolve under successive leaders. Each leader examined in this section introduced reforms that they believed would make Labor more modern, as well as more attractive to voters.

The Whitlam policy legacy

Assessing the legacy of the Whitlam government is actually very difficult, not least because of the circumstances of its dismissal, which tends to make Whitlam a somewhat heroic political figure.

His government's extensive reform agenda was also heroic to some, given that it embraced an agenda not usually, up to that point, associated with Labor. It included trying to achieve equal rights for women in the workplace, to advance the cause of the environment and to recognise the land rights of Indigenous Australians. Whitlam was also a great supporter of the arts. The Whitlam government withdrew Australian troops from Vietnam and ended military conscription, which had been introduced in 1964 under a Liberal government.

His government's major reforms in education and health, where a universal health insurance scheme (called Medibank, today called Medicare) was brought in, were entirely within the Labor tradition of supporting the welfare state, yet his government's decision to cut industry protection by 25 per cent in 1974 characterised a poor relationship with the union movement. The Whitlam government was particularly angry with the unions for their failure to exercise wage restraint.

As opposition leader in the 1960s, Whitlam took on the party organisation with a view to reducing the power of the affiliated unions and their delegates. Indeed, so angry with Whitlam was the Victorian branch of the ALP that it tried to engineer his downfall at the hands of Caucus. The move was rebuffed, and Whitlam retaliated by reorganising the Victorian branch with a view to diminishing the power of the left-wing unions.

See Chapter 16 for more on Whitlam's contribution to Australian politics.

WHITLAM: TOWARDS A MODERN ALP

The Whitlam government's policy legacy is also sometimes understood as modernising in that it sought to address the concerns of middle-class Australia. Universal healthcare and greater access to higher education were major parts of the policy platform, as was the pursuit of Indigenous land rights. These things are now seen as inextricably linked with the Labor policy tradition, even though they were of marginal relevance to the industrial wing of the party.

Hayden: Farewell the Socialist Objective

Labor experienced another long period in federal opposition between 1975 and 1983. After another landslide defeat in 1977, the federal Caucus eventually replaced Whitlam as leader with Bill Hayden. Hayden tried to recast the Labor Party's image to the voters as a party of moderate reform, more interested in working with private enterprise in a bid to secure economic growth.

To this end, the party got rid of the Socialist Objective, made possible after the change to the structure of National Conference to now include 99 delegates (refer to Table 9-1). The right-wing factions that now had the numbers in the larger Conference supported a motion to do away with the Objective on the grounds that it was obsolete.

The Hawke government

Assessing the Hawke government poses even more difficulty than assessing Whitlam's legacy. Elected to power in 1983, Labor had its longest-ever period in office, which stretched until 1996. Along the way, Bob Hawke was displaced as leader by Paul Keating.

Hawke was Labor's most successful federal leader, having won the 1983, 1984, 1987 and 1990 elections. Despite his success, it wasn't the voters who got rid of Hawke. That dubious honour rests with the Caucus, which voted to replace him with Keating in 1991. By that stage, however, Hawke's popularity had declined as economic recession took hold.

The controversy about the Hawke government revolves around its approach to economic policy. The Hawke government projected itself as a reform government, but the changes it made to the economy seemed to be closer to the agenda of the business community than the trade unions. In particular, the government deregulated the banking sector, floated the Australian dollar, set about instituting specifically targeted welfare, reintroduced a partial fee system for university education and began the process of selling off (that is, *privatising*) former government corporations — some, such as the Commonwealth Bank, that had been set up by former Labor governments.

VOTE 1

HOW LONG IS A YARD?

Bob Hawke is famous on the world stage for reasons other than politics. Long before he entered parliament, he established a beer-drinking record for the fastest consumption of a yard glass of beer — in 1954, while he was at Oxford University. For a time, this record stood in the *Guinness Book of Records*.

On the other hand, the government returned Medicare (it had been abolished by the previous Liberal–National government) and put together a major welfare program designed to assist poor families. It was this program that caused Hawke to declare that, by 1990, no child would be living in poverty. He had got his lines wrong. The hope was that by 1990 childhood poverty would have been seriously reduced.

The unions and business under Hawke

Hawke's biggest project was to try to bring the unions and business together in dialogue over a range of policies in a bid to find consensus. Before coming into parliament, Hawke had been president of the Australian Council of Trade Unions (ACTU) and had a long history of sorting out industrial disputes between unions and businesses.

Although he was a union man (albeit one with a First Class degree from Oxford University), Hawke was also very friendly with local business operators, especially those who had migrated to Australia and had become self-made successes. On this basis, Hawke argued that government should be about bringing unions and business together.

The Accord

The Prices and Income Accord was arguably the Hawke government's greatest policy achievement. This agreement was thrashed out at a summit, held at parliament between unions, businesses and some welfare advocacy groups, in which wage restraint was promised in exchange for price restraint. The Accord process soon became the method of policy creation preferred by Hawke. His ministers sought to find agreements between competing interest groups as part of the policy-making process.

In economic policy and industrial relations, the Accord process led to the ACTU agreeing to wage restraint and award restructure. In exchange, business promised to work with unions in working out wages and conditions. At the same time that his critics were accusing him of betraying the Labor tradition, Hawke had actually done more than any previous Labor leader to incorporate the union movement into the nation's policy-making process.

Hawke also had an interesting approach to Conference. Whereas Whitlam had tended to disregard the body, Hawke actually made sure that any major policy initiative his government wanted to take first had to be agreed on at National Conference. Of course, the factional system, which became quite rigid and disciplined at this time, helped make sure that the Labor leadership was rarely defeated on such matters.

See Chapter 16 for more on Hawke's contribution to Australian politics.

A TALE OF TWO CONFERENCES: 1984 AND 1986

The first National Conference held during Hawke's time as prime minister occurred in 1984. Plenty of arguments erupted at this meeting, including a major row over a Hawke government proposal to allow the sale of uranium to France. A party member jumped onto the floor of Conference and set fire to his membership card in protest — an action captured on television.

By 1986, however, such instances of dispute had disappeared. Thanks to the factional system, Conference became a highly stage-managed affair. Big decisions were made as a result of factional conveners meeting and reaching agreements behind closed doors. Out on the floor of Conference, meanwhile, debates were constrained and dignified.

Conference was clearly keen to be seen as a part of a functional government. Those who went to the 1986 Hobart Conference hoping to see conflict and histrionics went away disappointed.

Keating: From treasurer to prime minister

Paul Keating had been treasurer for much of the Hawke government's years in office, and, in that position, was a robust advocate of market-driven economic reform. In 1991, however, Keating finally realised his ambition to become prime minister when the Caucus elected him to replace Hawke. Keating won the 1993 election campaigning against a goods and services tax (GST) proposed by his Liberal opponent (in 1985, as treasurer, Keating had actually supported the idea of a GST).

Keating was prime minister until 1996. During that time, he changed his position on economic reform (mainly in the face of a recession), but also sought to project a new set of agenda items. These items included reconciling white and Indigenous Australia by issuing a declaration of apology for many of its policies (outlined in a particularly moving and powerful speech delivered in Redfern in 1995, outlined in Chapter 17), and by starting up the campaign for Australia to become a republic.

Keating's style had long been the basis for the accumulation of many admirers, but in 1996 the Australian electorate indicated what they thought of him and Labor by dispensing one of the biggest defeats Labor had ever experienced.

The rise of Rudd

Labor spent 1996 to 2007 in federal opposition. During that time, the federal party was led by former Hawke and Keating minister Kim Beazley. Beazley lost the 1998 and 2001 elections. After the 2001 defeat, Beazley was replaced by Simon Crean, who eventually gave way to Mark Latham. Latham lost the 2004 election, after which Beazley returned to the leadership. Just prior to the 2007 election, Beazley lost the leadership again, this time to Kevin Rudd. Rudd led Labor to the 2007 election and won.

Even in the early stages of Rudd's prime ministership, he demonstrated his style to be closer to the Whitlam reform agenda than to that of Hawke. The declaration of an official apology to Australian Aboriginal and Torres Strait Islanders was one of the first things the new Rudd government did, but the issues of global warming, the global financial crisis and the complex areas of health and education reform also preoccupied the government.

The Rudd government sought to ameliorate the anti-union elements of industrial relations laws put in place by the previous Liberal government, but the Accord process used by the Hawke government was not revisited. The Rudd government was soon in dispute with some building industry unions.

Rudd himself bore more resemblance to Whitlam in background than he did to Hawke. A former diplomat and someone with tertiary qualifications, Rudd didn't come from the trade union movement (unlike Hawke with his ACTU links). Rudd also fell outside of the factional system. Although aligned with the right wing, some of his most senior colleagues (his deputy prime minister, Julia Gillard, and finance minister, Lindsay Tanner) were aligned with the left.

After becoming leader, Rudd demanded — and got — an agreement that, when in government, he would choose his own ministry. This move changed Labor rules and traditions, where the ministry was chosen by Caucus — usually after a negotiated carve-up of positions among the factions. Ultimately, this was the beginning of Rudd's undoing. After a leadership spill in June 2010, Julia Gillard was made leader of the Labor Party and consequently Australia's first female prime minister.

The Gillard years

Julia Gillard had enjoyed a high public profile during Labor's years in opposition. Once Labor won the 2007 election, Gillard's stocks continued to rise. She held significant responsibilities between 2007 and 2010. For example, in addition to being the deputy prime minister, Gillard was minister for education, as well as social inclusion and employment and workplace relations.

Following a string of poor opinion polls, and growing frustration within the Labor party about Rudd's leadership, Gillard was chosen to replace Rudd as Labor leader and prime minister. She quickly called an election, but the result was poor for Labor as the party lost ground in the lower house.

Despite this, Gillard was able to construct a minority government and relied on the support of independents and the newly elected Australian Greens MP in the lower house.

The Gillard government was active in implementing a raft of new laws. These included new funding arrangements for schools, introducing the National Disability Insurance Scheme, and a Minerals Resource Rent Tax. The Gillard government also introduced the Clean Energy Bill 2011, which sought to establish a mechanism to price carbon. This, however, was quickly branded a 'carbon tax' by the opposition and Gillard's popularity started to fall.

Labor replaced Gillard with Rudd in 2013, who led the party to a heavy election loss against the Tony Abbott–led Coalition.

Pragmatism in Action: Labor in the States

Labor's record of electoral success in federal politics is patchy. It has also been a patchy performer at state level. Historically, Labor has lost many more elections than it has won in South Australia, Victoria and Western Australia. By the same token, it has tended to be the natural party of government in Tasmania, New South Wales and, up until the 1950s split, Queensland. Labor was a disaster in Queensland between 1954 and 1989, but, in more recent times, Labor has again dominated that state's politics. Also more recently, Labor has been more successful in some of its historically weaker states (especially Victoria), while greater volatility has occurred in Tasmanian politics due to the rise of the Greens in the late 1980s.

Interestingly, two recent periods have seen Labor dominance of state governments. The first coincided with the Hawke years in the early 1980s, with Labor holding government in all states except Queensland. The premiers who governed at this time were seen as *managerial* — that is, they were more interested in trying to manage the financial affairs of their states in a pragmatic way. This strategy was a bid to ensure the delivery of social services alongside the encouragement of private development and growth. In other words, nothing was quite as non-ideological as a state Labor government and its premier.

By the 1990s, international recession saw voters turn on their state Labor governments and vote them from office. By the mid-2000s, however, Labor was back in every state and in the two territories as well! Once again, the premiers and chief ministers proved to be pragmatists who tried to balance the idea that Labor governments provide good-quality public health and education outcomes against a desire to attract investment to their states and seek to encourage a vibrant private economy.

Labor in the Future

The Labor Party is famous for some wildly dramatic moments and having almost equal shares of historical successes and earth-shattering failures. It won government in 1904 for a short time but has spent most of its time in national politics as the party of opposition. The party has split three times, and been sacked from office by a state governor (Sir Phillip Game's 1932 dismissal of the Lang government in New South Wales) and by a governor-general (Sir John Kerr in 1975). Labor has been forced from office by defiant upper houses a number of times (in Victoria in the 1940s and in the national parliament in 1975), and spent periods of opposition in excess of 20 years in national politics, and in the politics of Victoria and Queensland.

The ALP has proven to be an enduring party, defying its own tendency towards self-destruction (the various splits), some terrible losses in federal and state elections, and even finding a way to manage its internal factional system. Labor is also responsible for producing Australia's first female prime minister — Julia Gillard, in 2010.

REMEMBER

The challenges for Labor in the future relate to its core base. Labor has always been supported by *blue-collar*, working-class voters. It has also always had a strong degree of support among some *white-collar* voters, especially from those employed in human services such as teaching, social work and the law, and in the public sector. Trying to balance the political outlooks of these two groups can be difficult, as debates over immigration, national security and the environment show.

Also on the agenda is the question of how the trade union movement fits in. The vast majority of Labor MPs have some background in the union movement, although recent Labor prime ministers such as Gough Whitlam, Paul Keating and

Kevin Rudd weren't from a union background at all. The affiliated unions provide a great deal of Labor's operating revenue, as well as anywhere between 50 and 60 per cent of delegates to Labor's various conferences.

Is this a fair division of the internal operation of the party, with a union movement that now covers less than 20 per cent of the workforce? On the other hand, can the party survive without the input of the very movement that created it back in the 1890s? If history is anything to go by, Labor seems destined to survive, even in the face of self-inflicted crises.

IN THIS CHAPTER

» Tracing the origins of Australian conservative parties

» Examining the birth of the Liberal Party

» Checking out the party's organisation and structure

» Exploring Liberal factionalism

» Reviewing the Liberal track record in national government

» Looking at the Liberals in the states and in the future

Chapter **10**

The Liberal Party

The Liberal Party of Australia is the youngest of the three main parties that dominate the Australian parliament, having been created in 1944 (although the party's antecedents go back further, to 1909, when a Liberal Party was created by the efforts of Alfred Deakin). The party has a mass organisation like the Australian Labor Party (ALP), but a number of subtle differences make the Liberal Party somewhat more complicated than its adversary. The nature of the Liberal Party's relationship with the National Party (formerly the Country Party) also raises a major question.

The Liberal Party is sometimes described as the party of the business world, but, as you find out in this chapter, this concept doesn't mean that business interest groups are incorporated into the party's organisation the way affiliated unions are linked to the ALP. On the contrary, the Liberal Party has a very strong philosophical commitment to individualism that even extends to Liberal members of parliament. Technically, this commitment makes the Liberal Party just a little less rigidly disciplined than Labor. This chapter also examines how Liberal philosophies translate to the party organisation and its internal politics and traditions.

The Liberal Party has been a very successful party in electoral terms in national politics especially, and also in the politics of a number of the states. In federal politics, the Liberal Party has been the party of government much more often than not since 1949. In this chapter, we examine some of the milestones that have marked that track record and how various leaders have influenced the party's direction.

Early Origins: Free Traders, Protectionists and Fusionists

Technically, the Liberal Party of Australia was created in 1944. The antecedents of the party can be traced much further back, however. At the time of Federation and the creation of the new national parliament — at the very time that the ALP had already been created and was running candidates — the non-Labor side of politics involved two broad groups of parliamentary members. These groups were the Free Traders (elected mainly from New South Wales) and the Protectionists (elected mainly from Victoria). The former New South Wales premier and newly elected member of the House of Representatives (MHR) George Reid was the leader of the Free Traders, whereas Victoria's Alfred Deakin was the leader of the Protectionists. (Refer to Chapter 3 for more on the Protectionists and the Free Traders.)

Both groups were really only loose coalitions of MPs who depended on their own individual support networks to campaign in their electorates. Interestingly, both sides were somewhat antagonistic towards each other and, in the first years of the new national parliament, the Protectionists and Labor sometimes voted together to form minority governments.

The brittleness of non-Labor politics resulted in instability during the first decade after Federation. How brittle were things for the non-Labor side? Very, because, as prime minister, the leading non-Labor politician, Alfred Deakin, often relied on Labor support in parliament to continue to govern. This fact also explains why Deakin had three separate terms as prime minister: 1903 to 1904, 1905 to 1908 and finally from 1909 to 1910.

By 1909, the non-Labor politicians felt they needed to do something to avoid this instability and identified the need to enhance their organisation if they were to tackle the Labor Party more effectively. The Protectionists and the Free Traders came together in 1909 under the party name Liberal. Because the party was actually a coming together of these two groups, it was also known as the Fusion Liberal Party. Alfred Deakin led this party and, indeed, served as prime minister under this arrangement. The party's efforts to form a more cohesive force were spurred on further when Labor won the 1910 election.

The Fusion wasn't necessarily a united group, however, and anti-Protectionist sentiment simmered to the point where Deakin resigned from the parliament in 1913. The collapse of the Fusion Party allowed Labor to form a ministry and regain government in 1914.

A new anti-Labor party: The Nationalists

The remnants of the Fusion struggled along for a short period, when a sudden implosion of the Labor Party completely altered the dynamics of non-Labor party politics. The Labor split led by Billy Hughes over conscription (refer to Chapter 9) resulted in a number of former Labor MPs crossing the floor to vote with the Fusion and install a new government, with Hughes as its prime minister. This event created the impetus for the beginning of a new political party, bringing the Fusion remnants and the Labor defectors into one party. This new party was called the Nationalists (not to be confused with today's National Party, which used to be the Country Party — more about the Nationals in Chapter 11).

The Nationalists were, in fact, a rather diverse lot politically, being ex-Liberal and ex-Labor members brought together mainly over their dismay at the way Labor had handled the conscription matter while, at the same time, becoming ardent supporters of the Great War. Their organisation outside of the parliament was almost non-existent. The party did win federal elections, however. It won a big victory in the 1917 federal election and remained in power until the fateful 1929 election.

The Nationalists also won government in some of the states, including Victoria, where a Nationalist government included a young man by the name of Robert Menzies, who was serving as attorney-general. In 1934, Menzies won preselection for the federal seat of Kooyong and was elected to the House of Representatives.

For all this electoral success, the party experienced great volatility. Ex-Labor man Hughes was not liked in conservative political circles, and he was eventually forced to resign the party leadership to the MHR for Flinders, Stanley Melbourne Bruce, in 1923. Hughes went to the backbench, where he would scheme his revenge. In the meantime, Bruce secured an agreement with the Country Party to form a federal coalition that allowed that party's leader, Earle Page, to be deputy prime minister.

In 1929, amid the onset of the Great Depression, the Nationalist–Country coalition was defeated in a national election — and Bruce himself lost his seat of Flinders, denying the Nationalist opposition a parliamentary leader. Hughes tried to regain the leadership, but was blocked by the Country Party. The whole anti-Labor side of politics appeared to be in total disarray, when another Labor split came to the rescue!

Anti-Labor Uniting (Sort Of)

In 1931, the federal Labor government, headed by James Scullin as prime minister, was in disarray (refer to Chapter 9). A division of opinion over economic policy responses to the Great Depression became a major split. A number of Labor MPs were alarmed at the influence of former New South Wales Premier Jack Lang over the party and resigned. Like Hughes and his supporters, the Labor defectors crossed the floor and joined their former political adversaries, the Nationalists.

Among the Labor defectors was a former Labor premier turned federal politician, Joseph Aloysius Lyons. Like Hughes, Lyons was an ex-Labor man but, unlike Hughes, the former Tasmanian premier was an easygoing character. As a practising Catholic, Lyons was socially conservative and was able to get along with the more conservative elements among the old Nationalists. He was also seen as a much less imperious and ambitious character than Menzies, who was also in the federal Nationalist ranks by now and who also showed leadership ambition.

United they stand: Creating the United Australia Party

With the infusion of Labor defectors providing an acceptable leadership candidate, the Nationalists were dissolved and a new political party created, the United Australia Party (UAP). In 1931, the UAP won a landslide federal election victory, and Joe Lyons became prime minister.

REMEMBER

The UAP was the most directly related antecedent of the modern Liberal Party. It was different from the Nationalists in that the party turned its attention to forming an organisation to operate alongside the parliamentary party. The new organisation included a Women's Auxiliary and a Young UAP, clearly with the intention of recruiting members in order to raise finances for campaigns.

Serious tensions in the emerging party organisation became apparent, however. First, tensions arose between the Sydney office of the party and its Melbourne counterpart. The UAP, meanwhile, found it really difficult to set up an organisation in Queensland, where the Country Party was proving to be very strong (see Chapter 11). An interesting tension also developed between the UAP executive and the parliamentary party. The party executive included some leading business figures, who began to agitate for a greater say over policy and preselections. The parliamentary leaders, meanwhile, were very hostile to the idea of being told what to do by the big end of town. They weren't too keen on being told what to do by the party executive either.

United they fall: The collapse of the UAP

The organisational tensions in the party weren't too much of a problem as long as the parliamentary party was functional, and tensions in this side of the party remained under control for as long as Joe Lyons was prime minister. In April 1939, as the clouds of World War II began to gather, Lyons passed away.

Lyons was succeeded by Robert Menzies, but this succession wasn't without its political risk. The Sydney-based arm of the party was very suspicious of Menzies' ambition and would've preferred a different candidate. More destabilising, however, was the presence of Billy Hughes, who personally loathed Menzies and began plotting against him almost immediately.

It was Menzies who was the Australian prime minister at the beginning of World War II and, as such, in 1941 travelled to London to participate in Winston Churchill's British war cabinet. While he was away on this duty, the UAP started to collapse. Hughes launched abusive attacks on Menzies, and the Country Party threatened to walk out of the coalition.

ROBERT GORDON MENZIES: A LIBERAL GIANT

Robert Gordon Menzies, or Bob Menzies (later Sir Robert when he was knighted by Queen Elizabeth II in 1963), was Australia's longest serving prime minister — a record he established as federal leader of the Liberal Party. Indeed, Menzies was a giant figure in the party, having been instrumental in the re-organisation of the UAP after the 1943 election defeat.

Menzies was born in Jeparit, Victoria, into a small-business family. A gifted student, Menzies excelled at primary school and later went to Wesley College (his father, apparently, wanted him to go to Scotch College) and then to Melbourne University to study law after his strong academic performance earned him a scholarship. He was involved in student governance and then went into the law. He was one of the barristers who participated in the Engineer's Case, in which the High Court's ruling allowed federal industrial law to apply to state agencies, in 1920.

Menzies joined the Nationalists and was elected to the Victorian parliament. He was preselected to the federal seat of Kooyong as a member of the Nationalists and then the UAP. He launched the Liberal Party in 1945, but the new party suffered a terrible defeat at the hands of Labor in 1946. The bank nationalisation controversy (refer to Chapter 9) saw Labor defeated in 1949, and the Liberals began a long period of national government. Menzies retired from politics in 1966.

On returning to Australia in mid-1941, Menzies resigned the leadership and the prime ministership. The immediate beneficiary was the Labor Party, when two independent MHRs decided to support the formation of a Cabinet headed by then Labor leader John Curtin. The UAP struggled on to the 1943 election with none other than Billy Hughes as its leader. The party was thrashed by Labor in the 1943 poll.

From the UAP Ashes: The Liberal Party

Non-Labor politics was completely in the doldrums after the 1943 election. Interest in reorganising non-Labor politics was high, however, with the former leader, Menzies, a prominent player in negotiations, especially between the Victorian and New South Wales divisions of the UAP.

In 1944, two conferences were held. The first, in Canberra, aimed at bringing the remnants of the UAP together to explore the possibility of putting a new party together — not as easy as it sounds. The collapse of the UAP had seen a number of other state-based non-Labor parties appearing, including the Liberal Country League in South Australia, the Queensland People's Party and a Liberal Democratic Party in New South Wales. An external organisation called the Institute of Public Affairs (IPA) also argued that it should be given affiliated status with any new party.

The Canberra conference succeeded in finding enough common ground to proceed with the next stage of trying to put a new organisation in place. It also agreed on the name Liberal Party. The next meeting took place in Albury, where the party's constitution was drawn up and agreed to, and an interim party executive was installed.

The various non-Labor parties in the other states were willing to align with this new organisation, although the Queensland People's Party took a little longer to join the new Liberal Party. This alignment was more relevant to state politics than federal politics, and reflected an early feature of the new party, where each of the state divisions had a degree of autonomy from the federal level. Still, the formation of functional organisations with large mass membership in each state — even those states that had previously been weak for the UAP — was a major achievement realised within the first ten years of the party's existence.

The Liberal Party Organisation

The Liberal Party operates in each of the states (except Queensland, where the Liberal and National Parties have merged) and in the Australian Capital Territory (the Northern Territory party is the Country Liberal Party). This state- and territory-based diversity points to a major point of difference between the ALP and the Liberal Party. Whereas the ALP has a strong degree of central authority placed in the hands of the national level of the party, the Liberal Party is made up of six autonomous state and territory divisions, based on a mass membership at the local level, and a federal division that attends to the affairs of the party at the national level, though it can't discipline its state-based components.

Because the Liberal Party's state and territory divisions are autonomous, they also have their own structures and constitutions. However, all divisions have a party headquarters that's responsible for the day-to-day running of the party, as well as supporting its election campaigns.

At a federal level, the party's Federal Secretariat is responsible for the party's operation, as well as assisting its state divisions when appropriate.

REMEMBER

Some other fundamental points of difference exist between the Labor organisation and the Liberal Party. Whereas Labor has affiliated unions, the Liberal Party doesn't allow the affiliation of any external organisation, be it companies, business advocacy groups or even policy think-tanks such as the IPA. The Liberal Party is a party that only individuals can join.

When the new party established this rule of not allowing the affiliation of any external organisation, it resonated with the best traditions of individualism and liberty associated with liberal philosophy, but it also had a pragmatic purpose. One of the things that annoyed Menzies was the attempts by business interests to use their financial contributions to the UAP to interfere in the parliamentary operation of the party. To that end, the ban on associations joining the Liberal Party was partly a means of constraining the influence of big corporate or associational donors on aspects such as policy-making and preselections.

VOTE 1

Liberal philosophy found expression in another form, and again the outcome was the complete opposite of the Labor rules. Labor, of course, was a party where discipline was based on pledges of loyalty. The Liberal Party would have no such pledge. The party's constitution declared that individualism and liberty of thought and action were essential parts of the party's philosophy. Consequently, members would not be asked to sign pledges of loyalty, and Liberal members who succeeded in getting elected to a parliamentary chamber would always have the right to vote according to their conscience if they wished to.

Getting together: State and Federal Council

The individual member is at the base of the Liberal Party organisation. Membership is organised in local branches in each of the states. Each state division of the party (the Liberal Party prefers the term state *division* rather than state *branch*) has a general body that meets regularly to transact party business and to which delegates are elected from the local branches, from a specific women's division and from the Young Liberals (which we cover at the end of this section). This body is called *State Council*.

State Council is the Liberal equivalent of Labor's State Conference (refer to Chapter 9), but with some very important points of difference. First and foremost, State Council doesn't have any direct authority to tell the parliamentary wing of the Liberal Party what to do. (Labor Conferences, of course, have the power to make binding policy.)

What Council can do, however, is elect office bearers to the state division's organisation, including the important positions of state party president, state party treasurer and state director. Of these, the position of state director is arguably the most significant, because it's actually the position of party secretary. The director is responsible for the party head office where the *State Secretariat* resides. As the party's state-based administrative arm, the Secretariat is expected to work very closely with the parliamentary leader of the party. Additionally, the director takes responsibility for the management of election campaigns when they arise.

State Council also elects delegates to its federal equivalent, Federal Council. Again, in a reflection of the party's federal nature, each of the state divisions sends an equal number of delegates, with representation also for the national presidents of the Women's Council and the Young Liberals. Like its state counterparts, Federal Council elects a federal executive that includes a federal president and a federal director. The Federal Secretariat provides support for the federal parliamentary leader.

The Federal Council is the national gathering of the delegates of the party organisation but, again like the State Councils, the body has no direct power over formulating party policy. Figure 10-1 shows how the structure works. The closest the Federal Council gets to formulating policy is to debate and perhaps amend something known as the *party platform*. The Liberal party platform is a general statement of principles that the party stands for. The assumption is that the parliamentary party uses these broad statements as a guideline to forming actual policy.

Liberal Party policy-making process

Parliamentary wing	**Extra-parliamentary wing**
Parliamentary leader	Federal Council
↑	↑
Parliamentary party	State Councils
	↑
	Branch members

Note: Policy decisions made by the Federal Council are not binding on the parliamentary party, which is ultimately responsible for making policy.

FIGURE 10-1: Federal and State Councils of the Liberal Party are important in debating policy but have no direct influence on the parliamentary wing.

VOTE 1

In the light of the restrictions that party rules place on their ability to impact on policy, it may seem that the various party Councils aren't particularly important or eagerly attended by party delegates. This isn't actually the case. Councils are important to the operation of the party and they can be an important forum for the membership to express ideas on policy — including specific policy proposals. Even though the rules don't allow Council to make decisions on policies that are binding on the parliamentary wing, delegates debate and vote on specific proposals nonetheless — and they expect their Liberal MPs to take these perspectives into account when formulating policy.

Follow the leader!

One of the main reasons Council doesn't have the power to make binding policy is because the party's operation is based on the idea that the power to make such decisions ultimately rests with the parliamentary leader. Indeed, the Liberal Party is sometimes described as a top-down or leadership-based party. Of course, you must remember that the power of the leader isn't unfettered. To be leader, a Liberal MP must have the support of the Party Room, and a wise leader is one who works with, rather than dictates to, the Party Room.

The Party Room

No loud music, dancing or frivolity here (usually). The *Party Room* is the technical term used at both the state and national levels in the Liberal Party to describe the coming together of all Liberal MPs from both the lower and upper houses. In effect, the Party Room is a caucus (the Liberal Party doesn't like this word because of its technical use in the Labor Party) but, according to the party rules, a Liberal MP does have the right to vote according to their conscience.

Because the parliamentary Liberal Party often operates in coalition with the National Party, a distinction is made between the meeting of the Party Room (Liberals only) and the *Joint Party Room* that occurs when all Liberal and National MPs from both houses meet collectively.

REMEMBER

The origins of this feature of the party's organisation go back to the type of party Menzies was trying to create in 1944. The idea of giving the parliamentary leader the right to determine policy had been part of the non-Labor party tradition, and the new Liberal Party maintained this idea.

The parliamentary leader was given other important powers. Unlike its Labor counterpart (where, traditionally, such matters were determined by Caucus), the Liberal Party expects the parliamentary leader to have the right to choose the ministry and to allocate portfolios. Not only can the leader stamp his imprimatur on policy, but he also has a free hand to choose the personnel for the Cabinet and the ministry.

By Menzies, of Menzies, for Menzies

Some analysts have argued that the Liberal Party organisation was put together by Menzies simply so that he would have a party structure to serve his political ambitions — a party by Menzies, of Menzies, for Menzies. In other words, the essence of the Liberal Party rests in the support it gives to the parliamentary wing generally and the parliamentary leader in particular. In such a model, the leader is assumed to know what the party's policy direction is, and the party organisation is required to do little other than provide candidates for election and raise the finance to fund election campaigns.

TECHNICAL STUFF

The real world of politics is a bit more complicated. The Liberal leader does have a lot of power within the party, but it's by no means without its constraints. Federal Liberal leaders, for example, have no power to direct or discipline state Liberal leaders (a reason, in fact, some state and federal Liberal leaders have actively disliked each other at various times in history).

The Liberal leader is under no obligation to take the mass membership's views on policy into account, but only a foolish leader would disregard the broader party view. Likewise, a Liberal parliamentary leader may have greater technical ability to direct her Party Room colleagues on contentious matters, but such a leader would probably fail to hold the position for too long — as one-time leaders Tony Abbott and Malcolm Turnbull were to discover during their time in the leadership. As former federal Liberal leader and prime minister John Howard once put it: Liberal leaders shouldn't forget that party leadership is 'a gift from the Liberal Party Room'.

A structure for government or opposition?

Analysts have argued that the Liberal Party organisation is better suited to being in government than in opposition. In government, Liberal leaders and their Cabinet colleagues can rely on input from the public service to help flesh out policy ideas. In opposition, however, this important source of input is denied. On the occasions that the Liberals have been in opposition, debates about policy formulation have sometimes become a problem. Sometimes the burden of formulating policy options falls on the party Secretariat and the director, which can prove to be a difficult task for such a small group of people to discharge.

REMEMBER

The Liberal Party has been more successful in federal elections than not, and the party's history in federal politics (and in states such as Western Australia and Victoria) since its official launch in 1945 has been peppered with long periods in government. The tensions in the relationship between the organisation and the parliamentary party are always present, but they tend to come to the surface more readily during periods in opposition.

The branch membership strikes back!

The Liberal Party organisation doesn't seem to guarantee ordinary members a great deal of influence over policy-making. The party rules do, however, give branch members one very substantial power and that is over the preselection of Liberal candidates. Although some variations exist from one state division to another, the general Liberal principle (consistent with the party's commitment to decentralising power within the party) is that the power to endorse Liberal candidates for election rests with the local branches.

The Young Liberals

The Liberal Party's Young Liberals organisation is designed to socialise young people into the broader party. It has always been a substantial organisation but, in the 1960s and 1970s, it was a very big and powerful body, especially in Victoria, where membership was very large. In those days, the Young Liberals was as much a social organisation as a political body.

Many Liberals who were to become prominent in state and federal politics in both the parliamentary wing and the organisation got their start in the Young Liberals. The body still exists but is much more political in its orientation these days. It also has a more conservative rival organisation in the form of the Liberal Students' Federation.

In 1983, the Liberal Party was defeated in a federal election. After this defeat, it convened an internal inquiry headed by the New South Wales party president, John Valder. The findings of the inquiry — contained in the Valder Report — were that some aspects of the party organisation needed review and reform. The Valder Report noted the problem of the Federal Council's lack of power over policy and recommended that parliamentary Liberals should take the body more seriously. Valder was also critical of some aspects of the autonomy of the state divisions, and argued for more power for the party's federal and state executives to discipline branches. Few Liberal divisions moved to enact such reforms, however.

Liberal women

The Liberal Party prides its record on incorporating women into its organisation. Soon after its creation, the Liberal Party established the Federal Women's Committee (FWC), in 1945. The FWC was incorporated into the official party organisation in 1946 and has been represented in the party's federal executive ever since.

The Liberal Party also explicitly provides positions for women in the party's organisation. The national level, for example, has a vice-president (female) position. Each division also has similar positions that can be filled only by women, as well as having a specific women's section, also referred to as the Women's Council.

Many people still highlight the need to address gender imbalance in the Party Room. (After the 2019 election, only 23 per cent of Liberal lower house MPs and Senators were women, compared with 47 per cent for Labor.) However, the Liberal approach tends to be constrained by both its organisational rules (it is very difficult to direct local branches on which candidate they should select) and the party's philosophical commitment to the idea of 'merit selection' — which they present as being counter to a concept such as 'affirmative action'. Such action is seen by many in the party as a left-wing approach to the issue.

Liberal Factionalism

The Liberal Party claims that it's not subject to factionalism — at least, not the sort of rigid and disciplined factionalism observed in the Labor Party. To a great extent, this claim is true, because the Liberal Party certainly doesn't have disciplined and organised factions. Factionalism does occur, however — hardly surprising given the breadth of the party's philosophies and ideas, the variety of people attracted to the party, and the tendency for all political parties to have some sort of factionalism (refer to Chapter 8).

Trying to tie down the Liberal Party's factional politics is somewhat difficult, however, because the alliances formed between members can be quite fluid. One political scientist identified as many as nine factional groups operating in the party during the 1980s. The fluidity of Liberal factionalism sometimes leads commentators to talk of factional tendencies in the party. The decentralisation of preselection powers to the local branches also works against disciplined factionalism because it becomes very difficult for aspiring factional leaders to control the choice of candidates.

Given these tendencies toward fluidity, some general trends in the way Liberals come together to try to influence the internal affairs of the Liberal Party are discernible.

Liberals versus conservatives

Like Labor, the Liberal Party has a range of ideological and philosophical traditions to draw on. Two main traditions have consistently underpinned the Liberal Party's approach to politics. The first is *liberalism*. Although it's possible to identify a number of variations in what liberalism actually means, generally it tends to value individual freedoms and take a progressive approach to social policy. The second tradition is *conservatism*, which seeks to maintain the status quo, especially in the area of social policy.

The Liberal Party aims to accommodate philosophical liberals and conservatives as part of a broad *centre-right* political party (usually concerned with limiting the role of government in society). The result can be something of a philosophical or ideological division within the party. As differences in philosophical viewpoints often lead to factionalism in any political party, the differences in opinion between liberals and conservatives can be the basis of the formation of internal alliances of party members and MPs. These alliances are particularly common when matters of morality or ethics arise, such as the regulation of human reproduction or the role of religion in society.

Moderates versus Hardliners

The terminology identifying Moderates versus Hardliners is very popular in media reports about internal Liberal politics, and is something of a modern variation on the liberals versus conservatives dynamic.

Moderates are usually understood to be those Liberals who have been very influenced by liberal philosophies of writers such as John Stuart Mill. They believe in individual liberty but can accommodate the idea of government intervention to achieve 'good' social outcomes. Moderates also tend to be a little less inclined to talk about the importance of religion to politics, and some may also argue the case for individuals to take responsibility for their moral choices.

The *Hardliners* are usually understood as conservatives and are willing to use their position within the party or the parliament to advocate views such as opposition to excessive liberty, advocacy of higher levels of censorship, the centrality of religion to politics and the need for government intervention to maintain moral standards in the community.

VOTE 1

The impact of the divide between Moderates and Hardliners tends to be greater in individual state divisions, where sometimes quite bitter rivalries exist. The South Australian division of the party, for instance, has a long history of quite severe division between its Moderate and Hardliner members. Similar divisions are discernible in New South Wales and, to a slightly lesser extent, Victoria.

Wets and Dries

In the 1980s, when the party was in opposition federally and in many of the states, a major debate about economic policy emerged. The Liberal Party appeared to divide between those who could see a role for government intervention in the economy (and especially in the form of protection for industry) and those who were advocating limited government intervention in the economy. This latter group were sometimes described as *neo-classical liberals* or *economic rationalists* because of their advocacy of a free marketplace.

Australian journalists, however, dubbed the economic rationalists as *Dries*, and the Liberals who advocated for greater government intervention, especially through welfare measures, as *Wets*.

State-based alliances

Factional tendencies along state lines are somewhat inevitable in a party that is so federal in its structure as the Liberal Party. State allegiances tend to be more important to federal parliamentary Liberals — a reflection, indeed, of the importance of the autonomous nature of the state divisions.

However, the rivalry between New South Wales (especially Sydney) and Victoria (especially Melbourne) is one of the most important state-based rivalries of all when it comes to non-Labor politics. The enduring nature of this rivalry, with its origin in the free trade versus protectionism debate of the early 1900s, can still be seen in the modern Liberal Party.

During the Howard government's term, for example, some significant debates flared up between the prime minister, John Howard (from New South Wales), and his treasurer, Peter Costello (from Victoria), on a range of issues, including immigration and reconciliation. Nowadays, state differences tend to be less noticeable in philosophical debates but more prominent in key parliamentary affairs, including the most important decision of all — who will be the leader?

Leadership alliances

Of all the factional configurations that affect the Liberal Party, the matter of how members and MPs align themselves with the parliamentary leader (and, when applicable, the main rival for the leadership of the party) is arguably the most important. The importance of this alliance also reflects one of the realities of the way the Liberal Party is organised and the primacy of the parliamentary leader to the structure.

REMEMBER

The importance of the leadership means factional politics in the party tend to be at their most intense when a leadership crisis occurs. By the same token, a strong and successful leader can count on a very low level of factional agitation in the party. Leadership-driven factionalism, therefore, tends to be most intense during times in opposition.

VOTE 1

LEADERS FROM THE BIG STATES

Very rarely have federal Liberal leaders come from any state other than New South Wales or Victoria. Of the 17 federal Liberal leaders since 1949, 10 were from New South Wales, 6 (including Menzies) from Victoria and only one was from another state — Alexander Downer from South Australia.

THE HOWARD VERSUS PEACOCK BATTLE

Nowhere was the politics associated with leadership factionalism more obvious than the protracted battle between federal leaders John Howard and Andrew Peacock between 1983 and 1996. Both men had two goes at being federal leader and, when they ran out of puff towards the 1990s, they found surrogate candidates to do their bidding.

The leadership battle then tended to cross over with other factional dynamics. Howard's candidacy tended to have support mainly among New South Wales and South Australian Liberals, while Peacock was favoured by Victorians, Queenslanders and Western Australian Liberals (who, in the 1980s, were bitter enemies of Howard). Peacock's supporters were also sometimes dubbed Wets because Howard sought to project himself as an economic Dry. Howard was also seen as a Hardliner, and so Peacock supporters were branded Moderates.

This division was also evident in more recent years, especially with the different approaches of Howard and his treasurer, Peter Costello, on social policy. For example, Costello's reputation as a more socially progressive Liberal was enhanced when he joined 300,000 people in the Walk for Reconciliation in Melbourne. Howard, meanwhile, refused to participate in such events.

The issue of same-sex marriage, which was resolved following a public postal ballot and then a vote in parliament in 2017, also highlighted the differing views of Liberals on social issues. Those who were in favour of same-sex marriage tended to be aligned with socially progressive Liberals such as Malcolm Turnbull, while those who disagreed with changing the law tended to be aligned with conservatives such as Tony Abbott and Scott Morrison, both of whom abstained from voting on the issue in parliament.

The Liberal Party in Government

Since 1949, when the party won the federal election and Robert Menzies began his yet-to-be-surpassed record of tenure as Australian prime minister, the Liberals have been in national government more often than not. Indeed, the federal Liberals governed in coalition in an unbroken stretch between 1949 and 1972. The Liberals also achieved record periods in government in Victoria and South Australia, although the party has historically been weak in Queensland, where the National Party has tended to be the main anti-Labor party. In short, the Liberal Party has been an extremely successful party.

Many reasons have been put forward to account for the party's record of success, among them:

» The Labor Party contributed to its own downfall, first with unpopular policies such as its attempt at bank nationalisation in 1947 and then by splitting in 1955. (Refer to Chapter 9 for more on the Labor splits.)

» While Labor had the unfortunate tendency to look as if it were caught up in the politics of ideology (thanks to the split), the Liberal Party took pride in being pragmatic and middle class.

Certainly, by the 1960s, it appeared as if the Liberal Party was the natural party of government federally and in a number of states.

Menzies retired from politics in 1966, after which the party endured a period of great instability when Menzies' successor, Harold Holt, disappeared while swimming off Portsea on Victoria's Mornington Peninsula in 1967.

An ugly skirmish followed Holt's disappearance as to who would succeed him, and the contest was between the New South Wales division, which backed William (Billy) McMahon, and the Victorian division, which backed John Gorton. Initially, the contest was resolved by the Country Party, which told the Liberals that it would walk out of the coalition if McMahon were to become prime minister. Gorton duly got the job (he was a senator at the time, but was quickly rushed in to represent Holt's seat of Higgins at a by-election) and stayed leader until 1971, when he resigned and allowed McMahon to gain the leadership. McMahon then became only the second Liberal leader to lose an election to the ALP (and the first to do so since 1949), when the government was defeated by Gough Whitlam's Labor Party in 1972.

REMEMBER

Within three years, the Liberals were back in government, this time under the leadership of Malcolm Fraser, who remained prime minister until the defeat of his government at the hands of Bob Hawke and the Labor Party in 1983. This defeat was the beginning of a long and difficult period of federal opposition until 1996, when Howard led the Liberals back into government, staying on as prime minister until 2007, making him the second longest serving prime minister after Menzies.

Pragmatism or programs?

The Liberal Party is clearly a broad centre-right party that tries to accommodate liberals of various types as well as conservatives, but in a way that is pragmatic enough to attempt to appeal to *middle Australia*. This notion of middle Australia may seem vague, but there is a sense that the Liberal Party has a feel for what constitutes the middle-class aspirations of Australian society and, in their moments of electoral success, responding to that sense.

REMEMBERING HAROLD HOLT

What better way to commemorate a prime minister who disappeared, and was presumed drowned, off the coast of Victoria than build a public swimming facility and name it after him? Such a facility can be found in the suburb of Glen Iris in Melbourne, where the Harold Holt Memorial Swimming Centre was opened by Prime Minister John Gorton in March 1969. There's a long list of other Holt memorials, including the US Destroyer USS *Harold E. Holt* and a sundial in Melbourne's picturesque Fitzroy Gardens, to name just two.

Yet, in more recent times, the Liberal Party has sought to project itself as much more conservative. This conservatism has been expressed partly in the support of conservative social policy, partly in defence policy and partly in embracing the idea that religion has a place in helping to form conservative values.

Liberals and the unions

The Liberals can argue about and disagree over many things, but implacable opposition to the trade union movement is one of the key values all Liberals agree on. Some liberal Liberals can accept the idea of unionism as a form of freedom of association, but all Liberals agree the unions have no legitimate role in the governing of Australia.

Some more conservative Liberals even argue that the unions have no legitimate role in the labour market or in industrial relations. This antipathy towards the union movement is important as one of the key political issues that keeps the Liberal Party together, as well as allowing them to form a coalition with the National Party.

Menzies in government

The Menzies government, which lasted for 17 years, revealed all the characteristics of its pragmatism towards economic policy on the one hand, and a certain conservatism on the other. (Chapter 16 gives a summary of Menzies' time in politics.) The government certainly did away with many of the regulations associated with the former Labor postwar reconstruction government. However, in their place came protection designed to assist the manufacturing industry (the Chamber of Manufacturers was based in Melbourne and was a big supporter of the Liberal Party) and to help protect the family farm in agriculture (at the behest of the Country Party, which Menzies governed with in coalition). The importance of coalition politics was reinforced by Menzies, who got on very well with Country Party leaders Arthur (Artie) Fadden and, later, John McEwen (see Chapter 11).

MENZIES' 'FORGOTTEN PEOPLE' SPEECH

In 1942, Robert Menzies made a speech that has served as an iconic oration that established what the Liberal Party (which had not yet been created, of course) would stand for. In outlining his criticism of the Labor Party's relationship with unions and its willingness to use state regulation and control, Menzies sought to weave notions of freedom to do business, freedom to own property and freedom from government regulation with a very Protestant notion of the importance of hard work, thrift and a secure nuclear family life.

Even though it would be three years before the party was formed, this speech seems to sum up the spirit of the Liberal Party's approach to politics. In essence, Menzies sought to represent what he identified as the 'forgotten people' in his new party. The forgotten people, according to Menzies, were the middle class; people who were salary earners, small-business owners and so on who, he believed, were not adequately represented in parliament.

These ideas of Menzies' 'forgotten people' continue to hold power in the Liberal Party today, with Prime Minister Scott Morrison echoing similar sentiments with his identification of the 'quiet Australians' — who he argued were behind his 'miraculous' 2019 election victory.

Check out Chapter 17 for more on this and other memorable political speeches.

THE LIBERAL PARTY AND PROTESTANTISM

In the rather sectarian politics that operated in Australia in the 1940s and into the 1950s, the Liberal Party appeared to be as Protestant-based as the Labor Party appeared to be Catholic-based. Menzies himself came from a Scottish Protestant background, although he was also known to have been quite opposed to any notion that the Liberal Party be an exclusively Protestant party. This sectarianism started to break down in the 1950s and 1960s as a result of the Labor split (refer to Chapter 9) and the upward social mobility of Irish Catholics in postwar Australia.

On the other hand, Menzies adopted a very conservative position on foreign policies that saw him get involved (somewhat embarrassingly) in the Suez Canal crisis in 1956. Menzies led an international delegation to persuade the Egyptian president to abort plans to nationalise the Suez Canal, which was the main oil supply channel for Britain and France. But Menzies' apparent support for French and, especially, British interests seemed to play a role in the negotiations failing.

Menzies then supported the disastrous British and French invasion of Egypt, which led to many commentators questioning his judgement on international affairs.

Menzies also signed Australia up to the Vietnam War in support of the United States. He sought to have the Communist Party of Australia banned, first by way of legislation (overturned in the High Court) and then by referendum (defeated in a vote). To the concern of some of his colleagues, the ageing Menzies also seemed to be increasingly enamoured with the British aristocracy, and younger Liberals were horrified when the Prime Minister proposed that the new Australian decimalised currency be called a royal. In 1966, at the age of 71, Menzies finally retired.

The post-Menzies period was one of turmoil brought on by the disappearance of Holt and the factional brawling over his replacement. The decline in the party's standing in the eyes of the electorate was reflected in the gradual recovery in voter support for Labor. In 1969, Labor came close to defeating the Gorton government, and in 1972 McMahon's Liberal government was defeated.

Malcolm Fraser's government

The Liberal Party returned to government in a landslide victory in December 1975, following the dismissal of the Whitlam government by then Governor-General Sir John Kerr (refer to Chapter 5). This series of events brought Malcolm Fraser to the prime ministership, and he remained in government until 1983 (winning elections in 1977 and 1980 along the way).

Malcolm Fraser was, at the time, considered to be a very conservative person who once famously declared that 'life wasn't meant to be easy'. His conservatism tended to express itself in foreign policy (where he aligned Australia closely to the United States) and in his attempt to reduce the size of government. He honoured a promise to do away with Labor's Medibank health insurance scheme. He also tended to be close to the Country Party and was a firm supporter of the coalition, despite the fact that, in 1975 and 1977, the Liberals had won such a big election landslide it could've governed in its own right.

Typically for the Liberal Party, the Fraser government also proved to be progressive in other policy areas. The Fraser government was a strong supporter of multiculturalism and brought in the Special Broadcasting Service (SBS). Fraser also opened Australia up to Vietnamese and Cambodian 'boat people', who were fleeing repression under the communist regimes in their home countries. See Chapter 16 for more on Fraser's contribution to Australian politics.

But the Fraser government struggled on economic policy. Initially trying to reduce government expenditure, the government, after 1980, began to increase expenditure to ward off a recession. One of the consequences of the increased spending was a falling out between Fraser and his treasurer, John Howard. Howard had urged the Prime Minister to stay true to the objective of reducing government expenditure. Later, Fraser became a constant critic of Howard as a Liberal prime minister on the grounds that the Howard government was insufficiently 'liberal', especially on some human rights issues. In 2010, Fraser became so disillusioned with the Liberal Party that he quit as a party member.

The Howard government

After a 13-year period in opposition characterised by seemingly endless leadership tensions, the Liberal Party was elected back into national government in 1996. The leader of the party was John Howard, who had lost the 1987 election and who had been reviled by a series of people supposedly on his own side of politics, such as former Queensland National Party Premier Joh Bjelke-Petersen (see Chapter 11). In one of these tense exchanges, Howard declared to the media that he was 'the most conservative man in Australian politics'. It was probably this utterance, rather than his equally famous statement during the 1996 election campaign that he would preside over a government about which people would feel 'relaxed and comfortable', that best captures Howard's legacy.

Assessing the Howard government can be difficult, given the sometimes controversial nature of his political beliefs. In some ways, Howard's record was consistent with the Menzies approach, whereby economic reform was welded to social conservatism.

GST AND WORK CHOICES

The Howard government prided itself on its ability to undertake economic reform. In 1998, the Howard government promised to introduce a new consumption tax — the goods and services tax (GST) — that would add 10 per cent to the cost of goods and services. This tax was brought in, but the Liberal Party nearly lost the 1998 election over it.

In 2007, the issue that was uppermost in the campaign was the Howard government's decision to legislate to remove the trade unions from Australia's industrial relations system under its Work Choices policy. The Liberals lost the 2007 election, and Howard was defeated in his seat of Bennelong.

History appeared to have repeated itself. When the Nationalists were defeated in 1929, and Prime Minister Stanley Bruce lost his seat, one of the issues on the agenda was the government's attempt to remove trade unions from the industrial relations system. As in 1929, the Howard government's Work Choices appeared to be a reform the Australian electorate wasn't prepared to accept.

Also like Menzies, Howard was a strong believer in Australia's British cultural heritage and was an opponent of the idea of an Australian republic. He was also a strong believer in the importance of the US alliance to Australia's defence, and was a very enthusiastic supporter of American military incursions into Afghanistan and Iraq. See Chapter 16 for a summary of Howard's leadership and Chapter 17 for an outline of his speech following the Bali terrorist attack.

Howard was often identified with the conservative and the Dry tendencies of the party (refer to the section 'Liberal Factionalism' earlier in this chapter), yet, during his time as prime minister, he displayed another Menzies trait of incorporating his factional adversaries into the government. All of the Howard ministries had a good selection of Wets or Moderates, including some who had a record of crossing the floor to vote with the opposition.

The Howard government's Liberal legacy appeared to be completely at odds with that of the Fraser government. Where the Fraser government believed in multiculturalism, the Howard government rejected the idea as divisive. The Fraser government opened Australian borders to Indochinese boat people. The Howard government, on the other hand, instituted a strict border control policy (with Howard famously claiming, 'we will decide who comes to this country and the circumstances in which they come'). The Fraser government continued the Whitlam government's policy of extending land rights to Aboriginal Australians. The Howard government, by contrast, sought to limit Indigenous land claims, and Howard was constantly at loggerheads with a number of Indigenous community leaders over matters ranging from the abolition of the Aboriginal and Torres Strait Islander Commission (ATSIC) through to the Intervention welfare policy the federal government employed in the Northern Territory in 2007. Formally known as the Northern Territory National Emergency Response, the Intervention saw the use of the army to carry out radical health and welfare checks in Aboriginal communities.

VOTE 1

Interestingly, just as he had been a problematic treasurer for Malcolm Fraser, Howard as prime minister was constantly looking over his shoulder to assess the leadership ambitions of his treasurer, Peter Costello. Even in government, the Liberal Party could factionalise over leadership matters.

Post-Howard: The Abbott, Turnbull and Morrison governments

After losing the 2007 election, the Liberal Party reverted to bad habits in opposition as it regularly changed leaders in the hope of finding one to lead the party back to government. Brendan Nelson had a short stint as opposition leader but, having failed to take the shine off the then-new Rudd government, was replaced by Malcolm Turnbull in 2008. Frustration quickly grew within the Coalition, however, as Turnbull appeared to side with the Rudd government on climate change policies, especially concerning a proposed emissions trading scheme (ETS). In 2009, the Party Room decided to replace Turnbull with Tony Abbott who was far more combative than his immediate predecessors.

This proved to be an inspired choice for the Liberal Party as Abbott led the Coalition to almost win the 2010 election. In 2013, the Coalition defeated the Labor Party (which had gone through its Rudd-Gillard-Rudd leadership phase).

The initial period of the Abbott government focused on dismantling key policies from the previous Labor government, especially concerning the pricing of carbon. The Abbott government also placed emphasis on asylum seeker policy and reducing government expenditure. Abbott also revised the Australian honours system and reinstated the knights and dames awards for prominent figures — the first of which was the late Prince Philip, who was awarded a knighthood. These decisions were described by Abbott as a 'captain's pick' and suggested he was happy to make these decisions without the input of his Party Room. This proved unpopular and motivated his opponents in the party to move against him. In 2015, Abbott was replaced by Turnbull.

Upon becoming prime minister, Turnbull promised to avoid the 'captain's calls' that typified the Abbot prime ministership. Moreover, Turnbull was a socially progressive Liberal, which meant he would be advancing different policy ideas compared with his socially conservative predecessor. He led the Coalition to a narrow win in the 2016 election, but speculation over his future as prime minister never abated, especially because he failed to implement a long-lasting solution to energy or environmental policy.

Highlights during Turnbull's prime ministership included the postal vote, and subsequent changes to the law, on same-sex marriage as well as changes to the Senate voting system (which we cover in Chapter 13).

Following a string of poor opinion polls, Turnbull was replaced as prime minister by Scott Morrison in 2018. Morrison sought to present himself as a pragmatic prime minister, similar to John Howard. Seemingly happy to be seen as 'an ordinary dad' from the suburbs, Morrison was given what many presumed to be the impossible task of leading the Coalition to victory in the 2019 election. After all, the government had disposed of two prime ministers and was consistently behind the opposition in published opinion polls. Despite this, Morrison led the coalition to its third election win in a row since 2013.

The Morrison government's policy agenda was sidelined in 2020 as the government sought to address the social and economic disruption caused by the COVID-19 pandemic.

The Liberal Party in the States

The Liberal Party has historically been very strong in a number of states, although it's also true that the party has been chronically weak in Queensland. Rather like the federal Liberal Party, some of the state divisions enjoyed long periods in government, with state premiers such as David Brand (Western Australia, 11 years, 11 months), Tom Playford (South Australia, 27 years) and Henry Bolte (Victoria, 17 years) achieving records in government commensurate with Bob Menzies' federal record.

In more recent times, however, changes in the pattern of state politics have been discernible. Both major parties have had turns at governing the states. The Liberal Party has at some time governed each of the Australian states except Queensland (in Chapter 11 we explain the complicated situation in Queensland, where the National Party has been the major anti-Labor party), as well as each of the territories.

In the main, the days of the authoritarian and patrician long-serving Liberal premier appear to have gone, although Victoria's Jeff Kennett looked like he was trying to emulate the feats of Henry Bolte, who spent 17 years as premier. (Kennett lasted seven years as premier.) The Kennett government's commitment to radical market reform also made his approach to Liberal governance look like something of a model. However, Kennett and his federal counterpart, John Howard, didn't get on very well, especially over issues such as multiculturalism. Interest in the Kennett model tended to wane, however, after his somewhat unexpected defeat in the 1999 Victorian election.

The Liberal Party and the Future

No doubt the Liberal Party has been a very successful party. But perhaps its most important achievement is the way the party has managed its internal affairs, to the point that the destructive instability that beset the Nationalists and the UAP hasn't been revisited.

The challenges for the Liberal Party include the problem of how to arrest a declining membership. Both major parties suffer from this problem, but because the Liberal Party doesn't have a revenue stream derived from affiliation fees paid by external associations, it's very dependent on membership fees for its financial viability.

REMEMBER

The Liberals also have to deal with the impact that the existence of the National Party has on Australian politics generally and on non-Labor politics in particular. Coalition politics are important to the non-Labor side, and a successful Liberal leader is invariably one who manages the relationship between the Liberal and National Parties well.

One possible option is for the Liberal and National Parties to merge, which has been on the agenda for many years. In 2008, the Queensland division of the Liberal Party agreed to merge with the Nationals and create a new party — the Liberal National Party (or LNP). (See Chapter 11 for more on the National Party.) The case for amalgamation rests on the argument that it's more efficient for the non-Labor parties to come together and fight Labor rather than fight each other.

IN THIS CHAPTER

» Exploring the origins of the National Party

» Looking at the politics of coalition

» Understanding the party organisation and policy traditions

» Examining the National Party in government and in the future

Chapter **11**

The National Party

The National Party of Australia was once called the Australian Country Party. Remembering this historical point is important for two reasons. First, it gives a serious hint about the importance of rural interests to Australian politics. Second, it makes the distinction that today's National Party is *not* the same thing as the party that emerged from the Labor split during the Great War, the Nationalists.

The National Party is sometimes called the *Murray–Darling Basin Party* because of the way its electoral support is concentrated in rural Queensland, New South Wales and, to a lesser extent, Victoria. In this chapter, we explain just how this trend enables the party to win lower house seats in the parliament, even though the party's national vote rarely gets into double figures. We also examine the Nationals' ability to, therefore, partake in coalition politics with the Liberal Party, a luxury denied to other non-major parties.

In fact, in Queensland, the Nationals have traditionally been the superior coalition partner, and this chapter takes a look at how the party is structured and how Queensland is different. Although the Nationals aren't known for the huge philosophical divides suffered by the major parties, we do examine the critical issues that cause some friction. And we give you the National Party leaders and their influence in government.

The Origins of Rural Party Politics: The Country Party

The National Party of Australia, formerly known as the Country Party, is the second oldest political party in Australia. It emerged in Western Australia in 1914, when a member of the state's Legislative Assembly declared that he was a member of a political organisation that sought to advance the interests of farmers.

The real impetus towards creating a national party to represent rural interests occurred after World War I, however, when, in 1919, some members of Billy Hughes's Nationalist Party, led by Tasmanian William McWilliam, declared they would join a new party called the Country Party. The Country Party then fielded candidates in the 1919 federal election, winning 9 per cent of the vote nationally and gaining 11 House of Representatives seats.

In 1922, the Country Party won 12 per cent of the federal vote and 14 seats — this result proved to be very important because it gave the party the balance of power in the lower house. In 1923, Country Party leader Earle Page agreed to a coalition proposed by Nationalist leader Stanley Melbourne Bruce, and the first — but by no means last — federal anti-Labor coalition was formed.

A farmer's party

The emergence of the Country Party was a reflection of how important agriculture was to the Australian economy and, indeed, to Australian society. By the time of Federation, in 1901, the vast majority of Australians actually lived in cities and towns. Farming, however, was one of the nation's most important activities, with agriculture providing an important source of export income, especially from the sale of Australian wheat, wool and meat to Great Britain.

REMEMBER

Farmers and graziers were very cognisant of their economic significance and formed what were known in those times as leagues (today they'd be called interest groups or producer groups — refer to Chapter 1) to convey rural demands to the political process. Rural Australians even back then were conscious of the problems of service delivery in areas such as health, education and transport, and the leagues were designed to lobby city-based decision-makers to ensure a flow of services to the bush. One of the main arguments put by these leagues was that rural Australia's shortfall in population was offset by the disproportional contribution farming made to the nation's wealth. This refrain has been a constant in Australian rural politics.

Soldier settlements

The dynamics of rural politics changed after the Great War. As part of its policy to demobilise returned soldiers, the Hughes government encouraged a *soldier settlement scheme*, where returned soldiers were able to obtain small landholdings to undertake intensive agriculture and horticulture. (The same scheme opened up irrigation farming, especially in the Riverina in New South Wales and in northern Victoria, and in very harsh environments such as the mountainous and isolated areas of Gippsland in Victoria.)

Very quickly, many of these settlements began to struggle, and farmers sought to gain more policy concessions by forming a political party to advance their agenda in the parliament. The creation of the Country Party was the result, and its job was to find ways of securing services and infrastructure for rural Australia.

A shared constituency

To assume that all farmers supported and voted for the Country Party (or the National Party today) is a mistake. Farmers and graziers see themselves as small-business people and, as a result, tend to support pro-business political parties. The rural constituency, therefore, tended to be shared between the Country Party and the other non-Labor parties going around (today, the rural constituency tends to be shared between the National Party and the Liberal Party).

Support for the National Party now tends to be strongest among small-scale intensive farmers such as fruit and vegetable growers, sugarcane growers in north Queensland, irrigation farmers in the Riverina and in Victoria's Goulburn Valley, and dairy farmers in Queensland and in Victoria's beef and dairying districts in the Gippsland region. Broad-acre farmers (those who tend to farm livestock or grains) in rural New South Wales and Queensland are also strong supporters of the party, but not in Victoria. Graziers in Victoria tend to vote for the Liberal Party, as do broad-acre farmers in South Australia and Western Australia. Intensive farmers in Tasmania also tend to align themselves with the Liberals.

REMEMBER

The question of who supports the National Party and who doesn't is very important. First, it reveals the degree to which the National Party's strength is specific to two states in particular — New South Wales and, especially, Queensland — and, perhaps a little less so, to Victoria. The party is much weaker in Western Australia, and weaker still in South Australia and Tasmania. Second, the fact that both the National Party and the Liberal Party share this electorate means that, for all the cooperation that goes on as part of their coalition agreements, an undercurrent of competitive strain exists in this relationship.

The National Party is one of a number of organisations that still seek to advocate the interests of rural Australia. Producer groups such as the various Farmers' Federations and all sorts of farmer and grazier groups also fulfil this role. No less important is the Country Women's Association — a venerable body that seeks to provide a social network for rural women. Young farmers groups are also formed to assist young people working in primary production.

The Country Party consolidates

During the very same period when first the Nationalists and then the United Australia Party (UAP) were in the process of emerging and declining, the Country Party succeeded in putting together an effective national organisation and consolidating as a coherent party.

The consolidation of the Country Party relied on some important changes to Australia's electoral system that served the party's interests. They certainly helped ensure that the Country Party would consistently win a strategically significant number of lower house seats.

The first advantage for the Country Party was the introduction of preferential voting. We explain the intricacies of this system in Chapter 13, but the main things to note are that the system requires voters to cast a preference for every candidate and that the result of the election is determined by the distribution of preferences. In 1924, this voting system meant that Country and Nationalist candidates could run against each other without splitting the non-Labor vote and helping a Labor candidate win the election.

The second of these advantages was the introduction of *rural weightage*, which allowed rural electoral divisions to have much fewer voters (up to 40 per cent, at one stage) than city electorates. This situation stayed in place in Australian national elections until 1974, when the weightage was reduced to a tolerance of 10 per cent, and then in 1984, when it was abolished altogether.

Coalition Politics

The formation of the Country Party initially posed a threat to the Nationalists. Because the two parties shared the rural constituency, the Country Party posed a danger of splitting the non-Labor vote — and helping Labor win more seats.

A sense of rivalry also existed between a farmer-based party that was becoming quite well organised with a strong ordinary membership and the Nationalists with its weak organisation.

By 1923, the Nationalists and the Country Party had come to an agreement (made possible after the Nationalists replaced as leader Billy Hughes — who hated the emerging Country Party and who, in turn, was hated back — with the more conservative Stanley Bruce). The two parties entered into a coalition. In exchange for supporting the Nationalist prime minister in the House of Representatives, the Country Party was given the deputy prime ministership and a number of seats in the ministry.

Coalition politics in Australian national politics has been based on this agreement ever since. The Country or National Party has, as a result, been a party of government for most of its existence. The few times it has been out of government have corresponded with the few times Labor has managed to win federal elections. Whenever the Liberal Party (or its predecessors) won national elections, it governed in coalition with the Country or National Party. This agreement has been such an article of faith in the non-Labor side of politics that the Liberals have gone into coalition even after elections when the Liberals had won enough lower house seats to be able to govern in their own right.

The coalition agreement

By being able to win lower house seats, the National Party is able to partake of a form of politics denied to other non-major parties. Even though the Nationals don't win a large number of lower house seats, they can be so strategically important that they hold the *balance of power* in the house in which government is formed, enabling them to cast the deciding vote on legislation. The Nationals can, therefore, be a part of coalition politics. In Australian political history, the party the Nationals have historically entered into coalition with has been the Liberal Party.

Coalition politics also allows the National Party to exercise political influence sometimes well in excess of the proportion of seats it holds. Coalition agreements have given the National Party access to the power to govern — a power the party has exercised extensively throughout its history.

The nature of the agreement between the National Party and the Liberal Party has varied from time to time since 1923, but, in a nutshell, the key features include:

>> A promise of exchange of support for the Liberals in the lower house for a number of positions in a coalition Cabinet (the number of National ministries is determined as a ratio of the number of seats they win)

>> A promise that the deputy prime ministership goes to the National Party leader

>> An agreement that the Nationals get the portfolios of trade and primary industries (although in recent times the Liberal party has taken back the trade portfolio)

>> An agreement that the parties won't run candidates against sitting members of the other coalition party

>> An agreement to run 'joint tickets' for the Senate in NSW, Queensland and Victoria

Limits to coalition

The coalition can continue between the two parties, even in opposition, although occasionally the coalition has been suspended during a period in opposition. Each of the states has a slightly different experience of coalition politics.

In Queensland, where the Nationals are the major non-Labor party, a coalition existed until 1983, when the Nationals were able to govern on their own. Poor relations between the Liberals and Nationals occurred after this time until 2008, when the Nationals and Liberals decided to merge.

New South Wales has always had a Liberal–National coalition operating in state politics. In Victoria, however, the Liberals and Nationals were bitter enemies until 1991, when a coalition agreement was finally reached. It was suspended again between 1999 and 2008 but has since been renegotiated.

FROM COUNTRY TO NATIONAL: THE DEMOGRAPHIC PROBLEM

The name change for the Country Party occurred in the 1980s and was part of a deliberate policy of trying to make the party more relevant to voters beyond the rural regions of the Murray–Darling Basin. The first step in the name change occurred in 1975, when the party's name was changed to the National Country Party (NCP). In 1982, the party changed its name to the National Party of Australia (NPA), or the Nationals.

Almost from the moment the Country Party was formed, critics and analysts have predicted its inevitable demise. The argument goes that, as Australia's urban population grows while the rural population falls, the Country Party would face being overwhelmed by Australia's urban reality — a demographic problem, indeed. The party has always been interested in finding ways to be more relevant to voters beyond the rural constituency. Changing the party's name was one such response.

The National Party Organisation

Like the other main Australian political parties, the Country Party (now the National Party) was set up to be a mass party, in that the point of the party was to provide a local basis for individuals to join the party, pay a membership fee and participate in its internal affairs.

Local membership occurs through the state divisions of the party, and the state divisions are autonomous, reflecting the importance of federalism to the National Party. Technically, the National Party is something of a top-down party, in that its rules give the parliamentary wing — and the parliamentary leader — a certain degree of autonomy from the organisation, especially with regard to policy decisions.

Each state division of the party has a Council to which delegates from the branches are elected, and each state division elects delegations of equal number to a Federal Council. Each State Council also elects office bearers and an executive, and the Federal Council elects a federal president, a federal secretary, a federal treasurer and an executive.

This structure so far sounds similar to the way the Liberal Party is organised, but the two parties differ in some very important ways. They also tend to operate and behave differently.

One example of these operational differences is that the National Party organisation is, first and foremost, a support mechanism for the parliamentary wing, with local branches being responsible for preselections. However, history shows that National MPs tend to have very long parliamentary careers, due partly to the fact that most National seats are very safe.

HANGING ON TO NATIONAL SEATS

The coalition agreement with the Liberals isn't altogether altruistic (remember, it's a coalition, not a friendship). Under the coalition agreement, neither party will run a candidate against a sitting member. But, if a Liberal or a National MP retires or vacates a seat, a *three-cornered contest* can take place, meaning that Labor, Liberal and National candidates can nominate. Most National MPs don't realistically fear Labor winning their seat, but they do fear the Liberal Party. So National MPs hang on as long as they can, especially if they hold seats that might go to the Liberals in a three-cornered contest.

Council meetings are rather different in their operation from the major parties, too. Federal Council meetings tend to involve delegates and MPs coming together and discussing things ranging from the operation of the party through to policy debates. Some analysts suggest that this role leads to a type of forum arrangement, where MPs and party members (who probably have very similar views on most matters) enter into discussions that tend to give rise to a strong sense of what the party stands for and what the party will do on specific matters.

A small parliamentary party

Federally, and in most of the states, the National Party tends to have very small parliamentary wings. Following the 2019 election, the federal National Party comprised 10 lower house and 5 upper house MPs — a total of 15. This is in addition to the Nationals who were elected as part of the Liberal National Party of Queensland. The parliamentary wing of some of the state divisions is even smaller, which means the group dynamics of the parliamentary party are very different from the larger parties. Federally, this trend has been reflected in the way in which National Party leaders have tended to hold their positions for long periods of time and in a comparative lack of persistent factionalism.

Queensland: A National Party heartland

The situation of the National Party in Queensland is a little different from the other states, which also has implications for federal politics. Basically, Queensland is the National Party's strongest state. In all the other states and in federal politics, the National Party was and is the junior member whenever it goes into coalition with the Liberal Party. In Queensland, however, the reverse has been true. In Queensland, the National Party has been the largest anti-Labor party, and the Liberals have been the junior partner.

REMEMBER

In federal politics, no Nationals get elected from Tasmania, South Australia or Western Australia, and Victoria these days usually returns only two or three National MPs to the House of Representatives. The vast bulk of the Nationals' Party Room, therefore, comes from Queensland and, to a lesser extent, New South Wales.

Just how different Queensland is from other Australian states involves two important factors in particular. First, Queensland is the most decentralised of the Australian mainland states — that is, the majority of its population resides outside Brisbane. This demographic improves the chances of election for a non-urban party like the Nationals. Second, Queensland is a big primary-producer state with a very large agricultural component. This preponderance of farming and farmers helps consolidate the National Party's dominance over non-Labor politics.

Joh Bjelke-Petersen: A National Party icon

The propensity for Queensland to be different and the dominance of the National Party over the state's politics from 1968 to the 1980s was personified in its long-serving Nationals premier, Sir Joh Bjelke-Petersen. Bjelke-Petersen was a farmer and land developer before being elected to the Queensland parliament. In the 1950s, he was appointed as a minister, with the collapse of the Labor government due to the 1955 split leading to the formation of a Country–Liberal coalition.

In 1968, Bjelke-Petersen became premier following the death of Jack Pizzey. Thought to have been put there to warm the seat for someone else, Bjelke-Petersen proved to be a popular and populist leader. He consolidated the Country–Liberal coalition and then, in the 1980s, began to engineer a situation where the Nationals could govern Queensland in their own right. This situation was achieved in 1983.

VOTE 1

Bjelke-Petersen was a serious opponent to Labor Prime Minister Gough Whitlam, and it was Bjelke-Petersen's decision to break convention and send an anti-Whitlam casual senate vacancy candidate that allowed the 1975 constitutional crisis to begin.

RISE AND FALL: JOH FOR PM

By 1987, Bjelke-Petersen had become something of an anti-Labor hero, especially during what would become Labor's longest term in federal government. Then, in complicated circumstances, Bjelke-Petersen announced he intended to become prime minister. No details of how he would achieve his aim were provided, but the onset of the Joh for PM campaign provided the basis for the Queensland National Party to launch an attack on the federal coalition, presumably to take control of at least the National Party side of it.

The Joh for PM campaign was a disaster for the federal coalition and probably led to the defeat of John Howard's Liberal–National coalition in the 1987 election. Bjelke-Petersen, meanwhile, tried to return to being premier of Queensland but was forced out of the job. Later, he was charged with corruption but was exonerated in the Supreme Court. In 1989, the National Party lost state government to the Labor Party — the first Labor victory in that state since the 1955 split.

Factionalism in the National Party

That the Joh for PM campaign could take such a grip on the party in 1987 indicates that factionalism does exist in the National Party, notwithstanding its relatively small number of parliamentary members and the community-minded approach of its organisation. Rural Australia tends to have a clear idea about the importance of rural outlooks and values, and the National Party doesn't have philosophical or ideological divides. The factions tend to cluster more around overt political matters, such as whether the Nationals should be in coalition with the Liberals, or on an economic argument about whether agriculture should be oriented towards domestic markets or export markets.

Coalitionists versus go-it-alone Nationals

By far the most contentious matter in the National Party relates to whether or not the party should be in coalition with the Liberal Party. Those Nationals who support the idea of a coalition tend to hold very safe seats and tend to aspire to a position in a coalition ministry. They also take the view that the National Party constituency is best served by having access to government.

The opposite view is that the National Party would be best served by standing alone as a separate party and not being subsumed by the Liberal Party. This view tends to argue that being in coalition makes the Nationals subservient to the major party partner. Among these advocates can be found Nationals sometimes described as mavericks because of their willingness to speak out against coalition activity.

Domestic agribusiness versus export farming

A bit of tension exists in rural politics between those who produce for domestic markets and those involved in export-oriented agriculture. The old Country Party was formed for the express purpose of protecting and advancing the interests of small-scale farmers. In the 1950s, the Country Party presided over a series of subsidies designed to protect the family farm.

Today, agricultural economics comprises one sector that produces for domestic consumption and another that produces for export. Domestic producers have tended to advocate subsidies and orderly marketing in order to protect family farms in particular. The export farmers, however, are more committed to free trade.

Amalgamation or a separate party?

Another potential divide within the party is over whether it should amalgamate with the Liberal Party. The strongest advocates of amalgamation tend to be coalitionists in the party (especially former federal parliamentary leaders). The fiercest opposition to amalgamation tends to come from the party's grass-roots members, who have the strongest sense of their party being very different from the Liberals. They also tend to be at the cutting edge of competition with the Liberals when campaigning in local electoral divisions. And they appreciate themselves as being the smaller — and potentially more vulnerable — party in the relationship and fear that the Nationals' identity would be overwhelmed by the larger party.

VOTE 1

In 2008, the Queensland Nationals and Liberals decided to amalgamate. The amalgamation occurred after a long period of poor relations between the two parties that appeared to assist the Labor Party in winning state elections in Queensland. The fact that the Nationals are the larger of the non-Labor parties in that state may have been the reason an amalgamation agreement was reached, because the Nationals appear to have the numerical advantage in the new Liberal National Party organisation.

The National Party in Government

The coalition agreements with the Liberal Party ensure that, even as a minor party, the Nationals have access to government whenever the Liberal and National Parties have a majority of seats in the lower house. The fact that Australia's political history has seen so many conservative governments means that the Country or National Party has actually had a very long record of policy-making activity. The Nationals have wielded influence over Australian policy-making far in excess of the share of the vote they win and the number of parliamentary seats they secure.

REMEMBER

The National Party is widely regarded as the least ideological of the main Australian parties, partly due to a consensus within the party about rural values. These values are unashamedly conservative and are so commonly held across the party that members find no need to discuss them, unlike the Labor and Liberal Parties, where debates about philosophy and tradition go on all the time. The National Party's total disdain for the unions — which are seen as a serious impediment to the economics of agriculture — is a very strong value that is shared with the Liberal Party.

The party is also famous for the way it pragmatically chases policy outcomes, particularly if they're tangible outcomes such as a new road, a new building, a new school, a new university for the bush or whatever. The party is sometimes accused of *pork-barrelling* — a term that refers to using the policy-making process to divert projects and programs to a particular constituency, even if it's inefficient or irrational to do so. The Nationals have also been keen advocates for rail and road programs designed to improve rural transport. In this section, you get to see that the Nationals have gone through some interesting times but have always attempted to implement policies that serve the interests of their core voting base.

The early coalitionists

The history of the National Party (and its Country Party predecessor) also tends to be linked with the very prominent political figures who led the party at various times. The two early federal leaders who established the coalition with the Nationalists, the UAP and, later still, the Liberals were Earle Page (1923 to 1929 and 1934 to 1939, see Chapter 18) and Arthur (Artie) Fadden (1940 to 1958).

In terms of policy, the Country Party demonstrated that it could strike a hard bargain in giving the major non-Labor party support. The party demanded ever-increasing diversions of government funds to rail and road programs, as well as buttressing the irrigation systems established after the Great War.

In political terms, Page and Fadden were also prone to trying to influence events in the Liberal Party. Page hated Billy Hughes, which helped bring Hughes down as leader. Page also hated Menzies, considering him to be something of an upstart, and helped bring him down in 1939. On the other hand, Fadden and Menzies got on very well, and Menzies' campaign to create a new party was given support by the new Country Party leader. When Labor was defeated in 1949, Fadden agreed without hesitation to re-establish a coalition with the Liberal Party.

John (Black Jack) McEwen: A Country Party giant

On Artie Fadden's retirement as leader after just under 18 years, in 1958, the leadership of the Country Party passed to John (Black Jack) McEwen. A patrician character from Victoria's Goulburn Valley area, McEwen was another of those long-serving Country Party leaders who profoundly influenced policy and meddled in the internal affairs of the Liberal Party. He remained as leader until his retirement in 1971.

McEwen is famous for a number of things. It was McEwen who, as trade minister, finalised agreements on the sale of export coal to Japan at a time when many Australians still saw that country as an enemy from World War II. McEwen also tried to establish a political relationship with the union movement in a bid to try to make his party more relevant to urban Australia. This attempt involved McEwen asking unions to agree to his proposal to have a complex system of subsidies and marketing arrangements designed to protect the family farm in exchange for agreeing to industry protectionism in order to protect manufacturing jobs. The economic outcome delivered was highly protected manufacturing and agricultural industries.

McEwen also meddled in Liberal Party affairs. Indeed, it was McEwen who stopped William McMahon from becoming Liberal leader and prime minister following the disappearance of Harold Holt in 1967. McEwen had never forgiven McMahon for the time when, as treasurer, he had appreciated the value of the Australian dollar — a decision that diminished the export income of Australian farmers. McEwen told the Liberals that, if they elected McMahon as leader, the Country Party would walk out of the coalition. The Liberals chose John Gorton instead. It was this incident in particular that led to the famous adage in Australian politics that the Country Party is the tail that wags the coalition dog. See Chapter 18 for more on McEwen's input to politics.

THE COUNTRY PARTY AND RURAL SOCIALISM

Critics of McEwen's approach accused the Country Party of 'rural socialism'. McEwen's ability to persuade coalition Cabinets to pursue his economic ideas resulted in Australia having a domestic-oriented rural economy buttressed by all sorts of subsidies, guaranteed minimum commodity prices (paid for by taxes and levies) and orderly marketing. Until the 1980s, for example, Victorians couldn't buy milk products made in New South Wales, so Victorian dairy farmers could be guaranteed of their market. The arrangements were eventually done away with by the Hawke Labor government in the 1980s.

Doug Anthony: A moderniser

Doug Anthony took over the party leadership on McEwen's retirement in 1971 and held the leadership until 1983. Anthony was something of a moderniser and was the leader who presided over the first name change of the party to National Country Party in 1975.

Anthony ran a very disciplined party and was known to be a close confidant of Prime Minister Malcolm Fraser, ensuring the National Country Party had strong influence in the Fraser Liberal governments between 1975 and 1983. Anthony tried to embrace the idea of free trade and became an advocate of the importance of export agriculture. He also tried to place the party closer to the interests of mining and mining companies. The defence of McEwen's schemes to protect small-scale family farming continued, however, which led to the first real signs of tension within the National Party membership. Some began to suspect that the party's traditional support of family farming was being eroded by the free trade agenda.

Tim Fischer: Back to basics

The 1983 election marked a period of opposition for the National Party that was to prove extremely difficult. Ian Sinclair took over as leader of the party in 1984 and was charged with the responsibility of heading the party in its dark days in opposition. As the Hawke government began to unravel the McEwen arrangements, the National Party constituency looked to their politicians to do something. Impotent in opposition, some farmers began to put their faith instead in interest groups such as the National Farmers' Federation. The Joh for PM campaign caused huge damage to the party in 1987 (refer to the section 'Rise and fall: Joh for PM', earlier in this chapter) and, by 1989, the party had a new leader — Charles Blunt. The party continued to feel the effects of the Joh for PM campaign during the 1990 election — a result so disastrous for the Nationals that Blunt lost his seat of Richmond.

Part of the blame for all of this turmoil was placed on those in the party trying to make the Nationals relevant to the city. After the 1990 disaster, the party installed Tim Fischer as leader, who immediately set about trying to re-establish the party's reputation as the party of the bush. In 1996, the Howard-led Liberal Party swept back into office, and Fischer and his colleagues were back in government by virtue of the coalition agreement.

The coalition was back in government, and Fischer got on well personally with Prime Minister Howard (who, in the Liberal tradition, was a strong supporter of coalition politics). The political situation in which Fischer found himself had changed somewhat from the days of Anthony, however. Under the previous Labor government, rural economics had been deregulated and oriented towards export.

Howard's government was an economic rationalist government, so there was no return to rural subsidies. Furthermore, some significant government services were privatised. A classic example was the privatisation of the nation's telecommunications provider, Telstra. One of the chief concerns of the Nationals was whether the privatisation of Telstra would lead to a loss of services in the bush. Despite these concerns, Howard had no intention of backing away from privatisation policies.

The Nationals in the ministry were bound to follow the privatisation policy. However, some backbench Nationals revolted, and one — Bob Katter from the Queensland-based seat of Kennedy — resigned from the party.

VOTE 1

As if this tension wasn't enough, the Nationals were also under attack from Pauline Hanson — an independent MP whose anti-Aboriginal and anti-globalisation rhetoric was gaining support in regional and rural areas. Hanson formed a party — One Nation — that, in 1998, helped defeat the Queensland National state government headed by then premier Rob Borbidge. (See Chapter 12 for more on One Nation.)

The National Party appeared to be under siege. Relief came in the form of help from Howard, who put together a major welfare and assistance package for regional Australia from the receipts of the Telstra privatisation, and whose party found a way of marginalising Hanson and One Nation.

Fischer appeared to have steered his party through a difficult period. His successors, John Anderson and, later, Mark Vaile, maintained the policy of staying in coalition and relying on the Liberal Party to direct economic policy. This tradition appeared to continue with Warren Truss who took over from Vaile in 2007.

From Barnaby Joyce to Michael McCormack and back to Joyce

In 2016, following Truss's retirement, Barnaby Joyce became the leader of the Nationals. Joyce had been a senator for Queensland since 2005, but contested, and won, the New South Wales seat of New England in the lower house in 2013. A socially conservative politician, Joyce became both leader of the Nationals and deputy prime minister.

Joyce enjoyed a very high public profile in this role. His contributions to the policy debate appeared to continually advance the interests of rural and regional communities, as well as primary producers. This sometimes caused friction between the coalition partners, but ultimately Joyce was regarded as an effective Nationals leader.

In 2017, Joyce was one of the MPs who had to resign from parliament due to his citizenship status, but was able to be returned in a subsequent by-election. Support for his position as leader, however, dropped when it was revealed that he had been having an extramarital affair.

Michael McCormack replaced Joyce in 2018. But Joyce did not relinquish his leadership aspirations. In 2020, following a sense of growing frustration from some Nationals about the party's leadership, Joyce challenged McCormack for the top job. While Joyce was defeated, he maintained support from some within the party. After another attempt, Joyce reclaimed the leadership of the Nationals in June 2021 and returned to being the Deputy Prime Minister of Australia.

Future Challenges

The National Party's resilience has been proven by its performance over time. Its share of the national vote has been declining slowly, but it's still able to win lower house seats, which puts it in a position to partake of coalition politics in the right circumstances.

REMEMBER

The party faces many challenges. The demographic problem of declining populations in rural areas has not gone away. The attempts by the National Party to make itself relevant to voters outside the Murray–Darling Basin have failed, however.

The Nationals and the Liberals have worked cooperatively over the years, often despite mutually felt resentment, especially among the ordinary members of both parties. The questions of whether the Nationals should be in coalition and whether the Nationals and the Liberals should merge will continue to nag away, especially at the branch membership level.

Meanwhile, the economics of Australian agriculture has been changing. The small family farm is in decline in the face of increasing corporate dominance of food production and retailing. Meanwhile, Australian farming has become concerned less with domestic consumption and more with exporting. In each instance, the National Party's core membership and electoral base have been eroded. In turn, the National Party has shifted its focus to mining, increasing ties with mining communities and companies. No longer are the Nationals the party of rural socialism; neither, indeed, are they the 'tail wagging the coalition dog'.

Chapter **12**

The Minor Parties and Independents

M any more political parties exist in Australia than just the Labor Party, the Liberal Party and the Nationals. A study of the Australian party system found that over 100 parties had been registered to contest federal elections since World War II. This diversity of parties helps buttress the notion of Australia being a multi-party democracy where voters have quite a substantial choice of parties they can vote for — even if the reality is that most Australians vote for one or other of the two major parties.

In this chapter, we look at how the electoral system, including preferential voting, influences how minor parties can win a parliamentary seat, usually in the Senate federally. We also let you ponder the impermanence of most minor parties and how their success can be rated.

Among the array of minor parties are a small number that have succeeded in getting elected to the upper house of an Australian parliament and, in many instances, have held the balance of power, enabling them to cast a deciding vote on legislation. Here we introduce you to those parties, as well as some of the independents who have succeeded in getting into parliament. We also look at the future of minor parties in Australian politics.

Minor Parties: People's Tribune or a Waste of Time?

Minor party politics tends to be quite diverse, and generalising about minor parties and how they approach the political debate is difficult. Some common themes do emerge, however. The role and impact of minor parties is inextricably linked with the electoral systems used for the two houses of parliament.

Minor parties are also distinguishable from each other by whether they originated as the result of a split from one or other of the major parties, or if they emerged from the pursuit of a set of policy issues. No sense of permanency is associated with minor parties, although it's also true that some minor parties have been a part of the parliamentary scene for some time.

Opinions divide when the topic of minor parties comes up. People associated with major parties are often very disparaging of minor parties. One Labor senator once described the Australian Democrats as 'fairies at the bottom of the garden', and a former Labor prime minister once described the Senate (the chamber where minor party representatives tend to get elected) as 'unrepresentative swill'. Major party people tend to see minor parties as annoying distractions from the main two-party-dominated struggle to win government.

Minor party activists, however, see themselves in a different light. To those who venerate them, or are involved with them, minor parties are the lifeblood of liberal democracy. They provide the 'multi' in multi-party politics, and they provide voters with a choice. They are also seen as a way in which the political debate can be widened beyond a debate simply about economic policy. Minor parties can help bring an array of issues to the political debate, especially if those minor parties have been formed to pursue radical or unconventional ideas and agendas.

The importance of the electoral system

The impact of minor parties on the party system is profoundly influenced by electoral systems. Because most Australian jurisdictions have bicameral parliaments, state and federal elections usually involve a combination of preferential voting and proportional representation systems (see Chapter 13).

Minor parties find it difficult to win seats in a parliament where single-member electorates are used, as is the case in the House of Representatives. The reason is that, to win the seat, a candidate needs to win 50 per cent of the vote cast in the electoral district. Because most minor parties rarely poll above 4 per cent, the chance of someone other than a Labor, Liberal or National candidate winning the seat is pretty slim.

The chances of getting elected in a system of proportional representation are much better, however. In states such as South Australia and New South Wales, getting elected to the Legislative Council is possible with about 4 per cent of the vote — this low percentage is the reason why, indeed, the New South Wales upper house has representatives from minor parties such as One Nation and the Shooters' Party (now known as the Shooters, Fishers and Farmers Party). Even in the Senate, where the quota to win a seat is 7.7 per cent or 14.4 per cent (depending on whether it's a full or half-Senate election), some minor parties have had success with less than 2 per cent of the primary vote. In 1987, for example, the Nuclear Disarmament Party won a Senate seat with less than 2 per cent primary vote, while in 2004 Family First also won a seat with only 1.8 per cent of the vote.

BY-ELECTIONS AND MINOR PARTIES

Minor parties may find that their vote increases in by-elections. The theory here is that voters use by-elections as an opportunity to convey a latent anti-major party sentiment in election contests that won't lead to a change of government. In more recent times, the tendency has been for one or other of the major parties to not field a candidate. Usually, in this case, a minor candidate may receive a huge share of the vote, even to the point where she can win the seat. This situation occurred in the 2002 Cunningham by-election, where the Liberal Party did not run a candidate in the normally safe Labor seat. With the help of the 30 per cent or so of Liberal voters without a Liberal to vote for, the Greens' Michael Organ received a strong enough vote to win the seat — the first time the Greens held a seat in the House of Representatives. Organ lost his seat in 2004.

MINOR PARTIES LOCKED OUT OF THE LOWER HOUSE?

While it's hard to do, some minor parties have been able to win seats in the House of Representatives.

In 2010, the Australian Greens won the seat of Melbourne — a remarkable achievement for a minor party. Moreover, the party was able to keep Melbourne and get close to winning other inner-metropolitan seats across the country in subsequent elections. Clive Palmer also made his party stand out from the many other minor parties by winning the Queensland lower house seat of Fairfax in 2013. In 2016, Rebekha Sharkie won the district of Mayo in South Australia for the first time as a representative of the Nick Xenophon Team (which then changed its name to Centre Alliance). She retained her seat in the 2019 election.

Minor parties are very important to Senate elections and to the operation of the Senate if and when they win seats.

Preference wheeling and dealing

The use of preferential voting does allow minor parties to have some indirect impact on lower house elections. Here, the way the preferential system requires voters to cast a preference for all candidates competing in each electoral division is the key thing to remember.

In really close contests, when no candidate has a majority of the vote, the count will *go to preferences* — that is, the count will look at the way each ballot has ordered its preferences and allocate votes accordingly. The second, third or fourth preference choice of those people voting for minor party candidates could be consulted and counted. In turn, the way minor parties advise their intending supporters to order their preferences can be crucial in determining who wins the seat.

This process of advising voters how to order their preferences is called *directing preferences*. Journalists often talk about the way minor parties direct their preferences, conjuring up an image of minor party people in smoke-filled rooms allocating ballots, which is *not* the way the process works. What does happen is that a minor party may decide to direct its preferences a certain way, and then print how-to-vote cards that are given to voters as they arrive at the polling stations to assist them in filling out their ballots. How-to-vote cards are advisory only. At the end of the day, it's up to individual voters as to how they order their preferences.

Analysts think that most Australian voters do follow how-to-vote cards when making their electoral choices, giving the minor parties some potential to influence the outcome of elections in individual seats. This potential can lead to negotiations and dialogue between major parties and minor parties to secure the direction of preferences. Policy commitments can be used in this horse-trading — in exchange for directing preferences, a major party might promise a minor party certain legislative or policy action on an issue important to the minor party. This process is known as *preference wheeling and dealing*, and it usually occurs during the campaign period in the lead-up to an election.

Measuring minor party success

How can the impact of a minor party be measured? Clearly, getting enough votes to win a seat in the parliament is a major criterion for success. Another may be a situation where minor party preferences help determine the outcome of a close lower house seat. A third measure involves a feature of the electoral system. In order to nominate, a candidate must pay a deposit that's refunded if the candidate wins 4 per cent of the votes cast in the electoral district.

INFLUENCING POLICY: THE DEMOCRATS AND THE GST

In 1998, the Liberal–National coalition contested the general election on a platform of bringing in a new goods and services tax (GST). The coalition won the election, but didn't win control of the Senate. The balance of power was held by the Australian Democrats, whose own policy was to support the idea of a GST but to exempt fresh food and certain other goods and services from the tax. The government didn't want exemptions, but, with the Democrats holding the balance of power in the Senate, eventually agreed to exempt fresh food from the new tax. Having won this concession, the Democrats agreed to pass the necessary legislation, and the GST became part of the Australian taxation system.

In achieving 4 per cent of the vote, a candidate becomes entitled to receive funding for every primary vote cast (about $2.76 per vote at the 2019 election), under Australia's regulations over public funding of elections. Of the many minor parties that contest elections, very few ever reach the 4 per cent threshold.

Senate-based minor parties

Of the many minor parties, only a few actually get into the parliament. When they do win seats, it's mostly via proportional electoral systems that are usually used for upper houses (Legislative Councils in the state parliaments, and the Senate in the federal parliament).

When they secure a place in the parliament, these electorally successful minor parties become very different from all the other minor parties that run for election but fail. This difference is particularly important if these minor parties hold the strategic number of seats that give them the balance of power between the Labor Party and the coalition. In such a situation, the minor party or parties are in a position to exercise real power — because, as we note in Chapters 4 and 5, a parliamentary bill doesn't become law until it has passed both the lower house and the upper house.

In this situation, minor parties become insiders in the process. The government, knowing it can't get legislation through the upper house without the say-so of whoever holds the balance of power, will open up discussion in a bid to negotiate a mutually acceptable outcome. The minor party or parties that hold the balance of power can then seek to have bills amended or to have the government take their policy perspective into account when drawing up legislation.

Here today, gone tomorrow?

The major political parties have demonstrated their ability to endure, surviving election defeats, internal ructions and even some major splits along the way. The survival record of minor parties has been a little patchier, however, with the overall dynamic being that minor parties emerge for a short period before disappearing. This short life span can even happen to minor parties that win representation to the Senate.

Some minor parties have been able to survive for a long time. The Australian Democrats, for example, was formed in 1977, and kept winning Senate seats until a failure to win a seat in the 2004 and 2007 elections meant there were no longer any Democrat senators. The party organisation, however, continues to survive (see the section 'The Australian Democrats' later in this chapter).

Some parties have been very short-lived. The Liberal Movement Party that won Senate representation from South Australia in 1974 was wound up a couple of years later. Some parties struggle on, even without parliamentary representation, and make a return to parliament. For example, Pauline Hanson's One Nation Party won a Senate seat in 1998. Six years later, the One Nation senator was defeated in an election. The party, however, made a return to the Senate when it won four seats in 2016.

Being able to continue to win seats in the Senate or state upper houses is critical to the health and wellbeing of parliamentary minor parties. Being in the parliament gives the minor party all sorts of benefits, such as:

>> Obtaining public recognition

>> Being the centre of media attention

>> Being able to participate in the policy-making process

>> Having access to parliamentary resources, perhaps the most important benefit of all

The generally accepted view of analysts is that a minor party that has had parliamentary representation but is unable to sustain its parliamentary presence is on a road to disintegration and, perhaps, oblivion.

Out on Their Own: Independents

Analysts and journalists sometimes group independents and minor parties into one category, but the reality is that they're very different phenomena. Minor parties may only have a small membership and/or win a minor share of the vote, but they're still political parties. They still have an external organisation and they still undertake the key functions of preselecting candidates and trying to get those candidates elected.

REMEMBER

Independents are not in political parties — they wouldn't be independent if they were. Independent candidates are individuals whose organisation is restricted to the local area where they're campaigning. They certainly don't have organisations that extend to other electoral districts (if they did, it would be tantamount to being a political party).

Independent success

For all the major party dominance over election outcomes, a sprinkling of independents have managed to win seats in lower and upper houses in national and state parliaments.

Of the states, the Tasmanian Legislative Council has the strongest and most consistent record of independent MPs, due mainly to the fact that the upper house electorates there tend to have a relatively small number of voters in them. Independents have been elected to the lower houses in both New South Wales and Victoria. Indeed, in 1999, three independents held the balance of power in the Victorian legislature and were involved in the process of deciding which of the major parties would be able to form a minority government. Of course, famously, three independents — Rob Oakeshott (NSW), Tony Windsor (NSW) and Andrew Wilkie (Tasmania) — were part of the balance of power that supported Julia Gillard's minority government following the 2010 federal election.

Independent MPs have been elected to the national House of Representatives for a number of years now, including a period after the 1996 federal election when six independents were elected. Some of the more notable independents to have won parliamentary representation are:

>> **Pauline Hanson:** The Liberal Party disendorsed Hanson just before the 1996 election. Despite this, Hanson was able to win the seat of Oxley from the Labor Party. She technically entered parliament as an independent (see the section 'The Who's Who of Minor Parties' for more on Hanson's time in the House of Representatives).

>> **Brian Harradine:** Australia's longest serving independent politician, Harradine, from Tasmania, sat in the federal Senate from 1975 to 2005, and from 1993 to his retirement held the title of Father of the Senate (jointly with Mal Colston from 1993 to 1999). Harradine passed away in 2014.

>> **Bob Katter:** The federal MP for the Queensland seat of Kennedy, Katter was once in the Nationals but, after resigning from the party in 1998, has held his seat ever since as an independent.

- » **Jacqui Lambie:** Originally elected as a senator from Tasmania representing the Palmer United Party (PUP) in 2013, Lambie continued to build a high public profile and national presence as an independent once she resigned from the PUP.

- » **Cathy McGowan:** In 2013, McGowan defeated Liberal MP Sophie Mirabella in the Victorian seat of Indi. McGowan decided she would not contest the 2019 election and supported Helen Haines who kept Indi as an independent-held seat.

- » **Andrew Wilkie:** Yet another Tasmanian who has been prominent in the national debate, especially on issues concerning national security and gambling reform. He has been representing the district of Denison, which was replaced by Clark, since 2010.

- » **Tony Windsor:** Elected as the independent member for New England in 2001 (having previously served as an independent in the NSW parliament), Windsor was a key player along with fellow independent Rob Oakeshott in organising crossbench support for Julia Gillard's minority government after the 2010 election. He was a strong supporter of climate change action and was a key advocate of Gillard's carbon pricing policy. He retired from the parliament just ahead of the 2013 election.

- » **Nick Xenophon:** In 2007, Xenophon won a South Australian seat in the Senate as an independent. Xenophon had already built a high public profile in South Australia, where he had been elected on a 'no pokies' platform to the state parliament. In 2017, Xenophon announced that he would resign from the Senate in order to contest the seat of Hartley in the 2018 South Australian state election. Xenophon lost this contest and left parliamentary politics.

Once were party people

The recent record of independent representation in the national parliament has been pretty strong, but some of those who've sat in the parliament as independents were once in the major political parties.

Pauline Hanson was elected in 1996 as an independent MP for the Queensland seat of Oxley, but had actually been first nominated for the seat by the Liberal Party. In 1996, Graeme Campbell won the massive Western Australian electorate of Kalgoorlie as an independent. The previous times he had won the seat, however, he'd done so as a Labor candidate. After 1996, a number of senators became independent, but that was because they resigned from the political parties they'd belonged to when they were elected.

Someone elected to a seat in parliament as a party-endorsed candidate does not have to resign from their parliamentary seat if they later resign from the party. Cory Bernardi from South Australia, for instance, was elected to the Senate representing the Liberal Party but, in 2017, decided to resign and start a new minor party, the Australian Conservatives. This new party, however, was wound up in 2019 and Bernardi left the Senate in 2020. He was replaced by a member of the Liberal Party, because he had originally won the seat as a Liberal candidate.

The Who's Who of Minor Parties

With each state and federal election, many new minor parties (and a few existing ones) get registered to have another shot at getting into the Senate or trying to influence outcomes in the lower house.

Of this plethora of parties, here we examine a handful that have won a seat in the Australian Parliament. Some of the parties mentioned here have either come and gone, or are in the process of decline. Still, some may be on the brink of being long-term participants in the Senate, while others have proven to be a bit like a shooting star — one moment you see it, and the next moment it's gone.

The Democratic Labor Party

The Democratic Labor Party (DLP) was the minor party created out of the split that affected the ALP in the 1950s (refer to Chapter 9). The party was originally formed in Victoria. The Queensland Labor Party (the party that split from the ALP in Queensland) joined the DLP a little later on.

VOTE 1

The DLP became a bitter opponent of the ALP — a reality that confuses some people who think that the DLP was simply an offshoot of Labor. Part of the bitter opposition was due to ideology, with the DLP accusing the ALP of being too influenced by 'left-wing ideas'. As a consequence, the DLP became ultraconservative. It reached into its Catholicism to oppose abortion, but it also became a strong advocate of a hardline anti-communist approach, especially to foreign policy. The party was a strong supporter of Australia's involvement in the war in Vietnam.

As part of its anti-ALP approach, the DLP did two important things in the electoral process. First, it ran candidates in all lower house electorates and issued how-to-vote cards that directed its preferences to the Liberal Party. For a small but not insignificant number of former Labor voters, this ploy was the way they transferred their voting alignment to the conservative political parties.

The second important strategy was to run Senate candidates. Here the DLP could succeed in winning enough support to get senators elected, especially from Victoria and Queensland. From the 1950s until the mid-1970s, the DLP held the balance of power in the Senate. This fact wasn't particularly obvious to the public because of the way the DLP supported the Liberal–Country coalition in government.

In the area of education policy, the DLP was to have a major success and a lasting impact. Concerned about the impoverished nature of the Catholic school system, the DLP succeeded in persuading the Menzies government to use federal funds to assist private (usually church-run) education. This policy continues to this day (sometimes to much contention).

The DLP in its original form collapsed after the party's failure to win any seats in the 1974 double-dissolution federal election. A new form of the party was resurrected in Victoria in the 1980s and, in 2006, a DLP candidate was elected to the Victorian Legislative Council. In 2010, the DLP returned to the national parliament when it won a Victorian Senate seat, but has not had further successes at the federal level since then.

The Australian Democrats

The Australian Democrats was a very significant minor party that had a presence in the Senate from 1977 through until 2007. The Democrats were put together in the aftermath of the 1975 constitutional crisis (refer to Chapter 5). The party was actually created out of the remnants of another minor party — the Australia Party, which was formed by moderate Liberals who opposed the war in Vietnam. The Australia Party's main strategy was to stalk the DLP at election contests, but, when the DLP collapsed after 1974, so did the Australia Party. The new Australian Democrats was put together using the old Australia Party membership lists.

HELLO MR CHIPP

Playing a role in the creation of the Australian Democrats was a former federal Liberal MP, Don Chipp. Chipp had been a minister in the McMahon government and was something of a leadership rival to Malcolm Fraser. Fraser refused to include Chipp in his ministry after the 1975 election, precipitating Chipp's resignation from the Liberals and from the parliament. Chipp then threw his support behind the Democrats and was successfully elected to the Senate from Victoria in 1977.

The Australian Democrats was a Senate-oriented party. The party's ethos was to try to win the balance of power in the upper house and use it to keep the government of the day in the lower house answerable and accountable for its actions. Don Chipp had a colloquial way of describing this ethos when he said that the party's main aim was to 'keep the bastards honest'.

The Australian Democrats won Senate seats in every election from 1977 through to 2001. During a lot of this time, the party also held the balance of power. If a government wanted to get legislation through the parliament, it had to deal with the Democrats. For their part, Democrat senators took an open mind to this process and sought to negotiate outcomes. The party's rules stressed that Democrat senators would never block supply, so the party didn't pose a threat to a government's tenure. This stand then led to a situation where governments bargained with the Democrats to get their legislative program through the upper house.

The idea of using the Senate as a genuine house of review struck a chord with a small but strategically significant number of voters. As a result, the Democrat vote in the Senate was always higher than its House of Representatives vote. The party's heydays coincided with the Labor governments of 1983 to 1996, which led to the Democrats appearing to be stronger on social progressive policies than Labor, as the minor party tried to capitalise on voter disillusionment with the major parties.

In turn, the Democrats appeared to be a left-of-centre political party as it made overtures to disillusioned Labor voters, appealed to emerging social movements such as the anti-uranium movement and the environmental movement, and took up causes such as Indigenous rights, women's rights and gay rights. The party also had some unique organisational factors. Party members had the right to influence policy debates and, more significantly, the power to elect the parliamentary leader.

VOTE 1

The party's leaders tended to be high-profile and charismatic politicians. Chipp led the party until his retirement in 1986, when the leadership was handed to Janine Haines from the key Democrat state of South Australia. Haines led the party to its best election result in 1990, yet, in a bid to win a seat in the House of Representatives, the leader had stepped down from the Senate. When the Haines bid for the lower house seat of Kingston failed, the party experienced leadership turmoil thereafter.

These leadership struggles undermined the party's reputation in the eyes of the electorate. Then, after the 1998 election, the party negotiated with the Liberal–National Party coalition to bring in the controversial GST. This split the Democrats and led to a major decline in the party's Senate vote. When the party failed to win any seats in both the 2004 and 2007 Senate elections, it lost its parliamentary representation. The party was formally deregistered in 2016 for not having the required 500 members. However, in 2019 the Australian Democrats re-emerged and was once again registered as a political party by the Australian Electoral Commission. The party continues as an organisation, and has contested some state and federal elections.

The rise and fall of the Democrats has been quite interesting. At the party's height, some analysts described them as the 'third force' in Australian politics, with some even speculating that the party could displace one or other of the major political parties. Threats to the party came from all directions, however. In addition to their internal fights, the Democrats became concerned about the rise of environmental parties such as the Australian Greens and, at one point, floated the idea of a merger between the Democrats and the Greens. This merger did not eventuate, however.

REMEMBER

The Australian Democrats shouldn't be confused with the Democratic Party in the United States. Although they share a similar name, they're completely different political entities.

The Australian Democrats were also interesting on the matter of preferences. Whereas so many minor parties sought to influence politics by wheeling and dealing on preferences, the Australian Democrat party rules forbade any direction of preferences, especially to one or other of the major parties. The Democrats would instead issue split tickets (see the sidebar 'Splitting the ticket' for more information), although, later, the party issued split tickets that directed preferences to the Greens.

The Nuclear Disarmament Party

Back in 1982, before it was elected to government, the ALP had an anti-uranium policy that committed Labor to stopping uranium mining and supporting nuclear non-proliferation. In July 1982, National Conference abandoned the mining policy. Then, when Hawke became Labor prime minister in 1983, the new Labor government went out of its way to ensure close military relations with the United States were maintained.

Labor's approach enraged the left wing of its own party and other left-wingers outside party politics. One of the consequences of this anger was the formation of a new political party to champion the anti-nuclear cause. The Nuclear Disarmament Party (NDP) was formed in time for the 1984 federal election and included such luminaries as the then lead singer of rock band Midnight Oil, Peter Garrett, as one of its New South Wales Senate candidates.

VOTE 1

Garrett won nearly 9 per cent of the vote but, because Labor refused to direct preferences to him, the rock star failed to win a seat. In Western Australia, however, a virtual unknown by the name of Jo Valentine did win a seat for the party.

SPLITTING THE TICKET

A split ticket occurs when a party issues a how-to-vote card that doesn't direct preferences to any parties, or perhaps directs preferences to other minor parties but not to any major party. A how-to-vote card is produced that says 'how to vote giving your preferences to Labor' on one side of the ticket and 'how to vote giving your preferences to Liberal' on the other side (hence the term *split*). Arguments used to arise about the Democrats' decision to publish split tickets that ranked preferences to Labor on the left-hand side of the card on the grounds that it somehow advantaged Labor over the Liberals.

The NDP, then, was to have had a place in the Senate but, before the upper house could meet, the NDP had a national conference at which large numbers of people — including senator-elect Valentine — resigned. Valentine took up her seat as an independent, although she later registered the Valentine Peace Group as a party with the Australian Electoral Commission. Under this banner, she was re-elected in 1987.

The failed NDP conference looked as if it had destroyed the party but, in New South Wales in 1987, the NDP won another Senate seat (with about 1.8 per cent of the primary vote). Senator-elect Robert Wood was to have joined the upper house but, before he could do so, Elaine Nile — wife of Reverend Fred Nile, who was to later create his own Christian Democratic Party (another minor party with a presence in the New South Wales upper house) — challenged Wood's candidature in the High Court. Wood, it appeared, was not an Australian citizen. The court overturned Wood's election and the seat went to the second-placed person on the NDP ticket, Irina Dunn, who then resigned from the NDP and took her seat as an independent.

After all this turmoil, the real legacy of the party, however, was to act as a catalyst for a reshaping of the minor party scene generally, and of the green-tending political parties that were to emerge in particular.

The West Australian Greens

Talking about the various environmental parties in Australia is difficult because they're literally a collection of autonomous state-based parties that, in 2003, agreed to enter into a loose confederation. For a long time, two main green parties existed — the Australian Greens (see the next section) and the West Australian Greens. What was more, these were two competing parties — the West Australian Greens were the last and the most reluctant of the state parties to come into the confederation.

The NDP was directly linked with the West Australian Greens. After leaving the NDP to form the Valentine Peace Group (the VPG) and being re-elected to the Senate, Jo Valentine tired of parliamentary politics and resigned from the Senate.

Under Section 15 of the Constitution, someone from the VPG had to fill this casual Senate vacancy. The second person on the VPG ticket was Christabel Chamarette. Chamarette duly became the next VPG senator. By the time this happened, however, the VPG had been replaced by a new party — the West Australian Greens.

In 1993, Chamarette was joined in the Senate by a second West Australian Green, Dee Margetts. Margetts had defeated the Australian Democrat candidate to pick up the Western Australian seat with the help of ALP preferences. This success was the high point of the party's Senate results, however. Chamarette was to lose her seat in 1996 and Margetts in 1998. By this stage, Bob Brown of the Australian Greens was in the Senate, and green politics had a new leader to focus on. The West Australian Greens tried unsuccessfully to win back its Senate position in 2001. It then became part of the green confederation.

The Australian Greens (the Greens)

Between 1996 and 1998, two distinct and separate green parties were identifiable in the Australian Senate. The 1996 election was very significant as the poll that finally brought Dr Bob Brown to the federal parliament. He was an environmental activist from Tasmania, made famous by the anti-Franklin Dam campaign, who then served in the Tasmanian Legislative Assembly.

Brown had run for a federal election once before, when, in 1993, he unsuccessfully ran for the lower house seat of Dennison. Although not enough to win him a lower house seat, Brown's vote was strong enough to get him into the Senate in 1996. After 1998, Brown was the sole Green in the national parliament.

VOTE 1

GREENING A STATE PARLIAMENT

Environmental issues have been very important in Tasmanian state politics, and a dispute over a proposal to build a new pulp mill in the state's north-west helped mobilise the Greens as an electoral force in Tasmania. In 1989, five green independent candidates were elected to the Tasmanian House of Assembly. The green independents held the balance of power and, after negotiating an agreement with the Labor Party, eventually voted to allow a minority Labor government to be formed.

This agreement between the Labor Party and green independents was known as the *Green–Labor Accord*. Two of the leading personalities in this accord were Bob Brown and anti-pulp mill activist Christine Milne. Brown was to bring this experience of minority government and wheeling and dealing with the major parties to the Senate in 1996. In 2004, Milne was also elected to the Senate. Tasmania's green political movers and shakers were together again in the Senate.

The Greens have become a consistent feature of the Senate, though the party is often described (sometimes as an attack) as either an extremist party, mainly because of the propensity for their adherents to use ecological concepts to explain what they believe in and how they see the political debate, or as a single-issue party, because of its connection with the environment.

In the parliament, however, the Greens tend to operate in ways closer to the Australian Democrats, especially in their relationship with the Labor government. With the Democrats being absent from the Senate, and with the policy debate becoming increasingly preoccupied with environmental issues, the Greens have emerged as the next largest and most significant political party after Labor, the Liberals and the Nationals in the Australian party system.

Pauline Hanson's One Nation

In 1996, a former Liberal candidate for the Queensland-based federal seat of Oxley, Pauline Hanson, was quoted during the election campaign as saying that, in her opinion, a 'reverse racism' was operating in Australia, where Indigenous Australians were getting a disproportionately greater share of welfare assistance than non-Indigenous Australians. Amid the controversy arising over her comments, the Liberal Party withdrew its endorsement and Hanson contested — and won — the seat as an independent.

Hanson's presence in the parliament was to cause constant controversy, especially as she used the House of Representatives to opine on a range of subjects. As part of the plan to get re-elected and increase her influence, Hanson and some supporters established a political party — called Pauline Hanson's One Nation Party, or just One Nation for short — to raise funds, preselect candidates and run the campaign.

One Nation's first big electoral success was in the Queensland state election in 1998, when the party won 12 lower house seats in the unicameral parliament — a result that helped bring down the National Party government of Premier Rob Borbidge. This result actually galvanised the Liberal and National Parties to attack One Nation, by issuing how-to-vote cards that put One Nation last in the list of coalition preferences in time for the next federal election, held in 1998.

This decision to 'put One Nation last' denied Hanson the chance to be re-elected in the lower house and stopped the election of One Nation senators in Western Australia, South Australia and New South Wales. In Queensland, however, support for One Nation was strong enough (almost 15 per cent) to elect a senator. The successful candidate, Heather Hill, was challenged in the High Court, where it was revealed that she wasn't an Australian citizen. In her place came the second-placed One Nation candidate, Len Harris.

Almost from the moment it was formed, One Nation started to fragment. All the One Nation MPs elected to the Queensland state parliament resigned from the party and formed a new party, the Country City Alliance. The national version of One Nation also started to fall apart — a process exacerbated by the fact that Hanson failed to win re-election.

Later, the Queensland Electoral Commission alleged that One Nation had lodged fraudulent returns, and Hanson had to face court and a period of imprisonment before an appeal exonerated her. One Nation struggled on and actually won some upper house seats in the Western Australian parliament in 2017.

VOTE 1

While Hanson was out of parliament, she was not out of the public debate and became somewhat of a minor celebrity. In 2010, Hanson announced that she wished to emigrate to the United Kingdom, but then changed her mind. In yet another twist to the One Nation story, Hanson returned to the national parliament in 2016 when her party won four seats in the Senate (for herself, Malcolm Roberts (QLD), Brian Burston (NSW) and Rod Culleton (WA)).

Family First

In the 2004 election, a candidate for the Senate in Victoria by the name of Steve Fielding, representing a minor party called Family First, won a seat. The fact that he did so with only 1.8 per cent of the primary vote caught everyone's attention and was a reminder of how important preference deals could be in getting people elected under the system of proportional representation.

Fielding's success also drew attention to the Family First Party, which many commentators tended to describe as a religious party. This description was due partly to the allegation that the party drew many of its candidates and a lot of its money from some evangelical churches — although, it must be said, Family First personnel have always denied that such a relationship exists.

Family First struggled to maintain a spot in the Senate. While it won a seat at the 2013 election, and again at the 2016 double-dissolution election, the party merged with Cory Bernardi's Australian Conservatives party in 2017 and deregistered as a national party shortly after.

Clive Palmer United Party

In 2013, Queensland businessman Clive Palmer shook up Australian politics by launching one of the most well-resourced campaigns ever seen by a minor party at the national level. Leading his newly formed party (the Palmer United Party), Palmer achieved remarkable results. Not only did he win the lower house seat of Fairfax in Queensland, but the party also won a Senate seat in Queensland and

Tasmania (where its candidate was Jacqui Lambie). The Palmer United Party also won a Senate seat in Western Australia following the re-election in 2014 that was caused by missing ballot papers during the original election count in 2013.

The party promoted a range of policies such as reducing taxation while seeking to increase the age pension. Internal divisions, and the fact that the party struggled to replicate its initial success in subsequent elections, meant the Palmer United Party had a short, but sharp, impact on Australian politics. The party later changed its name to the Palmer United Australia Party, and then in 2018 to the United Australia Party. The party contested every lower house set in the 2019 election. Although failing to win a seat in either chamber, the party's campaign (which reportedly cost approximately $60 million and was mostly anti-Labor) was seen by some to have influenced the coalition's subsequent win.

Liberal Democrats

The Liberal Democrats also won their first Senate seat in 2013. The party was focused on trying to reduce government intervention in social and economic policy. For example, the Liberal Democrats promoted principles such as lower taxation and greater individual freedoms.

The party's senator from New South Wales, David Leyonhjelm, decided to leave the Senate in an ultimately unsuccessful tilt at winning an upper house seat in his home state in 2019.

The party also won representation at state level when it won two seats in the Victorian upper house in 2018.

Minor Parties of the Future

When the Australian Democrats appeared on the scene and managed to win seats in a number of Senate contests, it appeared as if a form of orderly pattern had emerged in the minor party system. However, since 1984 — the federal election that saw the size of the Senate increased — the minor party system for the Senate has become more volatile.

The volatility also extends to the parties themselves, however. The volatility and short life span of the NDP, the West Australian Greens and the Palmer United Party stands in contrast to the long period in which the Australian Democrats and even the old DLP were around. It remains to be seen if new and reconstituted parties, such as One Nation, will be able to keep their seats in the parliament in future elections.

4

Citizen Power!

Chapter **13**

Elections: A Festival of Democracy

The electoral process is the cornerstone that democracies are built on. For electoral results to have legitimacy, elections must be free, fair and regular. Voting is a crucial part of any democracy and, when it comes to elections in Australia, one is just not enough. Separate elections are held for federal, state and local governments, with different methods used to elect representatives, which this chapter explores.

Elections channel the will of the people, as citizens decide who will represent them in the parliament. Because political parties play a major role in elections, voters tend to choose candidates according to the party the candidates belong to, with the assumption that they're choosing which party they wish to see win government.

In this chapter, you also get to delve into the background of the ballot papers and how the votes are counted, as well as some of the challenging outcomes that can result.

Democratic Origins

For a nation that was originally founded as a penal colony, it's perhaps remarkable that Australia is also one of the older liberal democracies. From 1855 onwards, Australia developed the idea of parliamentary government based on *manhood suffrage* (that is, that all men over the age of 21 could vote, regardless of whether they held property or not). Indeed, Australian colonies led the way in the adoption of *universal suffrage* (that is, that both men and women should have the right to vote) when, in 1894, the colony of South Australia legislated to allow women to vote.

When the Australian national parliament was created at Federation in 1901, the Constitution explicitly stated that the two parliamentary houses — the House of Representatives and the Senate — would be directly elected. The number of lower house seats would be allocated to each state proportionally (New South Wales would have the largest number of seats), with the original states (so not including the Northern Territory and the Australian Capital Territory) being guaranteed at least five lower house seats (the reason Tasmania today has five seats despite its small population). In the Senate, however, each original state would have the same number of seats regardless of population.

The Constitution left it to the parliament to decide on how the election rules would be drawn up, with these rules taking the form of the *Commonwealth Electoral Act 1918*, which has, of course, been regularly amended since then. The parliament decides on what electoral systems are used and how elections are conducted. Over the years, some changes have been made to the composition of parliament. Most notably, the Senate was expanded to allow for the two territories to have two senators each.

The first national election for the Australian parliament was held under its own electoral laws in 1903 (as distinct from the 1901 election that was held under colonial franchise laws). All men and women of 21 years of age and above who weren't Indigenous Australians and who weren't excluded because of their being in prison at the time were entitled to vote, making Australia one of the first nations to adopt near-universal suffrage. Refer to Chapter 3 for information on voting rights for Australia's Indigenous population.

HOW MANY SEATS?

The first federal parliament had 62 members of the House of Representatives and 6 senators for each of the original states (a total of 36 senators). Both houses have been expanded. Today there are 151 members of the House of Representatives (47 from New South Wales, 38 from Victoria, 30 from Queensland, 16 from Western Australia, 10 from South Australia, 5 from Tasmania, 3 from the Australian Capital Territory and 2 from the Northern Territory) and 76 senators.

EXTENDING THE FRANCHISE

In 1962, the Commonwealth Electoral Act was amended to allow Indigenous Australians to enrol, although it was not compulsory, as we outline in Chapter 3. In 1967 a constitutional referendum was passed that made responsibility for Indigenous Australians a concurrent federal and state power. The Commonwealth now had the power to make Aborigines and Torres Strait Islanders to be full national citizens and be expected to conform to the national electoral laws. It was not until 1983, however, that this expectation took legal form after the overhaul of Australia's electoral laws by the Hawke government just ahead of the 1984 election.

In 1974, meanwhile, and as part of its overhaul of the electoral system, the Whitlam government again extended the franchise by lowering the voting age from 21 years to 18. The Whitlam government also legislated for the Northern Territory and the ACT to have Senate representation.

Federal and State Elections

Elections are complicated things, partly because they're about politics (political parties, leaders, election campaigns, party workers and so on), and partly because they're subject to a host of laws and regulations that guide everything from the way an election can be called all the way through to how far from a polling booth a party worker must stand when handing out how-to-vote cards.

Elections are great media events. The political media love them because they have all the hallmarks of a sporting contest such as horseracing (and you can now even bet on election outcomes). Check out Chapter 15 for more on the media and politics. The election count itself is also a major media event, with television networks employing computer whizzes to construct televisual graphics to track the vote and political experts to comment sagely on the *swing*, which is the difference between the percentage of votes for a candidate in a particular seat in the current and previous elections. (See Chapter 14 for more on percentage swings in marginal electorates.)

As a political commentator once noted, elections are so important precisely because they're the closest most citizens come to experiencing the day-to-day rigours of modern politics.

A term that conjures images of an old tyre tied to a grimy rope hanging off a big old tree, the swing in politics can be as much fun. It's a term used among political commentators that simply refers to the difference in the vote for the parties from one election to the next. Remember, you need to look at two swings — the swing on first preferences, or the *primary vote*, and the all-important *two-party swing*, when combined preferences are counted, which determines election outcomes.

Australian elections: Compulsory democracy

Australians actually have to participate in elections — it's the law! In 1911, after a particularly poor turn-out at a Senate election, the federal parliament enacted compulsory voting. The law actually requires Australian citizens (previously 21 year olds but, after 1974, 18 year olds) to have themselves placed on the electoral roll. When an election is called, citizens are expected to attend a polling station, have their attendance recorded and then cast their vote.

In 1924, the federal parliament went a step further, and enacted laws to make it compulsory to register your name on the electoral roll and to attend elections. Compulsory voting applies to all federal elections, and all state and territory elections. Compulsory voting also applies for local council elections in New South Wales, Victoria, Queensland and the Northern Territory.

REMEMBER

The Australian Electoral Commission (AEC) will fine you if you don't vote. Keep an eye on election dates, polling booths and other useful pieces of information about voting on the AEC's website at www.aec.gov.au.

VOTE 1

The fact that voting is compulsory can polarise opinion. Some believe that voting is a civic duty (similar to paying taxes) and that it draws the government and citizenry closer. Others, however, argue that compulsory voting infringes on individual rights and forces citizens who have little interest in politics to vote.

Conducting elections

Independent authorities are responsible for the conduct of elections in Australia. Among other tasks, these authorities are responsible for counting the votes that ultimately elect the government and for maintaining the *electoral roll* — the list of all eligible voters and their addresses.

The AEC is responsible for running federal elections, while state electoral commissions conduct state elections. These authorities actively promote Australia's democratic processes through their websites and regular advertisements. They employ professional staff, who must always remain apolitical to ensure the integrity of the authorities' decisions. The Australian electoral system just wouldn't be the same without them.

Drawing up electoral boundaries

The AEC and state authorities are also responsible for the crucial task of setting the geographic boundaries for electoral districts. They take into account population size and geographic divisions (such as rivers and roads) and try to keep common communities together in creating, or modifying, district boundaries.

TECHNICAL STUFF

In Australia, the term used to describe the process where electoral authorities draw up electoral districts is a *redistribution*, which happens periodically in order to keep the number of voters in each electorate roughly equal within each state. In the past, rural electoral districts were allowed to have fewer voters than city electorates, but this situation was changed in 1983. Now, electorates are permitted to be slightly over-enrolled or slightly under-enrolled only when the AEC tries to accommodate what it thinks population growth will be in between redistributions.

Counting up the votes and declaring the result in each electoral district is also an important function that's carried out by the AEC and its state counterparts.

Naming electorates

Naming Commonwealth electoral divisions is also the responsibility of the AEC. Generally, it names divisions after noteworthy Australians who have contributed to society and have since passed away. For example, the seat of Bruce was named after Lord Stanley Bruce, who was prime minister between 1923 and 1929; Bradfield was named after engineer and bridge designer John Bradfield; and Dawson in Queensland was named after Andrew Dawson, who was the state's first Labor premier, elected in 1899.

But Aboriginal and geographic names are also used. For example, Canberra is based on the Aboriginal word that translates to 'meeting place'. Eden-Monaro in New South Wales, on the other hand, is named after the geographic area it covers — and not a two-door sports car.

Different electoral systems

If variety is the spice of life, then Australia's electoral system is quite zesty indeed. Different methods are used to elect representatives in different levels of government. For example, at the federal level, each district in the House of Representatives is represented by a single member who has won a majority of votes in the district. This contrasts with the Senate, which relies on candidates securing a certain proportion of the statewide vote in order to win a seat.

Electoral systems also differ between states. For example, the lower houses of the mainland states mirror the electoral system of the federal House of Representatives. In each case, a single member is elected to represent a specific locality. But the Tasmanian lower house uses a system of proportional representation and bases its electorates on the state's five federal electorates.

Elections for each state's upper house are now similar to that of the Senate, in their use of proportional representation. The only states to vary from this are Tasmania, which has single-member districts and uses preferential voting, and Queensland, which abolished its upper house in 1922.

Local government elections can also use different electoral systems. Some councils rely on voters attending a polling station to vote, whereas others may conduct their elections entirely through postal voting. Local government is a state responsibility, and the different states have different laws on local elections. Three states (Victoria, Queensland and New South Wales) have compulsory voting, and the state electoral authorities run these elections. The other states have voluntary voting or property-based voting and allow councils to run their own elections.

Many elections

Australians can go to the polls three times in a year to elect the three levels of government. All states have four-year parliamentary terms. New South Wales, Victoria, Queensland, Western Australia and South Australia have fixed parliamentary terms, whereas early elections can be called in Tasmania in certain circumstances.

The situation in federal elections is complicated by a series of factors, including the presence of the Senate and the restrictions on the way in which Senate elections may be called, which are outlined in the Constitution (refer to Chapter 3).

REMEMBER

The Constitution outlines that the House of Representatives is elected for a three-year term. The Senate, however, has six-year terms, with terms for half the Senate staggered to coincide with the House of Representatives. A normal election situation, therefore, occurs when all the House of Representatives seats and half the Senate are up for election every third year.

Because Australia is a Westminster system and because Westminster prime ministers have the right to call elections whenever they see the need (refer to

Chapter 4), Australian prime ministers can also seek to have the House of Representatives elections held early — that is, before the three-year term has expired.

TECHNICAL STUFF

Section 13 of the Constitution, however, says that an early Senate election can be called only 12 months ahead of when half the Senate seats are due to expire. So, a prime minister wishing to have an early lower house election occurring at the same time as a half-Senate election would have to call the early election within the 12-month expiry period for the Senate.

Of course, the prime minister can call an early election for the House of Representatives without having a half-Senate election. In this event, the lower and upper house elections would go out of sync, and a separate half-Senate election would have to be held later. A stand-alone half-Senate election last occurred in 1970.

Double-dissolution elections

If you've read the previous section, you may be feeling a tad confused. Well, it gets worse. Section 57 of the Constitution is called the *deadlocks provision* and allows for what's known as a *double-dissolution election*.

Section 57 is covered in more detail in Chapter 5 but, in short, this mechanism deals with bills that the Senate refuses to pass. Under the Constitution, a parliamentary deadlock can be resolved by the governor-general dissolving both the House of Representatives and the Senate at the same time.

Double-dissolution elections have important electoral consequences, for the Senate in particular, because a double dissolution requires the election of all 76 senators at the same time. When this situation occurs, the percentage of the vote required to win a seat falls quite dramatically compared with a half-Senate election.

LAST ON, FIRST OFF

Double-dissolution elections for the Senate introduce the problem of which senators get to enjoy their full six-year terms and which senators are left with three-year terms and contest for re-election at the next half-Senate election. This situation is dealt with under Section 13 of the Constitution. Under the current system, the AEC is able to determine the order that senators are elected from each state. The first six senators elected in each state are known as the *first-class senators* and get a six-year term, and the second lot of six senators are called the *second-class senators* and serve a three-year term. Senators from the territories have three-year terms regardless.

Calling elections: Who has the power?

The problem of Australia being a Westminster system with a written constitution again arises with the question of who has the power to call federal elections. Under Westminster practice, the power to call elections is in the hands of the prime minister. According to the Constitution, however, the power to call elections rests with the governor-general and, in some instances, with the state governors.

TECHNICAL
STUFF

The governor-general is the person with the authority to start the federal election process. (For state elections it's the governor.) The governor-general does this by signing a legal document authorising an election, called a *writ*, which brings the election laws into play. These laws outline:

>> The length of time allowable for people to register or amend their enrolment details

>> The date for nominations to be lodged with the AEC (or the state electoral authority for state elections)

>> The date of the election

>> The date at which the writs declaring the winner of each electoral contest must be returned to the governor-general for authorisation

The minimum amount of time for the conduct of a federal election is 33 days, and the maximum is 110 days, from call to declaration of the winners.

When a Senate election is called, authorising writs is the responsibility of the state governors, because the Senate is officially the house of the states.

The role of the prime minister

Although the Constitution technically puts the governor-general at the centre of the election process, for all practical purposes the power to call elections rests with the prime minister. This practice is a reflection of the importance of the prime minister in a Westminster system, and the situation in Australia is that elections are usually called by the governor-general on the advice of the prime minister of the day.

Even for double-dissolution elections, the prime minister has the call. Technically the power to call a double dissolution resides with the governor-general. However, the convention in Australian parliamentary practice is that the governor-general only uses Section 57 of the Constitution when advised to do so by the prime minister. Indeed, as we outline in Chapter 5, a prime minister can stockpile defeated legislation as the basis for asking for a double dissolution, providing the opportunity for such an election to be called for politically strategic reasons.

Fixed-term parliaments?

The issue of why the federal government doesn't have fixed terms has been a hotly debated topic over the years. Instituting a fixed parliamentary term would deny prime ministers the power to call early elections (and, indeed, would deny the governor-general the ability to dismiss a parliament the way Sir John Kerr did in 1975), but its achievement would require dramatic change to the Constitution.

In 1988, Prime Minister Bob Hawke argued fixed terms would give certainty to election timing and proposed a referendum to provide for fixed terms for the national parliament. The Australian voters overwhelmingly rejected the referendum, with only one in three voters supporting the change.

The Importance of Electoral Systems

Electoral systems work to convert the choices of the voters into representation. The type of system or systems used in the electoral process can have a profound effect on the culture of the political process. It determines which parties win seats and, as a result, which parties can affect who'll be in government and who'll be in opposition.

In Australian national politics and in those states that have bicameral parliaments, two different electoral systems are used.

In the case of the national parliament (and in all the states except Tasmania, and the Assembly for the Australian Capital Territory), the lower house electoral system — and the unicameral house in Queensland — uses single-member districts and the preferential voting system. In the case of the upper houses (with Tasmania the exception here because it uses the preferential system), proportional representation is used.

Up the majority! Preferential voting

As the maxim goes, majority rules. Preferential voting seeks to elect the candidate who has the support of the majority of voters in a given electoral district.

REMEMBER

Majority-oriented systems are based on the idea of a single person being elected from each electoral district. In Australia, *electoral districts* are also called *electoral divisions*, *electorates* or — most popularly of all — *seats*, because the person who wins the contest in the electoral division wins the right to sit in the House of Representatives.

Majorities can be determined by having a simple poll, where whoever gets the largest number of votes wins. In election parlance, such a simple system is known as *first past the post*. Australian elections used to be first-past-the-post affairs until 1918, when the system was changed.

TECHNICAL STUFF

Preferential voting requires voters to cast a numerical preference for all the candidates appearing on the ballot paper. The aim of the system is to elect a candidate who achieves 50 per cent plus one vote of the total formal vote cast in that electorate. If no candidate achieves this threshold on the total of first votes (the *primary* vote), then the count eliminates the candidate with the lowest primary vote and reallocates the second preferences from this candidate's votes to the next preferred candidate at full value. This process is repeated until a candidate eventually achieves the threshold of 50 per cent plus one.

To illustrate how preferential voting works, say three candidates, Terry, Cherry and Merri, stand for election in a district with 10,000 voters. One of them must win at least 5,001 votes to be elected. Terry wins 4,000 votes, Cherry wins 2,500 votes and Merri wins 3,500 votes. As the candidate with the lowest votes, Cherry's votes are distributed. Out of her 2,500 votes, 500 voters gave their second preference to Terry but 2,000 voters gave their second preference to Merri. So, in this example, the final votes stand at 4,500 for Terry and 5,500 for Merri, which means she is elected — making her very merry indeed.

PREFERENTIAL VOTING: MAXIMISING THE ANTI-LABOR VOTE

In 1918, the Nationalist government, headed by Prime Minister Billy Hughes, was worried that a split in the non-Labor vote between urban anti-Labor parties and rural anti-Labor candidates was helping the Labor Party. In order to ensure that the collective anti-Labor vote would eventually be counted together rather than be split, the government enacted laws that brought in preferential voting. The first general election to use preferential voting was in 1919.

For a ballot paper to be deemed valid by the AEC it must *number* all candidates in order of preference — a tick or a cross is a vote that's lost. In Australian elections, such lost votes (and any other errors in voting) are called *informal votes*. See Figure 13-1 for a sample House of Representatives ballot paper.

This requirement leads some to describe the system for federal elections as compulsory preferential voting, because a voter must cast a preference for all candidates. In some states (New South Wales and Queensland), a system of optional preferential voting applies, where voters are permitted to cast preferences for only as many candidates as they wish to vote for.

FIGURE 13-1: Preferential voting for the House of Reps means all candidates must be numbered in order of preference.

REMEMBER

The matter of preferences is obviously important to Australian elections, especially in closely contested electoral districts. This is one reason election commentators make a distinction between the *primary vote* and the *two-party-preferred vote* in election contests. The two-party vote is the important vote, because that is the result that determines which candidate wins the seat.

Lowering the electoral bar: Proportional representation

Proportional representation revolves around the idea of multi-member electorates in which candidates need to win only a proportion of the formal vote to win a seat. This is somewhat different from preferential voting (refer to the previous section), which is all about electing a single person from a single-member electoral division who has won an absolute majority of the valid vote cast.

In theory, the proportional system aims to allocate seats to candidates and/or parties in proportion to the share of the vote they win. This aim isn't quite achieved in Australian Senate contests, but proportional representation does give minor parties and independent candidates a much greater chance of winning a seat in the Senate than they might expect in the House of Representatives.

The basics

Each Australian state is represented by 12 senators, half of whom are elected every three years. Each state then is a *multi-member electorate* — that is, each state returns more than one representative. Since 1948, the method of electing senators has been a type of proportional representation known as the *single transferable vote (STV)* method.

As with lower house elections using preferential voting, voters in an STV system must numerically order their preferred candidates starting with their most preferred candidate (who gets a 1) through to the least preferred candidate. This practice allows the AEC to allocate preferences to candidates after one candidate reaches the necessary quota and is therefore elected. Preferences from candidates who have been eliminated from the count can now also be distributed.

Between 1949 and 2013, preferences had to be cast for every candidate contesting the Senate in each state. However, between 1984 and 2013, electors could utilise the 'Group Ticket Vote'. This allowed an elector to cast a primary vote above the black line on the Senate ballot, and the AEC would then assume that all preferences were to be allocated as per that party's how-to-vote card.

The Group Ticket Vote was abolished in 2016, as was the requirement that electors cast a preference for every candidate. Since 2016, electors can now cast at least six preferences for party lists above the black line on the Senate ballot paper, or cast at least as many preferences for individual candidates as there are vacancies to be filled (at least 6 preferences in a half-Senate election, or at least 12 preferences in a full-Senate election) below the black line.

Voting in the Senate is clearly a complicated affair. So, too, is counting a Senate result. Those people who count STV elections need endless patience and a good grasp of mathematics (or at least a very good calculator), because this system involves a lot of mathematical calculations in the process of electing candidates.

The quota

The first thing that needs to be calculated is the *quota*, which is the number of votes a candidate must get in order to win a seat. The quota is calculated by dividing the total formal vote cast by the number of vacancies to be filled plus one, and then adding one to that. (Got it?)

Fortunately, in Senate elections, you already know what the basic quota is, even before a vote is cast. In half-Senate elections, candidates need to win 14.4 per cent to secure a seat. In full-Senate (that is, double-dissolution) elections, the quota falls to 7.7 per cent.

The quota doesn't need to be achieved on primary vote alone. The quota can also be met through the distribution of preferences and the surplus.

REMEMBER

The surplus

The next major mathematical task is to calculate what is known as the *surplus*, which is the vote won by a successful candidate in excess of the quota. If a candidate wins 28.8 per cent, a surplus of 14.4 per cent occurs, given that the candidate needed to win only 14.4 per cent to secure a seat.

Because voters are required to indicate who their second, third, fourth (and so on) preferred candidates are, the question of where a surplus goes is determined by the voter's preference choices. The AEC then needs to work out the value of the surplus vote, because it's transferred to the next preferred candidate at a fraction of its value. If you're really keen to check out how the calculation is done, see the sidebar 'Calculating the surplus'.

DON'T FRET — IT'S JUST PSEPHOLOGY

VOTE 1

If you enjoy the electoral process — especially during election time — you may have a case of psephology fever. But don't be shocked. *Psephology* is the technical term used to describe the study, and analysis, of election results.

MINOR PARTIES LOVE DOUBLE-DISSOLUTION ELECTIONS

Indeed they do. At 7.7 per cent, the threshold to get elected is a little more than half that required for half-Senate elections, and much lower than for lower house elections. Under the STV system (refer to the section 'The basics'), the quota may include votes won as a result of preferences and/or the surplus. A minor party can then win a seat even if it wins a very small primary vote. In 1987, the Nuclear Disarmament Party (NDP) won a seat in New South Wales with 1.7 per cent of the primary vote as a result of a favourable flow of preferences (refer to Chapter 12 for more on the NDP).

TECHNICAL
STUFF

CALCULATING THE SURPLUS

Get your abacus out for this one. The surplus is calculated by dividing the total number of votes in excess of the quota (the total formal vote cast divided by the number of vacancies to be filled plus one, and then add one) by the total number of votes won by the candidate, giving a fractional outcome. Each vote cast for the successful candidate is then reallocated to the next preferred candidate at the fractional value. If you can follow all of this, you could well qualify for a Bachelor of Mathematics.

This process allows the AEC to determine the order in which senators are elected — an important consideration when electing a Senate after a double dissolution because it determines which senators will serve a six-year term and which senators will be up for election at the next general election.

The Senate ballot paper: It's a whopper!

The Senate ballot paper has many, many more candidates than a House of Representatives ballot paper, and the reasons include:

>> Parties other than Labor, Liberal and National have a greater chance of winning seats, so they often field candidates.

>> Senate contests occur statewide rather than as a series of contests in smaller electoral divisions, so the candidates are for the whole of the state.

>> All parties nominate lists of candidates usually in excess of the number of positions vacant.

Because of the greater number of candidates in Senate elections, Senate ballot papers are much bigger and much more complicated than House of Representatives ballot papers (see Figure 13-2 for a sample). In the 2019 election, for example, 105 candidates stood in New South Wales, with 458 candidates nationally contesting 40 Senate vacancies.

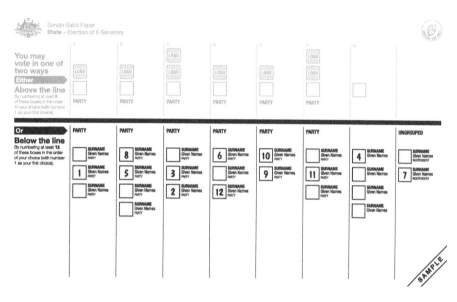

In the old days (that is, before 1983), all ballot papers had lists of names clustered in groups, but no party identifiers, making it pretty difficult for voters to remember who was who, especially for the Senate. The rules also required voters to number their preferences for every candidate. These requirements created two features of the Australian electoral process.

The first of these features was the tendency for Senate election results to be characterised by very high rates of informal voting. Confronted with so many names and needing to enter sequential numbers to indicate their preferences, very many voters made mistakes and their votes were considered informal and weren't counted.

The complexity of the electoral process before 1983 also led to the creation of the how-to-vote card, which is still used in most elections, despite reforms to the voting process. Because neither the Senate nor the House of Representatives ballot papers had any party identifiers on them, voters had to rely on the political parties to let them know who the party-endorsed candidates were. The parties mobilise their workers to hand out bits of paper identifying their candidates — how-to-vote cards, which the parties produce themselves.

In addition to identifying the party-endorsed candidate, these how-to-vote cards also advise voters how to cast their preferences. This last point is a crucial part of the politics of Australian elections. We return to that theme in the section 'Who Wins and How?' later in this chapter.

DON'T WORRY IF YOU MAKE A MISTAKE!

It can get a bit tricky if you decide to number each candidate in Senate contests individually rather than voting *above the line* (choosing only six preferences). No matter how much you concentrate, you may make a mistake. If you do make an error, you can get a replacement ballot paper from one of the electoral officials. So you have no excuse for submitting an incomplete or informal ballot paper.

THE POLITICS OF CHANGING THE SENATE BALLOT

Labor was the party that sought to alter the Senate ballot. Labor strategists believed that the high degree of numeracy required of voters to successfully fill in the old ballot papers tended to disadvantage some of Labor's core blue-collar and overseas-born, non-English-speaking constituents.

Moreover, in the 1974 double-dissolution election, a record 75 candidates nominated for the Senate in New South Wales. That election saw a very high informal vote, and Labor strategists were of the opinion that many of those informal votes had been cast by Labor voters.

Labor strategists believed that, had that informal vote been counted, Labor would have won an extra seat and would have controlled the Senate, and the subsequent 1975 crisis (refer to Chapter 5) would never have happened.

Reforming the Senate ballot paper

In 1983, the Hawke Labor government made changes to the law that had major consequences for the Senate ballot paper. The new laws allowed for party identification to occur on all ballot papers. In the case of the Senate, voters were also given a choice as to whether they wished to cast their own preferences or to vote for a party-approved list of preferences. This was known as the Group Ticket Vote (GTV).

This was a successful reform in that over 95 per cent of Senate ballots were cast as GVTs and this, in turn, helped to eliminate a very high rate of informal voting. It also seemed to lead to a number of minor parties winning seats with very small shares of the primary vote. This, in turn, seemed to alarm some commentators who called for reform. In 2016, Malcolm Turnbull's Liberal–National coalition government changed the Senate voting system to do away with the GVT by allowing for optional preferential voting. The black line continues to feature on the Senate ballot, while the Turnbull reforms also allowed party logos to appear on the ballot paper.

Who Wins and How?

Because Australia follows the Westminster model, it adheres to the convention that the party (or coalition of parties) that wins a majority of seats in the House of Representatives forms government. The result for the vast majority of lower house seats using preferential voting is known by about 10 pm on election night, and the political parties probably know by then who's able to form a government.

Some individual seats are always very close, and the count for these seats may take up to another two weeks to complete. The electoral law allows for a number of days to lapse for postal votes and votes cast in other electoral divisions to arrive and be counted.

When the AEC is satisfied that the result is known, the returning officer declares the seat. Later, the governor-general signs the returned writ for the electoral division, to give legal authority to the election. Refer to the section 'Calling elections: Who has the power?' earlier in this chapter for more on the process.

Recounts and disputed returns

Very close results are usually subject to review. In such cases, the AEC completely recounts the ballots in seats where the result is very close (candidates have the right to ask for a recount).

Some close outcomes are disputed on the grounds that some breach of the law or some improper behaviour during the conduct of the election may have affected the result. In such circumstances, an aggrieved candidate can appeal to the High Court, sitting as the Court of Disputed Returns, to deal with such matters.

These days, the High Court tends to deflect the task of adjudicating such disputes to the Federal Court. The courts have a number of options in resolving disputes, including verifying the result, overturning the result and declaring who will hold the seat, or ordering a fresh election.

Exaggerated majorities

Australia's preferential voting system, used in single-member electoral districts, is deliberately designed to achieve what is known as an *exaggerated majority*, when the winning party wins a proportion of seats much greater than its percentage of the vote. For example, even if a party wins a slender majority of the national vote, it usually wins a comfortable majority in the House of Representatives.

TECHNICAL
STUFF

In 2004, the coalition won just under 53 per cent of the two-party preferred vote to Labor's 47 per cent, a result that suggests a close electoral race. Yet, in terms of seats won, the coalition won 86 to Labor's 60 seats in the lower house. In 2007, the results were reversed, with Labor winning 53 per cent to the coalition's 47 per cent. This translated to 83 seats for Labor to the coalition's 65.

HOW CLOSE CAN IT GET?

Before 2010, the closest election result in Australia was in 1961, when the coalition led by Robert Menzies won 49.5 per cent of the two-party vote to secure 62 seats, against Labor's 50.5 per cent for 60 seats. The coalition won government with a majority of just 2 seats in the House of Representatives.

The 2010 election results were even closer. Labor won 72 seats, while the coalition won 73 seats of the 150 in the chamber. On the two-party preferred vote, Labor won 50.12 per cent of the vote to the coalition's 49.88 per cent. This resulted in a hung parliament — which we cover in more detail in Chapter 6.

Such close outcomes are rare. An election where the majority is 15 seats or fewer is a close outcome.

This system of exaggerating majorities helps reinforce stable government, because elections are usually won by a relatively comfortable majority by either major party. The preferential voting system used for House of Representatives elections is responsible for this phenomenon.

Paradoxical outcomes

A majority wins, right? Well, in the case of Australian federal elections, this may not be entirely accurate. A party can win a majority of votes across the nation, yet lose an election. The reason for this outcome is the failure of parties that have won a majority of votes to win a majority of seats in parliament. The problem of *wasted majorities* arises here (see the sidebar 'What a waste!').

Paradoxical outcomes are elections when a party wins government with less than 50 per cent of the two-party-preferred vote. Such results aren't uncommon in Australia and have occurred in 1954, 1961, 1969, 1990 and 1998. In every election (other than 1990), it was the coalition that won government.

TECHNICAL STUFF

In 1998, the most recent paradoxical election, Labor won 51 per cent of the two-party preferred vote to the coalition's 49 per cent. But Labor won just 67 seats compared with 80 seats won by the coalition. So, despite winning a majority of votes, Labor couldn't win a majority of seats and so didn't win government.

Paradoxical outcomes generally occur as a result of regional variations in the national vote, where a party performs well in some states, but very poorly in others. They may also occur because a party's vote increases in seats that it already holds, or in seats that it's so far behind in that a jump in its vote doesn't threaten to overthrow the incumbent. That's why winning the marginal seats (see Chapter 14) is so crucial to a party's chances of winning government.

WHAT A WASTE!

Wasted majorities are a feature of single-member electoral systems and occur when a successful candidate wins a vote in excess of the majority required to win the seat. Under the preferential system, a candidate needs to win only 50 per cent plus one of the formal vote cast. If she wins a vote of 52 per cent, or more, the votes additional to the 50 per cent plus one vote are wasted. This outcome commonly occurs in very safe seats for the major parties. By the same token, a party is better served when it wins a lot of seats with very slender majorities rather than a few seats with very large majorities.

So, in Australian politics, winning a majority of the national vote isn't enough. To win government, parties must win a majority of seats. Usually, either the Liberal–National coalition or Labor will win a majority of lower house seats and form a majority government. In the 2010 election, however, neither side won an absolute majority of lower house seats. The balance of power was held by the crossbench, made up of three independents and two minor party members. All but one of these crossbench members agreed to support a minority government led by Labor's Julia Gillard (refer to Chapter 6).

Minority governments are rare in Australian politics, but they can occur and they are allowable under our constitutional practice. A minority government survives for as long as it can get its supply bill through the House of Representatives, or it is not subject to a successful motion of no confidence in the lower house. If it fails either of these tests, the minority government must resign. The opposition then gets a chance to see if it can get crossbench support. If this is not forthcoming, the governor-general would dissolve the House of Representatives and call for fresh elections for that house only.

Ransom-holding minorities

In the Senate, the prospect of one or other of the major parties winning a majority, let alone an exaggerated majority, is remote. Under the STV proportional system used in the Senate (refer to the section 'Lowering the electoral bar: Proportional representation', earlier in this chapter), non-major party players have every chance of ending up holding the balance of power, enabling them to cast deciding votes on legislation.

The first minor party to enter the Senate after the move to proportional representation in 1949 was the Democratic Labor Party in the 1950s. By the time fondue dinner parties had swept the world in the 1970s, the Liberal Movement and Australian Democrats had won Senate seats.

But it wasn't until the early 1980s that the Senate saw a rise in the number of minor parties winning representation. Indeed, the Nuclear Disarmament Party, the Greens, One Nation and the United Australia Party have all won seats in the last three decades. (Chapter 12 gives more on minor parties.)

Some notable independents have emerged over the years. One major figure was Tasmanian Brian Harradine, who held the balance of power for a short period in 1999. In 2007, South Australian Nick Xenophon won a seat as an independent. Some senators have been elected on party tickets but then resigned from their party to sit as independents. (Refer to Chapter 12 for more on independents.)

VOTE 1

The election of minor parties to the Senate ties in with notions of democracy, because it allows a greater range of views to be represented in parliament. However, the election of some minor parties may be criticised for allowing fringe, or minority, views to impact on broader government decisions, especially if they hold the balance of power.

Minor parties and independents may gain influence if they hold the balance of power in the Senate, where the government must rely on their support to pass a bill.

After the election is over

The one immediate consequence of an election is that members of parliament are elected, form government and opposition, and get on with governing. While all that's happening, some of the last procedures of the election also take place.

First of all, the AEC publishes a report on the election. In addition to outlining the results, the report publishes the declarations of gifts and donations made to the parties to help them fund their election campaigns.

The AEC also reports on how much money the taxpayers will pay the parties to help offset their election costs. These publicly funded elections have been a part of the Australian electoral process since 1983. The electoral law says that the parties will be paid a certain amount for every primary vote won by their candidates in electoral contests for both houses of parliament (see Chapter 14 for more on party funding).

The parliament, meantime, convenes a *Joint Select Committee on Electoral Matters (JSCEM)*. Made up of parliamentarians from both houses and from all of the parties, it investigates the conduct of the election and makes recommendations to government about ways in which the Electoral Act may be reformed.

DAMNED IF THEY DO, DAMNED IF THEY DON'T

Minor parties and independents holding the balance of power are often the target of harsh criticism. If they yield to the government's demands to support a bill, they're seen as weak and ineffective. If they block a bill, they can be criticised for being hostile and not respecting the government's right to govern. Therefore, minor parties and independents have the tough task of allowing governments to govern while trying to advance their own causes in parliament.

In between elections: By-elections

Occasionally, members of parliament vacate their seats, sometimes by retirement and sometimes due to ill health or even death. In such situations, a *by-election* is required.

The rules for by-elections vary from state to state, but the basic rule is that by-elections occur in single-member systems. In multi-member systems using proportional representation, however, countbacks (a recount of ballot papers cast at the last general election) or appointments (with a vacant seat filled by a member of the same party that originally won the seat) can occur.

By-elections in the House of Representatives occur usually when the Speaker of the House requests that writs for a by-election be issued. Senate vacancies, however, are filled by the nomination of a replacement by the governor of the state that the vacating senator came from. Since a referendum change in 1974, the Constitution requires that a replacement senator also come from the same political party.

By-elections can be difficult for governments. They give voters in a seat an opportunity to pass judgement on the government of the day without actually having to change the government. The intense concentration on a by-election also raises the profile of the candidates themselves, and by-elections can result in non-major party successes, all the more so when a major party chooses not to put up a candidate.

Chapter **14**

Let the Campaign Begin!

rmed with the knowledge of how the system works (and especially the preferential and proportional systems used for the House of Representatives and the Senate respectively, which we outline in Chapter 13), you can delve deeply into the conduct of elections.

In this chapter, you get to examine the many rules and regulations that guide the way candidates and parties should conduct themselves during the official campaign period and the election itself, and in the aftermath of election day. These rules also extend to the way elections are funded, how the media may perform their duties, and how the parties and candidates are able to advertise themselves.

This chapter also guides you on how to be an expert at understanding how people vote and how election outcomes are predicted and then interpreted. In the technical world of political studies, this phenomenon is sometimes described as *electoral behaviour* or, even more esoterically, *political sociology*. Basically, analysts simply try to understand the reasons people vote as they do and what impact this has on election outcomes. In this chapter, you get to share that knowledge.

The Rules of the Game

Each state and the Commonwealth has its own election rules, and so variations exist in some of the finer points of the conduct of elections. In Tasmanian state elections, for example, candidates aren't permitted to hand out how-to-vote cards at polling booths. In New South Wales, voters are able to use *optional* preferential voting in state elections for the lower house. In federal elections, however, all voters must cast a preference for all candidates for their vote to be deemed as *formal*.

Federal elections are run by the Australian Electoral Commission (AEC). The legal bases for federal elections are the Australian Constitution and the *Commonwealth Electoral Act 1918* (as amended). The Electoral Act is the critical document because it sets out all the intricate details of how *writs* are issued (legal documents authorising an election and its results), which voting system is used for each chamber, how nominations are lodged, how the election is conducted and so on.

The electoral laws also require the AEC to coordinate functions including registering political parties, nominating candidates and overseeing the process that the parties and candidates use to lodge their how-to-vote cards. All printed material used in an election campaign, including how-to-vote cards, which we describe in Chapters 8 and 13, and with a little more detail in the section 'Directing preferences' later in this chapter, must have proper authorisation and must be lodged with the AEC. Any failure to lodge this material actually constitutes a criminal offence.

TIP

The AEC publishes the *Candidate's Handbook*, which explains the laws and procedural requirements that apply to Australian national elections. This material is available on the AEC website at www.aec.gov.au.

CARETAKER GOVERNMENT

When the writ is issued for an election, a convention of Australian parliamentary practice sees the incumbent government go into what is called *caretaker government* mode. Technically, the government stays in place and continues to exercise executive power up until the return of writs after the election.

During the campaign period, government is expected to continue, but in a very minimal form. In short, the idea is that the executive continues to meet and attend to essential tasks to ensure that the process of government goes on, even during the election. Under the convention, a caretaker government makes no new policy decisions and doesn't undertake any initiatives or make any appointments.

Elections: It's Party Time!

For some, election day culminates in an election-night party. Indeed, David Williamson, the Australian playwright, penned a famous play called *Don's Party* about a party held on the night of the 1969 election count. The play was later made into a film and is part of Australian political folklore.

But long before people get to cool their drinks ahead of a long night in front of the television, parties — that is, the political parties — have already played crucially important roles in the electoral process.

REMEMBER

Thinking about politics without political parties is almost unimaginable. Not surprising, then, is the fact that the vast majority of Australians vote for a party-endorsed candidate and more than 75 per cent vote for the Labor Party, the Liberal Party or the National Party.

A number of important administrative functions usually occur ahead of the election campaign, including registration of political parties, preselection and formal nomination of candidates, and the directing of preferences. These functions all revolve around the idea of the political party being the primary organisational means through which individual candidates contest an election.

Show me the money

The importance of the political party to the campaign process rests on two important considerations. First, most nominees for an election come from political parties, so the whole electoral administrative process needs to accommodate them, particularly in the authorisation of campaign material, including how-to-vote cards.

The second reason relates to an important electoral reform introduced for federal elections in 1983 and now applied to all state elections also. Arguing that the cost of running elections had become too great, in 1983 the then federal Labor government introduced public funding for elections. Candidates receive a payment for the total number of primary votes they win if they poll more than 4 per cent. In 2019, candidates received $2.76 per primary vote.

VOTE 1

Because most of the candidates who receive the largest share of the primary vote are party-endorsed candidates, the way the funding rules work means that the money is actually paid to their political party. In other words, the allocation of taxpayer funds that subsidise the cost of campaigning for elections goes to the political parties.

VOTE 1

HOW MUCH DOES AN ELECTION COST?

Democracy doesn't come cheap. In total, the cost of the 2019 federal election was just over $372 million. This figure includes the AEC's staffing expenses, as well as advertising and additional costs (such as printing) associated with holding the election. From this amount, approximately $69 million was paid to political parties.

The Liberal Party not only won government but also won the most money from public funding. It received a windfall of just over $27 million, while the Labor Party was paid in excess of $24 million. Of the minor parties, the various Greens parties received over $8 million, while Pauline Hanson's One Nation was awarded over $2.8 million.

The AEC publishes details of public funding after each election on its website at www.aec.gov.au.

REMEMBER

In order to claim the benefits that can be accrued, a political party must first register with the AEC. The criteria by which the AEC registers a party vary from time to time, depending on changes made to the Electoral Act by parliament. Party membership tends to be the main criterion, however. In the 2019 federal election, for example, a party could register with the AEC provided it could demonstrate that it had 500 bona fide financial members (members had to also be on the electoral roll).

When accepted and registered by the AEC, a party is then able to lodge its candidates collectively, ensure that the party's name appears on the ballot paper for both the House of Representatives and the Senate, and — if more than 4 per cent of the vote is won — become entitled to public funding.

Preselections and nominations

The most important task the parties perform ahead of an election (often well ahead) is to select their candidates. This function is called *preselection*. Each party goes through this process in a different way, but the end result is the same. Candidates are then nominated by their political parties as party-endorsed candidates, and the political party backs these candidates by campaigning on their behalf.

Two important sets of preselections must occur — the first for lower house seats and the second for the upper house.

In the lower house

Lower house seats are usually single-member electoral districts, so the parties select an individual to be the party-endorsed candidate for each particular seat. Because of the strong notion of local representation associated with single-member districts, these party preselections usually involve the local branch of the party. After preselection, the party's head office facilitates the nomination.

In the upper house

Preselection for the upper house is slightly different where proportional representation is used. Take the Senate as an example. Under the current rules, each party sends a list of candidates to the AEC. The order of the party list is determined by the party itself, which is important.

The way the system works, the top two Labor and Liberal candidates for a half-Senate election are guaranteed to win seats. As a result, winning the first or second positions on the *party ticket* (the candidate list) is eagerly sought. Likewise, the third position is important too, because the chances of the third-placed major party candidate getting elected are fairly strong. Meanwhile, for any minor party that aspires to winning a Senate seat, the top position on that ticket is also eagerly sought.

Because Senate contests are conducted within each of the states, the state executives of the various parties, rather than the local branches, tend to have the power and responsibility to determine who will be a Senate candidate and what order the party ticket gives.

Directing preferences

How preferences are directed is a hot topic, and relates to both the how-to-vote cards that are handed out at polling booths across the country on election day.

Before election day, all the parties must tell the AEC what their how-to-vote cards look like. In particular, they need to indicate how they intend to advise people about the order they should cast their preferences for candidates. Given that the majority of Australian voters rely on how-to-vote cards when completing their ballot papers, the advice parties give on how the preferences should be ranked is of crucial importance.

In House of Representatives elections, the way minor parties advise their voters to order their preferences may be crucial in determining which of the major parties (Labor or Liberal) wins very close seats. The minor parties know this, and some use their decision on directing preferences as a bargaining chip, especially on matters of policy.

YOU DON'T HAVE TO BE FIRST TO WIN

In the 2004 federal election, Family First's Steve Fielding won a Victorian seat in a half-Senate election with a primary vote of only 1.8 per cent. Fielding was able to win his seat because of favourable preference outcomes. All the parties in this election put Fielding as their next preferred candidate, giving him a surplus from the Liberal Party and the Labor Party, as well as preferences from the Australian Democrats. As a result of these preference flows, Fielding was able to achieve the 14.4 per cent quota.

Preferences are critical in the Senate contest too, and all the more so with the advent of optional preferential voting. The more complicated a system is, the more voters rely on how-to-vote cards to help them cast a formal vote. Since 2016, voting for the Senate has become very complicated indeed. Voters can now order their preferred party ticket from first preference to sixth above the black line, or they can cast their preference for as many individual candidates below the black line provided they cast enough preferences to match the number of seats to be filled (six in a half-Senate election, twelve in a full-Senate election). In such circumstances, voters will likely consult how-to-vote cards, so the decisions made about advice on how preferences should be directed can have a major influence in determining which party — including minor parties — secures seats.

REMEMBER

The practice whereby the parties make strategic decisions on how they advise their voters to order their preferences via the how-to-vote card is known as *directing preferences*. The crucial point, however, is that how-to-vote cards are advisory only — at the end of the day, the individual voter takes responsibility for how she orders preferences on the ballot paper.

The Campaign

While the members of the party machine negotiate and bargain with each other over preferences, the candidates are out and about campaigning. In theory, an election campaign is conducted in every lower house seat and in every state and territory for the Senate. In reality, however, campaigns tend to be run from the central office of the political parties, and the party leader becomes the main focus.

Raising money and conducting campaigns

The political parties are basically responsible for campaigning. The parties need to raise the finance required to conduct a full-blown modern advertising campaign.

An endorsed party candidate becomes part of a campaign that utilises the party name, the party logo and the party leader. The party also provides human resources for the campaign. Party workers and volunteers maintain social media, deliver pamphlets, put up posters and hand out the all-important how-to-vote cards on election day. These important activities all cost money.

One of the major burdens on the financial resources of the parties is the need to undertake political advertising. Political advertising involves a range of media, but by far the most important — and expensive — is television advertising, which can chew up millions of dollars. Although both minor and major parties are able to take advantage of online and social media, the major parties, in particular, base their campaigns around themes that are transmitted to potential electors via their television sets. The party organisations feel that, in order to be able to run a strong campaign (and to avoid being outflanked by their opponents), raising the money needed to pay for extensive advertising is essential.

VOTE 1

Strict rules surround the way parties raise money to pay for their election campaigns. At the end of the election, the parties have to lodge their fundraising returns with the AEC. Electoral law also requires individual and corporate donors to disclose what they've donated to the parties contesting the election.

Battle of the leaders?

The Australian political process revolves around parties, yet election campaigns seem to be almost entirely about leaders (and, following from an American habit, increasingly the leaders' spouses too). This phenomenon is partly the consequence of advertising and marketing, although usually leaders are also keen to be identified with the major political parties they lead.

VOTE 1

Very few Australians actually get to vote for the party leader directly because the major party leaders all come from the House of Representatives and all stand in their own individual electorates. The only people who got to vote for Scott Morrison in 2019, for example, were the electors of Cook — the electoral division in New South Wales Morrison represents in the lower house.

Campaigns require something that can provide a national focus, however, and the party leaders are able to bring that to a campaign. What's more, many of the key features of the modern election campaign revolve around the party leaders, further enhancing the idea that the contest is between leaders rather than between political parties.

The television campaign:
The Great Debates

Many American campaign techniques have made their way into Australian electioneering. The ritual of televised debates between American presidential candidates is now a part of the Australian campaign — although Australian Liberal and Labor leaders often end up agreeing to only one debate and the leaders of other parties rarely feature in this aspect of the campaign.

The Great Debates are usually preceded by all sorts of negotiations and bargaining. The campaign managers for the two major parties wheel and deal over formats, over the journalists who will play the role of inquisitors and moderators, and whether or not 'the worm' will be used (see the sidebar 'Beware the worm'). Before the 2019 election, for example, three debates were held, and these were split between being hosted in Perth by the Seven Network, in Brisbane by Sky News Australia, and in Canberra at the National Press Club.

VOTE 1

A pattern has emerged over these debates. In every election, opposition leaders become great proponents of debates and offer themselves for as many as the media can handle. Prime ministers, on the other hand, are reluctant to do any more than one debate and, as the media are really only interested in these things as a head-to-head event, the prime minister usually gets his way.

Launching the campaign

Despite the dominance of televised political advertising, some old-fashioned campaign techniques are still employed. Local appearances at shopping centres by the leaders hark back to the old notion of town hall meetings, and sometimes interesting contests between high-profile local candidates take place.

BEWARE THE WORM

The Great Debates are the forum in which 'the worm' has figured prominently. The worm is actually a graph line. Thanks to modern technology and the pervasiveness of market research, opinion pollsters can get a room full of people to give instant feedback on whether they like or dislike what they're seeing or hearing. In the Great Debates, the worm tracks audience reaction to the aspiring prime ministers, and this, in turn, can become a major part of the media coverage of a campaign — especially if one or other leader experiences significant downward-trending worms. In recent election debates, however, the worm has disappeared from our screens. Its loss may be missed by some, but probably not the party leaders.

One other interesting throwback is the official party campaign launch, which involves the party leader fronting a hall full of party faithful and delivering a campaign speech. These launches tend to go for about half an hour, and press coverage of them dominates the evening television news and the following day's newspapers.

REMEMBER

A critical issue arises from the scheduling of the official party campaign launch. Because of the large number of sitting members of parliament among the total number of candidates seeking election, parliamentary resources (printing allowances, travel allowances, staff allowances and so on) can be used as part of the campaign effort. However, the major parties may not use these resources after the campaign has officially begun — and the campaign doesn't officially begin until the official campaign launch. For this reason, these days, the official party campaign launches seem to happen at the end of the campaign rather than at the beginning!

Also, by law, political advertising in federal elections must cease two days before polling day. In the old days, a total media ban on election coverage for two days used to apply.

At the Press Club

The federal election campaign always finishes off with addresses by the prime minister and the leader of the opposition at the National Press Club in Canberra. These speeches are covered by the nightly news services, so the voters actually get to see snippets of the addresses and the question-and-answer sessions that follow.

By this stage, the travelling media has an idea of how the campaign has gone and who they expect to win. A probable election outcome sometimes becomes quite obvious in the way the leaders and the travelling media corps interact with each other at this campaign highlight. (See Chapter 15 for more on the media's role in politics.)

The Big Day! Sausage Sizzles and More

At last, polling Saturday comes around. The night before, party activists would've decked the fences and light poles around the polling stations (usually school, church or public halls) with party bunting and posters. Before the polls open, party workers stake out their positions outside the polling station where they prepare to hand out their how-to-vote cards.

Inside the hall, the AEC officials are sitting at their tables with the electoral roll to mark off the names of people coming in to vote and give ballot papers to voters. Voters retire to polling booths set up inside the hall to record their vote. They then deposit their ballots into a ballot box — green ballots for the lower house, white ballots for the upper house.

Considering how serious the event is, election day is usually something of a festive occasion. Party workers tend to chat with each other, and the people who have let their halls out to the AEC for the day often run a sausage sizzle and maybe a bric-a-brac stall. (Indeed, for many voters, the 'democracy sausage' goes hand in hand with voting.) Candidates tour the various polling stations to meet and greet both party workers and prospective voters. In the key marginal seats, party heavy-weights also call by. The party leaders themselves tour the marginal seats in their home states.

VOTE 1

When the polls close at 6 pm, the local count commences. The parties are allowed to appoint *scrutineers* to observe the count. The scrutineers report back to their party officials to advise on the progress of the count and how the preferences are running. The candidates' staff members sometimes forward this information to journalists, who then give running commentaries on what the insiders are saying about the count.

The candidates, meanwhile, retire to a function with their supporters and workers for refreshments and to await the results. In the capital cities of the states where the party leaders reside, the parties hire a major function centre or hotel, where the official party function is held. The party leaders come to this function at some point in the night either to claim victory or to congratulate their adversary.

Counting the vote: Saturday night fever!

Cancel all engagements, stock up on party supplies and get ready to watch history being made right before your eyes! Nothing's quite like an election night that decides who governs for the next few years. But as you bask in the warm glow of the TV coverage knowing you've contributed to Australian democracy by voting, the electoral staff are just starting the hard work of counting the ballot papers to find the winners in each of the lower house districts.

Unless the election is a very close affair (unusual, but not unknown), the result of the lower house contests are known within a few hours. By 10 pm on election night, the nation usually knows whether the government has been returned or defeated.

Although a result is usually known on election night, the count, in fact, may go on for weeks and weeks. In the 2019 election, which saw the trend in early voting continue to rise, only about 60 per cent of the votes were cast by voters at polling stations in the electorates where they live. These votes are counted on election night, and in the past usually gave a fair indication of what the result would be. In the 2019 election, the other 40 per cent of ballots were still out there somewhere — cast as pre-poll votes, absentee votes or even provisional votes.

Pre-poll votes

Pre-poll votes are cast before the election day. In the past, these votes were usually made by people who had a valid excuse for not being able to vote on Saturday (they may have been going overseas, or perhaps their religious beliefs don't allow voting on a Saturday). The 2010 federal election saw the introduction of *pre-poll ordinary votes*, which don't require a voter to provide a reason for not being able to get to a polling place on polling day. In the decade since, the number of votes cast as pre-poll ordinary votes has continued to climb.

These pre-poll votes are bundled up and sent to the state head office of the AEC for counting.

ABSENTEE VOTES

Some voters cast an *absentee vote*, often as a postal vote — that is, the voter has filled in the ballots and then mailed them back to the AEC. The AEC allows these votes to appear for up to two weeks.

In among the people voting at the polling stations are those who live in other electorates. These voters also cast absentee votes. Meanwhile, in the United States, Britain and other overseas countries, Australians turn up to the Australian Embassy or Consulate to cast their votes. These, too, are returned to Australia for counting.

PROVISIONAL VOTES

Sometimes voters turn up at a polling booth unsure as to where they're enrolled to vote. These electors cast what's known as a *provisional vote* by lodging ballots and providing their residential details. If their details are bona fide, the votes are counted.

This process takes time — up to two weeks, in fact — and in very close seats the result may hang on a handful of ballots making their way via the postal system.

Counting the Senate

The complicated nature of the Senate voting system means that it can take even longer to count. Senate counts can sometimes take up to a month to complete.

Who Votes How and Why?

Debates rage in Australian politics about the reasons people vote the way they do. Sociologists agree that voting behaviour is a subset of political behaviour, and that a person's attitude to politics (and voting) is influenced by important socialising influences. These factors include family, the workplace, education, perhaps even religion and/or ethnic background.

Of all of these socialising influences, one in particular stands out — namely, economic background. Generally, people's political outlooks, and the way they vote, are influenced by the work they do (or don't do) and the income they earn. In very basic terms, those employed as blue-collar workers are more likely to vote Labor, while those who are white-collar professionals earning substantial income are more likely to vote Liberal, and those primary producers who live and work in the Murray–Darling Basin are more likely to vote National Party.

REMEMBER

This simple guide to electoral behaviour assumes a link between socioeconomic status and political attitudes. Some analysts don't like this approach to politics, especially when examples of behaviour exist that run counter to the given wisdom. What does it mean when the Labor vote is high in an area of affluence? Why do blue-collar electorates sometimes return Liberal MPs? Some writers suggest that class is a declining influence in modern politics — a fact sometimes reflected in the sense that the two major parties appear to have converged on so many major economic policy debates.

One alternative view of elections is based on the idea of elections being akin to a political marketplace. The argument is that the major parties offer their policy manifestos, and voters make rational choices by asking, 'What's in it for me?' The assumption here is that voters act as consumers and make a consumer-based decision when choosing between parties.

Electing oppositions in or voting governments out?

One of the enduring debates about election behaviour centres on the length of time a government has held office. The reality of Australia's electoral history is that government is shared between both major parties.

This fact leads some analysts to argue that elections when the incumbent government is voted out represent a moment when a fair proportion of electors no longer support the government and, shifting their vote to the opposition, give the alternative party the opportunity to govern. The assumption here is that governments eventually lose office, usually as a result of being in power for too long.

Seats: Safe, marginal and swinging

Election commentators usually refer to three types of seats — safe, marginal and swinging. The margin that one or other of the major parties won the seat by in the last election is the starting point. Here's a rundown on how they're classified:

>> **Safe seats:** Usually considered to be seats where Labor or the coalition won 55 per cent or more of the two-party vote. In many instances, Labor and the coalition have won seats with two-party votes between 60 and 70 per cent! Safe seats are the seats the parties win election after election. Wasted majorities occur in safe seats.

>> **Marginal seats:** Won with the narrowest of margins. Some analysts consider 5 per cent to be marginal, but remember that the two-party swing in most Australian elections rarely goes above 3 per cent! In 2007, for example, the Victorian seat of McEwen was won by the Liberal candidate with a majority of 6 votes in an electorate where over 100,000 votes were cast.

>> **Swinging seats:** Also tend to be marginal, but they occasionally 'swing' from one party to another in consecutive elections. The parties tend to target swinging seats in campaigns in the hope of attracting crucial votes and winning the seat. These seats actually make or break governments. They're usually electorates that cover the outer suburbs of the major cities or regional areas.

VOTE 1

Analysts are interested in the swing (see the next section for just how important it is). A swing is simply the variation of the two-party vote compared with the last election. The issue of a swing is very important in marginal seats. Continuing the previous example of a marginal seat, if less than 0.05 per cent of the voters of McEwen changed their voting alignment from the slender 2007 result, then the seat would be won by a candidate from the Labor Party.

Predicting election outcomes: The pendulum

Analysts have found a way to understand and/or predict election outcomes without becoming bogged down in academic debates about why people vote the way they do. In this task, analysts are assisted by the electoral pendulum that looks at the percentage of change in the vote needed in particular seats for the sitting members to lose their seats, known as the *percentage swing*.

Elections that use single-member districts involve a battle between the major parties (Labor and the Liberal–National coalition) to win enough seats to have a lower house majority. The battle to win government is thus a battle to win just over half of the available lower house seats. Elections are a battle to win seats — especially *marginal* seats that could go either way (refer to the preceding section).

The idea of an electoral pendulum was developed by Professor Malcolm Mackerras. Just before each federal and state election, a 'Mackerras pendulum' is published that gives commentators an idea of what swing is needed for government to change by the opposition winning enough lower house seats to obtain a majority. Figure 14-1 shows an abbreviated, fictitious sample of an electoral pendulum (in reality many more seats would be included) for the governing Party A in a contest with Party B.

TECHNICAL STUFF

The pendulum lists the seats from least marginal to most marginal for the government on one side, and least marginal to most marginal for the opposition on the other side. The theory is that a uniform swing should see the very marginal seats change and, with this change, the question of which of the two major parties will govern should be revealed. The pendulum works for preferential voting and single-member districts. It doesn't work for proportional representation elections, such as for the Senate.

The pendulum is based on some realities of geography through the existence of seats, or electoral divisions. Electoral divisions are really just clusters of communities — usually similar communities.

The pendulum shows that the total number of seats tends to divide into three groups, safe, marginal and swinging, as we discuss in the previous section. In the real world of Australian politics, some interesting dynamics can be observed about each party's safe seats.

Labor's safe seats tend to cover the more industrialised, less affluent and more ethnically diverse suburbs of the capital cities and the larger regional cities. The safe seats for the coalition tend to be electorates made up of two sub-types — the very affluent, well-to-do city suburbs and regional areas dominated by primary industry, which are very safe for the Liberal Party. A collection of seats in the Murray–Darling Basin are very safe for the National Party. These safe seats are often referred to as a party's *heartland*.

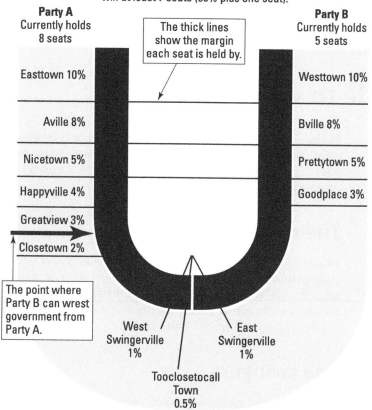

Total seats: 13
To win the election a party must
win at least 7 seats (50% plus one seat).

Party A
Currently holds
8 seats

Party B
Currently holds
5 seats

The thick lines
show the margin
each seat is held by.

Easttown 10%

Westtown 10%

Aville 8%

Bville 8%

Nicetown 5%

Prettytown 5%

Happyville 4%

Goodplace 3%

Greatview 3%

Closetown 2%

The point where
Party B can wrest
government from
Party A.

West
Swingerville
1%

East
Swingerville
1%

Tooclosetocall
Town
0.5%

FIGURE 14-1:
The electoral
pendulum assists
in predicting
election
outcomes by
examining the
percentage swing
required to win
marginal seats.

In this example, Party A holds a majority of three seats. At the next election
Party B must win at least three seats to win government. The pendulum shows
that Party B needs a uniform swing of at least 3 per cent in order to win the
ultra marginal seats of Tooclosetocall Town, West Swingerville and Closetown.
The citizens of East Swingerville, Tooclosetocall Town, West Swingerville and
Closetown can expect a vigorous campaign by the parties for their vote.

Focusing on the marginals

Apart from marginal seats being make-or-break electorates, the major parties
concentrate their efforts on the marginal seats as a reflection of the impact of
compulsory voting on the system.

The major parties rely on the electoral laws to ensure that voters in the safe seats
come out to vote, allowing the parties to concentrate their campaign effort on the
marginal seats. The major party leaders spend a lot of time touring marginal
seats, and residents in these seats are inundated with leaflets, posters and candidates accosting them at railway stations and shopping centres.

Out in the safe seats, meanwhile, campaigning activity is much less intense. The party that holds the seat sends some material out, while the other major party probably won't waste its time or resources on a campaign. Some voters in the very safe seats sometimes complain that they feel left out of the campaign circus.

A Guide to Voter Types

Election commentators often use jargon to identify and explain different voter types. Although this categorisation isn't an exact science by any means, understanding what the commentators are referring to is a useful exercise. This section covers the standard voter types.

The rusted-ons

This term is a short-hand reference to partisan voters who vote for one of the main parties in every election. The *rusted-on* voter is aligned to one party and votes for that party regardless of all circumstances. Interestingly, analysts suspect that between 75 and 80 per cent of the Australian electorate are partisanly aligned to Labor, Liberal and/or the National Party.

The swingers

The antithesis of rusted-on voters, swingers change their party alignment from one election to another. The reasons for this may vary, but analysts think these are the sort of voters who ask 'What's in it for me?' when assessing the parties or who to vote for in order to cast their verdict on the performance of the party in government. Swinging voters make or break governments, especially if they live in marginal seats.

The donkey vote

The Australian Constitution makes no mention of equine voters, but commentators sometimes refer to the 'donkey vote'. A *donkey vote* is when a voter sequentially numbers candidates in order of appearance, rather than of preference. Although a donkey vote is regarded as a formal vote, it may not reflect the real wish of the voter. Rather, it is just a way for the voter to cast a formal vote. Generally, candidates on the top of the ballot have an advantage in attracting up to 3 per cent of primary votes from donkey voters. A reverse donkey occurs where a voter casts ordered preferences from bottom candidate to top.

AAAA VOTE FOR ME!

In the old days when the ballot order was alphabetical, some parties began to look for candidates with surnames beginning with A. One party scoured the books looking for people with names like Aanensen and Aardvark to be their candidates. All this foolery stopped in 1983, when the Electoral Act was changed to allow the order of candidates on the ballot paper to be drawn at random by the AEC.

Informal voters

Some people attend the polling booth sporting relaxed, casual dress — in fact, thongs and shorts are the outfit of choice for many — but these aren't informal voters. No, *informal voters* are those who cast votes that don't count, either because they didn't cast preferences or because they made a mistake in filling out their ballot paper.

Studies on informal voting by the AEC have found that the vast majority of informal votes are, in fact, ballots with errors. The AEC also found that the informal vote rises the more complicated a ballot is — if, for example, it includes a lot of candidates. Informal voting also tends to be higher in blue-collar electorates.

Battlers

An often used and abused term, no-one really knows what a battler is, although it resonates with notions of economic struggle. *Battlers* used to be considered blue-collar voters and, therefore, Labor-tending but, in more recent times, both Labor and the coalition have claimed to be the natural choice of battlers. Moreover, a battler now seems to be anyone who's struggling with some aspect of their financial reality, including those trying to pay for their suburban mortgages, their fleet of four-wheel-drive vehicles, and private health and education fees!

Working families

When the coalition managed to appropriate the battler terminology during the years of the Howard government (1996 to 2007), the ALP had to come up with some sort of alternative. The term Labor came up with was *working families*. This group is actually the battlers by another name, although with one interesting and subtle variation. 'Battlers' has a somewhat macho feel to it, implying a traditional family structure where Dad is the main breadwinner. Working family, on the other hand, makes indirect reference to the role of Mum as a breadwinner too.

Doctors' wives

This term made its appearance in the 2004 election, amid interest in the rise of support in affluent inner-city electorates for the Greens on the back of their anti-war stand when Australia supported the US invasion of Iraq. The phrase *doctors' wives* was used by journalists in a bid to simplify a complex sociological development that identified areas where well-paid, human-services-employed people with high levels of education were clustered and appeared to be voting for either the Labor Party or the Greens.

Post-materialists

We are getting into serious stuff here. This complex term comes to us from American sociologists who observed the rise of a well-educated and affluent socioeconomic cohort who seemed to be more radically left wing than blue-collar workers. In particular, they noted the fervent commitment of this cohort to issues such as the environment, their commitment to feminism, their support of refugee rights and the importance of animal welfare. This cohort looks a bit like the Doctors' Wives from the previous section, although for this group our sociologists observed a gender balance, the tendency to youthfulness, and if this cohort were doctors it was because of their tertiary education.

In Australia at least, this cohort is now also associated with inner metropolitan electorates and may be the reason formerly safe Labor and Liberal inner-city seats have become vulnerable to the Greens or to independents who share post-materialist values.

IN THIS CHAPTER

» **Exploring the role of 'the press'**

» **Assessing different media platforms and their impact on the political debate**

» **Analysing the influence of political journalists and commentators**

» **Questioning the role of the Australian Broadcasting Corporation**

» **Examining the interaction between the media, spin doctors and opinion polls**

Chapter **15**

The Fourth Estate: The Media

The media plays a crucial role in politics. This chapter looks at the role of the media as the reporters of political events and as providers of a forum for debates about politics and government. Here, we focus on political journalism in particular, but also deal with the role of political commentators and non-journalist media people such as radio talkback hosts, whose programs can have a big impact on the political debate.

In this chapter, you get to consider how the media — including the Australian Broadcasting Corporation — observes and reports the processes of government on your behalf (or, to put it another way, on behalf of the media's readers, listeners and viewers). You also look at why in some democratic theory, the media is said to be a watchdog — that is, the media is understood to be casting a critical, as well as an analytical, eye over the operation of government institutions.

By examining these features, this chapter considers the idea of the media as the *Fourth Estate* — a standalone democratic institution alongside the other three estates (the legislature, the executive and the judiciary) that keeps them answerable and accountable to the people.

The Role of 'the Press' in Politics

Ordinary citizens don't have the personal resources to keep a constant view on the operation of government, even though liberal democratic theory assumes that citizens are well informed and fully engaged with politics and government. In the real world, citizens interact with the political debate indirectly, and usually through the media.

In theory, the media should provide a form of two-way communication involving, primarily, news and information about the operation of government to the citizens, as well as conveying community opinions back to the political process by way of public debates. The media also have the resources and professional ability to play a watchdog role on the decisions of government.

Many things qualify as media — and many of these media platforms can be, and are, used in day-to-day politics. The main media forms include television, radio, newspapers (and various other printed publications) and, these days, modern technological platforms such as the internet and mobile phones.

Media interaction with the political world can be varied as well, including new developments such as the use of blogs on the internet and social media as a means for people to express opinions about political matters. Indeed, part of the appeal of social media is the way citizens can use it to directly convey their opinions back to the political process. The more traditional and conventional approach, however, involves the idea that politics interacts primarily with journalism.

The coincidence of mass democracy with the emergence of mass-production technology in the form of printed media during the mid-1800s meant that the closest relationship between politics and the media has historically been between politics and *the press* — that is, newspapers. This development has a legacy in the terminology that has stayed with political journalism, through the press corps and the press gallery.

Press corps and press galleries

The importance of press journalists to the reporting of politics is revealed by the inclusion of political journalism in the operation of the legislature. In the United

States, for example, both the Congress and the presidency are observed and reported by the *press corps*.

In Westminster parliaments, journalists assigned to the coverage of the operation of the parliament (and, by extension, the performance of the parliament-based government) are allowed a gallery of their own where they can observe the operation of each of the parliamentary chambers. Located above the floor of the house but behind the presiding officer is the *press gallery*.

Both the press corps and the press gallery are based on the notion that reporting of the parliament is a specialised journalistic function. The inclusion of the corps or the gallery in the structure of the parliament is an acknowledgement of the crucial role the press plays in acting as a link between a key governing institution and the citizenry.

The Australian press gallery

Because Australia's parliaments are Westminster parliaments, political journalism conducted from the parliament utilises a press gallery. These galleries include not just an area where journalists can observe the operation of the parliamentary chambers, but also facilities adjacent to the chambers where journalists can file their copy and the electronic media can conduct interviews.

In the national parliament, the media facilities located alongside the House of Representatives and Senate press galleries are quite extensive and allow for the major print organisations, television networks and the Australian Broadcasting Corporation (ABC) to put their reports together and transmit them to their newspapers or electronic platforms. The courtyards around the national parliament are also wired to allow for transmission of live sound and images.

The ABC's News Radio network actually broadcasts the federal parliament when it is in session.

The Media

Political reporting tends to be referred to as 'the press' mainly as a result of the importance that newspapers have historically had in the coverage of politics. In more modern times, of course, the press also includes journalists from the electronic media. Indeed, you can now assume that television has replaced newspapers as the primary medium where citizens obtain their political information — a fact also reflected in the way the major political parties see television advertising as being so important to their election campaigns. Social media, however, is providing the biggest challenge to newspapers and even television. This is a reflection of the proliferation of computers and mobile phones across society.

Newspapers

Newspapers were once the dominant platform for the coverage of politics. In the mid-1800s, mass-production technology was applied to printing, and mass-produced, cheap newspapers became available to the masses.

Australia once had a large number of publishers producing a variety of newspapers. In more recent times, however, the newspaper industry has been reduced to two main players — Rupert Murdoch's News Corporation (of which the Herald and Weekly Times company is a subsidiary) and Fairfax Media. In recent times, the financially challenged Fairfax company was purchased by Nine Entertainment Co, which also owns Channel Nine Television. These two corporations produce the vast majority of newspapers published across Australia. News Corporation has a virtual newspaper monopoly in Adelaide, Hobart, Brisbane and Darwin. A duopoly exists in the other capitals.

The publishers produce two types of newspapers — broadsheets and tabloids.

Broadsheets

The term *broadsheet* actually refers to the paper size of a newspaper (broadsheets are the larger newspapers that are a nightmare to read on the train). In the language of newspaper politics, however, broadsheet also implies a newspaper of quality, gravitas and substance. Such newspapers are usually read by better educated, higher income-earning and human-services-employed readers.

These papers are characterised by their emphasis on the written word and on the importance of contributing to a political debate based on quality and reflection. Broadsheet newspapers tend to take the political debate very seriously and place strong emphasis on political reporting and commentary.

VOTE 1

The one remaining broadsheet newspaper (by actual paper size) in the Australian market is *The Australian* (News Corporation's national paper). In 2013, the two traditionally broadsheet papers of *The Age* (from Melbourne, owned by Nine Entertainment Co) and *The Sydney Morning Herald* (Sydney, also owned by Nine) went to tabloid size. They argue their content, however, remains in the broadsheet tradition. Nine also publishes the *Australian Financial Review (AFR)*. Although the *AFR* is also a tabloid-sized newspaper, its targeting of the Australian business community with high-quality reflective journalism covering both business and politics places it as part of the broadsheet cluster.

Tabloids

Tabloid newspapers aim to satisfy the mass market. The whole point of tabloid-sized paper was to produce a paper that could be read quickly and easily, especially by a blue-collar readership. Tabloid newspapers tend to place greater emphasis on photojournalism, while the written word in tabloid journalism seeks to be plain and easy to follow.

Tabloid readers tend to be less well educated than broadsheet readers and more likely to be employed in blue-collar activities. Tabloid newspapers tend to be very widely read and have the highest circulation.

VOTE 1

Nearly all Australian newspapers other than the aforementioned broadsheets are tabloids, including a number of News Corporation metropolitan dailies such as *The Advertiser* (Adelaide) and *The Mercury* (Hobart) that were broadsheets before the Murdoch organisation purchased them. The most significant tabloids in Australian politics, however, are *The Daily Telegraph* (Sydney) and the *Herald Sun* (Melbourne) — both News Corporation newspapers. The influence of these papers derives in no small way from the fact that they're the papers read by the masses in Australia's two biggest cities.

Television

Television is critically important to politics, even though politics isn't that important to television! Most television networks see entertainment as their primary interest, although all Australian networks have dedicated news and current affairs departments, and at least one subscriber network has a dedicated Australian news service (Sky News).

RUDD AND TURNBULL VERSUS MURDOCH?

Having been the centre of political news coverage for years, former prime ministers Kevin Rudd and Malcolm Turnbull became highly critical of News Corporation once they left office. Kevin Rudd started a vigorous campaign against News Corporation media outlets, claiming the organisation was too powerful. He also started a petition to gather support for a royal commission into media diversity in Australia, which was also signed by Malcolm Turnbull.

Television is important to politics because studies have shown that the vast majority of Australians learn what they know about politics from this medium. Television news is understood by politicians to be the main medium where they can communicate with the masses — it's as simple as that. For this reason, politicians tend to speak in short *sound bites* (short statements that can be easily slipped into a news story) and sporting metaphors when they're interviewed by journalists. Their main aim is to get their messages out to the voters by way of the television news as quickly and effectively as possible.

Door-stop interviews

The most obvious legacy of how the demands of television have affected the way politicians interact with the media is the *door-stop interview*. Designed specifically for television coverage, the door-stop involves a politician arriving at a designated area (say, in the case of a parliamentarian, the parliamentary entrance), being asked a question and then giving a short, often metaphor-based response that has been carefully thought about beforehand with a view to having these clever remarks broadcast on television.

Variations on the door-stop involve premiers or prime ministers, or opposition leaders or ministers, giving short statements filmed for television at a pertinent site. A premier announcing a major works project may be filmed in a fluorescent vest and hardhat on a works site surrounded by similarly attired associates. The assumption here is that television news must have pictures if a story is going to be selected to run.

VOTE 1

Television also comes to the fore during moments of political importance such as election campaigning or election coverage. Parliament is also covered by television, but Question Time from the lower house (refer to Chapter 6) is usually the only time parliament ever really makes it onto the evening television news.

TIP

Parliament also has its own television service, which feeds into its internet site. Check it out at www.aph.gov.au.

VOTE 1

THE AIR IS ALIVE WITH THE SOUND OF SOUND BITES

A *sound bite* (or grab) is a term used to describe a short and sharp message, often used by politicians. Because of the dynamic nature of the media, much time is invested in distilling an important argument or message into a few short sentences that can be easily used in news coverage and quickly understood by all voters. The most effective sound bites are those where a politician concisely puts forward a view in plain language.

In-depth interviews

Political journalism isn't all short 'n' sharp. While much effort goes into crafting a sound bite, politicians have many opportunities to engage in lengthier appearances, also providing the media with a chance to engage in greater scrutiny of elected representatives. Perhaps the clearest examples of these lengthier interviews can be found on the ABC's *7.30 Report*, and the ABC's *Q+A* (aka, questions and answers) also provides a forum for a more in-depth approach to issues.

Radio

Similar to television, radio's primary reason for existence is to entertain. Like television, most radio networks have a news service, although very few stations do anything other than use syndicated material. The exceptions are ABC stations, and their contribution to Australian politics is considered later in this chapter.

One exception to the general tendency for radio to be devoted to entertainment (and pay scant attention to politics) is the so-called talk radio stations. These stations fill their airtime with talkback conversations between listeners and announcers. The announcers can become quite significant political players in their own right, especially if they choose to make political issues the topic of the day.

Talkback hosts tend to fall into one of two categories. One type is the host who tries to bring journalistic values to the process and uses the talkback forum to quiz politicians and to allow debates on policy issues. In the second group is the host who uses the forum to precipitate controversy and uses the medium as a platform to make pronouncements on political matters. This second group is sometimes referred to as the *shock jocks* because of their practice of trying to attract listeners by encouraging reaction to controversies.

The internet and social media

The personal computer has emerged as one of the most important items of communication in recent times. All major media outlets now have websites, and much of the media output from newspapers now ends up on the internet.

The internet has become interesting for another phenomenon — the *blog* (short for web log). Political bloggers include people who aren't journalists but who set up sites where political matters can be discussed. Virtually all politicians and parties now use the internet for political purposes.

Sites such as Twitter, Facebook and Instagram give those who seek to comment on issues the internet space to do so. Politicians are particularly sensitive to these platforms, and some politicians are quite famous for their extensive 'posts'.

REMEMBER

Some internet and social media sites have been associated with a lot of controversy, not least because of their lack of accountability and tendency to increase division rather than encourage debate. Anyone can get on these platforms and say anything, and if they do it anonymously, it is difficult to hold them to account via more traditional means such as defamation laws. The reliability of some of these sites and some of the information circulating on social media has also been called in question, with the rise of what people on both sides of the political divide dub *fake news* — false or misleading information presented as news.

The political parties all maintain websites and have recently begun to run political advertisements on sites such as YouTube and on social media as an alternative to buying television advertising. What happens here is that the parties run their advertisements online not only in the hope that they reach voters more directly. They're also hoping journalists will watch them and report on them via the more established platforms (TV and newspapers). This way, it's hoped, the electorate becomes aware of the advertisement and goes online to see it — thereby saving the parties the expense of actually buying advertising time on the commercial networks.

King and Queen Makers? Journalists and Commentators

Political journalists can be important players in the political process by virtue of their close proximity to the parliament and parliamentarians. In theory, political journalists are supposed to practise their craft on behalf of the citizenry. The community's dependence on journalists for information and perspective puts reporters in a quite influential position in the political debate, however. Journalists are able to significantly influence the formation of opinions about politics and politicians, and often determine what does and doesn't get talked about as part of the political debate.

Journalists

Journalism, like any profession, is subject to hierarchy. The press gallery contains a number of relatively junior journalists who are required to keep a watching brief on the operation of the parliament and conduct interviews with politicians and various other political players.

REMEMBER

Journalists themselves have strongly held professional values that, in liberal democracies at least, see the profession as being independent of partisan politics. Journalists are expected to report without fear or favour and to undertake a critical reflection of the functions of government.

The press gallery recognises and respects hierarchy and seniority, and senior political journalists are given respect for their knowledge and experience, as well as their ability to influence the political debate. Another important source of significance granted to senior press gallery journalists is that their media organisations allow them to *comment* on politics as well as report on it. Senior journalists can, therefore, become major political players, especially when they express opinions on the conduct of government, the performance of leaders, or what should or shouldn't be done in the area of policy-making.

Opinion writers

Not everyone who has something to contribute to the political debate is a journalist, although their offerings are transmitted by the media. Many newspapers also have columnists and opinion writers who seek to affect the political debate.

OPINION: MASS OR ELITE?

Whose opinion is being influenced by the media? Obviously the media try to influence broad community opinion, but the politics of opinion formation identifies mass and elite opinion as two distinct subsets of community attitudes towards politics.

Elite opinion is usually associated with notions of social elitism, especially where people are in important positions of power and influence. Leaders in industry, in public administration and other such parts of the community whose decisions and actions have important economic and social consequences make up elite opinion. The broadsheets and the ABC tend to be the media outlets of choice for this social group.

On the other hand, *mass* opinion becomes important on those occasions where the community in its broadest sense is required to make a political decision — during an election, for example. In such a situation, mass media outlets such as commercial television networks and the tabloid press stand out as important channels of communication between politicians and the masses.

Some of these opinion writers are former journalists or essayists, or even former politicians; some may be experts in a particular field of politics and be associated with institutions such as universities. One common feature of this group of writers is that they aren't part of the press gallery. They're effectively outsiders to the parliamentary process looking in.

Political cartoonists

Political cartoonists can have a major impact on the political debate by bringing wit and humour to the task of interpreting the day's political events or in contributing to a political leader's image. Cartoonists are often able to get away with a much more polemical comment on the political events of the day than journalists, sometimes giving a political cartoon an enduring place in the memory of Australian political folklore for much longer than any written piece. Check out renowned cartoonist Bruce Petty's marvellous take on politics leading up to the 2007 federal election in Figure 15-1.

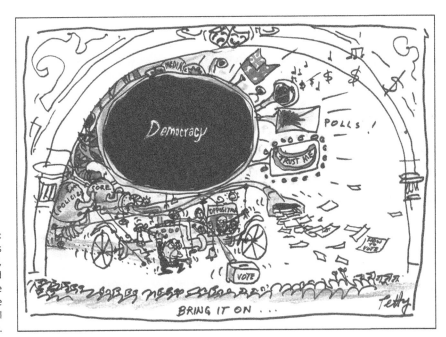

FIGURE 15-1: Bruce Petty's 'Democracy', which appeared in *The Age* in the lead-up to the 2007 federal election.

Opinion pollsters

In recent times, all the major newspapers have contracted opinion poll organisations to undertake polls to determine how people may vote at the next election, how they respond to the political leaders and what they think of the policy issues being debated by the government and the opposition. Usually these polls are in the form of short surveys or questionnaires.

The heads of these polling organisations can become very important participants in the debate by virtue of their expertise about opinion polling and what they're able to reveal about the most recent poll they conducted. The polling undertaken by Newspoll, Morgan and Galaxy tends to be reported on widely, especially during election campaigns. See the 'Opinion polling' section later in this chapter for more on the polls themselves.

Government Broadcasting? The ABC

The Australian Broadcasting Corporation (the ABC) is a major part of the media landscape in Australia. The ABC is an extensive cultural institution, as well as being a sizeable corporation that covers all aspects of electronic broadcasting — television, radio and, increasingly, the internet. It even has a publishing arm, although none of the ABC's magazines actually deals with parliamentary politics.

Like other electronic media networks, the ABC seeks to provide entertainment for its audiences. Unlike most of its private competitors, however, the ABC tends to put a lot of its resources into covering politics and government. ABC Radio, in particular, devotes a lot of time and resources to politics through its ABC NEWS networks (Radio National and local radio). ABC NEWS covers live sessions from the House of Representatives and the Senate, along with a delayed broadcast of question times during the evening.

REMEMBER

The ABC is a public organisation, although it's not entirely correct to describe it as a government broadcaster. The ABC is a part of the public sector, but it operates as a statutory authority rather than as a government department. Were it a government department, the ABC would be directly answerable to a government minister. But, because it's a statutory corporation, its management is actually undertaken by a CEO who is answerable to a board of directors and not the government directly, although the government of the day has the power to make appointments to the ABC board. However, ABC board members tend to take the idea of the ABC's independence from government very seriously when they're appointed. The ABC's relationship with the government of the day, then, always tends to be underpinned by mutual suspicion.

Balanced or left-wing bias?

The ABC takes its news and current affairs responsibilities very seriously, and it's acknowledged by politicians and commentators as making a major contribution to keeping the community informed about politics and government (and many other political and social issues in addition to local politics). The effort it makes in covering politics and society, however, often leads to tense debates about whether the ABC is inherently biased.

The most common accusation is that the ABC has a natural left-wing bias. Admittedly, such accusations tend to come from self-declared conservative commentators or politicians who attack not only the corporation's political journalism but also the transmission of programs about social issues that conservatives have issues with, although occasionally ABC listeners or viewers vent their displeasure as well.

REMEMBER

The ABC has responded to such accusations of bias with the development of internal editorial policies that require journalists to give equal time to both of the major political parties whenever politics is discussed. It has even gone so far as to require that someone keep a tally of the amount of time each of the parties receives on radio and television during election campaigns. Editorial guidelines, meanwhile, serve to remind journalists working for the corporation of the need to be independent and balanced when undertaking their craft.

Covering elections

The ABC's commitment to covering Australian politics comes to the fore during election campaigns and on the night of the election count itself. In addition to its own coverage, the ABC is the media outlet on which the various political parties are allocated time to broadcast *party politicals*, segments where the parties, in particular the leaders, get to put their positions forward (see the nearby sidebar for more). The ABC, meanwhile, maintains an extensive ABC NEWS website that deals with all manner of elections and election campaigns, and the ABC is guaranteed to cover the election count without any advertising.

The Power of the Media?

By virtue of the strategic role they hold in the transmission of news and information from the parliament and the other institutions of government, and in relaying public opinion back to these institutional players, the media are, potentially, powerful actors in the political process. The professional values of political journalism that seek to stress the importance of balance, objectivity, political independence, and ethical gathering and dissemination of the news seek to mitigate the power of 'the press' to a certain extent.

Agenda setting

One of the major struggles that occurs in Australian politics is over the *agenda* — that is, the issues that are considered so important to the political community they require some form of governmental response. The battle is really one between the media, the government and the opposition.

The opposition wants the debate to focus on the alleged deficiencies of the government. The government wants the debate to focus on its alleged achievements and what it hopes to do in the future. The media, meanwhile, can have their own agendas, ranging from interest in particular policy issues through to assessing the merits or deficiencies of the major parties and/or their leaders.

Spin doctors

With both government and the media cognisant of each other's ability to set the agenda, the media politics associated with government these days is increasingly influenced by spin doctors and spin-doctoring.

BRINGING DOWN THE OPPOSITION?

One of the criticisms often made of the press gallery is that it tends to focus on the things that are easier to report rather than on the more difficult issues. The way the media can get preoccupied with the seemingly endless leadership turmoil that can go on in an opposition party is seen as a symptom of allegedly lazy reporting.

Because oppositions in Westminster parliaments have little else to do with their time, they're often on the verge of a leadership challenge. The media seem to follow this with great interest, thereby allegedly failing in what's supposed to be their primary task — that is, keeping the government answerable and accountable for its performance.

Spin-doctoring is a colloquial way of referring to efforts made by politicians to have certain decisions and/or actions interpreted in ways favourable to themselves and their party. As part of this process, governments (and oppositions) employ *spin doctors* — primarily people trained in advertising and public relations — to advise the government (or opposition) on how to sell its message.

This effort is aimed in no small way at the public, but is also meant to target journalists and journalism. Mindful of the pressure journalists are under to get on top of stories and file their reports before deadline, public relations and media advisers associated with the government or opposition try to ensure they provide information and influence journalistic interpretations of decisions and events.

The rise of the spin doctor in Australian parliamentary politics has been linked with the growth in the number of ministerial staff and available resources. Policy-specific spin-doctoring is coordinated from a minister's or politician's office, sometimes with former journalists or other media experts filling dedicated media advisory roles.

Meanwhile, Australian state and federal governments have developed large media liaison units within the respective public services. Ostensibly there to help inform the public about policy, controversy arises when these units seem to be more involved in undertaking advertising about policy programs that praises the government of the day. This notion of taxpayer funds being used to promote the government drives oppositions mad, although they tend to become much more sanguine about this practice when they become the government.

Opinion polling

Media interest in opinion polling represents another form of agenda setting — this time in the form of media outlets regularly publishing the findings of polls conducted on their behalf by polling organisations. These polls track all sorts of things, but the polls that really have impact are those that seek to gauge voting intentions and the approval ratings of the major party leaders (the prime minister, or premier, and opposition leader).

These polls can have a political dynamic of their own. In recent times, opinion polls have sometimes become the catalyst for a major political event. Poll findings may encourage a prime minister or a premier to go to an early election, for example. The most usual consequence of poll findings, however, is the onset of leadership turmoil, usually in the opposition ranks, but occasionally poor opinion poll results can precipitate a leadership crisis in the government. In 1991, after a series of poor poll outcomes, the federal Labor Caucus decided to replace Bob Hawke as leader and prime minister with Paul Keating.

Some critics argue that preoccupation with the polls on the part of the main political parties also affects policy-making, where the fear of adverse poll reactions stops a government from undertaking important policy reform.

Polls published in the media tend to reveal two results — the primary vote for each major party and the all-important two-party-preferred vote, which shows which party would gain the most votes after the distribution of preferences. Although politicians publicly dismiss polls (their general response is 'polls come and go'), the results provide some indication of trends in how people intend to vote. Indeed, a series of polls that are consistent is usually a good measure of how voters are feeling towards a party, leader or issue at a particular point in time.

UNLEASHING THE ANIMALS

During the 1980s, then Prime Minister Bob Hawke set up the Australian National Media Liaison Service (known around the place as Animals through a loose approximation of its acronym). This body was required, among other things, to monitor media coverage of speeches made particularly by the opposition. This monitoring was then used by the government in a bid to highlight inconsistencies in the opposition's approaches to debates or to flush out controversial statements. Media monitoring is now done by private companies, but, at the time, the establishment of this unit caused much controversy, again on the grounds that it was utilising taxpayer resources to fund activities that actually assisted the political party in government.

VOTE 1

In recent times, the reliability of polls has come into question, with some election results that went against polling prior to the election. For example, the coalition was consistently behind the Labor opposition in opinion polls prior to the 2019 election, but Scott Morrison managed to secure another coalition victory.

Whatever their impact, opinion polls are now an integral part of the political debate. They're certainly an important part of the way the media, especially the broadsheet newspapers, cover politics. The commentary on the polls can assist in giving something for the political debate to focus on, and it can even become the catalyst for other political events, including leadership crises.

5

Part of Tens

Explore ten politicians who had an impact in Australian politics, and speeches worth listening to (again and again)

Enjoy ten acts of political bastardry.

Get to know ten women who made history in Australian politics.

Chapter **16**

Ten Politicians Who Made an Impact

Sometimes it may be easy to forget, but politicians are people too. The actions of individual politicians can shape the political landscape. This chapter looks at ten Australian politicians who made an impact on the political system. Sure, the merits of their contributions are often the subject of debate, but the people noted in this chapter acted in ways they believed were in the best interests of the country.

John Christian Watson (1867–1941)

Here's a little-known fact: John Christian Watson was actually born in Valparaiso, Chile, and spent his childhood in New Zealand. He migrated to New Zealand with his family as a child and later moved to Sydney, where he worked as a compositor on the *Daily Telegraph* and *Sydney Morning Herald* newspapers. Watson became active in the union movement, and he won the New South Wales lower house seat of Young in 1894 after standing as the Labor candidate.

Watson shifted from state to national politics following Federation in 1901. In doing so, he became the first-ever parliamentary leader of the Labor Party. The non-Labor parties struggled to gain a majority in the lower house and relied on the Watson-led Labor Party for support. But when the Deakin government resigned in 1904, Watson became prime minister. This triumph wasn't only a personal one for Watson, but also for the Australian Labor Party because it held government for the first time. Watson's prime ministership lasted just a little over three months, but his place as a pioneer of the Labor Party continues to this day.

John Curtin (1885–1945)

John Curtin was Australia's 14th prime minister. Elected to represent the seat of Fremantle in 1928, Curtin eventually became the leader of the Australian Labor Party (ALP) and led the party to win the 1941 election.

Curtin's time as prime minister coincided with World War II (refer to Chapter 2). Unlike the first war, Australia seemed directly threatened. Rather than rely on the United Kingdom for defensive support, Curtin sought, and gained, the support of the United States. Throughout the war years, the Curtin government continued to plan for the postwar period and introduced a range of welfare reforms. But the stress took its toll on Curtin. He died in office on 5 July 1945. The war in the Pacific ended just six weeks later.

Robert Menzies (1894–1978)

The record for the longest serving Australian prime minister belongs to Robert Menzies. He was first prime minister from 1939 to 1941 as leader of the United Australia Party. After losing the 1941 election, Menzies went about creating a new non-Labor party. In 1944, the modern Liberal Party was born. He led the new party and won the 1949 election.

A devoted monarchist, Menzies was characterised as 'British to his bootstraps'. He remained as prime minister until 1966, when he resigned. In total, Menzies was prime minister for 18 years and 5 months. By creating the Liberal Party, Menzies made a huge impact on shaping the modern Australian political landscape. (Refer to Chapter 10 for much more on Menzies and the Liberal Party.)

Gough Whitlam (1916–2014)

Despite having been prime minister for a relatively short period, from 1972 to 1975, Gough Whitlam has a special place in Australian politics and is regarded as a demi-god by some Labor partisans. Before entering parliament, Whitlam had served in the RAAF and later became a barrister.

In parliament, Whitlam was regarded as a top performer. He led the ALP to electoral victory in 1972 (with the iconic 'It's Time' slogan) and ended the coalition's 23 years in government. The Whitlam government seemed to be trying to make up for lost time because it introduced a record number of bills. But Whitlam's bombastic style and his government's reformist agenda were seen by some as trying to do too much too soon.

In 1974, Prime Minister Whitlam won a double-dissolution election. But, in 1975, his government was dismissed by the governor-general. Whitlam, however, remained as leader of the ALP until 1977. (Refer to Chapter 5 for more on the dismissal and Chapter 9 for more on Whitlam in government.)

Whitlam's approach to government and the fact that his time as prime minister was ended by the governor-general rather than voters make him one of the most significant politicians in Australian history.

Malcolm Fraser (1930–2015)

Malcolm Fraser entered parliament at the age of 25 but remained a backbencher for ten years. His first stint as a minister occurred in 1966, when he held the army portfolio in the Holt government. He remained a minister until the coalition was defeated by the Whitlam-led ALP in 1972.

Fraser became a critical Australian politician when he became opposition leader in 1975 — a job he held briefly. Thanks to the governor-general's intervention, he became caretaker prime minister when the Whitlam government was dismissed (refer to Chapter 5).

Fraser then led the coalition to victory at the 1975, 1977 and 1980 federal elections. In 1983, the Hawke-led Labor party regained national government. The controversial circumstances in which Fraser first became prime minister sometimes overshadow his contribution to national politics. His regular criticism of John Howard's prime ministership (1996 to 2007), over reconciliation, multiculturalism and immigration, didn't endear him to large sections of the Liberal Party. Indeed, in 2010, Fraser announced his resignation from the party. (Chapter 10 addresses Fraser's years in government.)

Bob Hawke (1929–2019)

Bob Hawke was a record-setter before entering parliament. He entered the *Guinness Book of Records* for the fastest consumption of a yardglass full of beer in 1954. In terms of political work, Hawke served as the president of the Australian Council of Trade Unions (ACTU) from 1969 to 1980 and built a high public profile with his consensus-based approach to negotiation.

Entering parliament in 1980, Hawke became leader of the ALP in 1983, just weeks before the election. He led the party to victory, which was a remarkable achievement considering the ALP was still grappling with the constitutional crisis of 1975 (refer to Chapter 5).

As prime minister, Hawke relied on consensus and negotiation in building his government's policies. With Paul Keating as treasurer, the Hawke government introduced a number of important economic reforms that, some argued, abandoned Labor tradition. For example, the government reduced tariffs and ended a number of industry subsidies. Despite being the most successful of all Labor prime ministers (refer to Chapter 9), Bob Hawke was replaced by his party with Paul Keating in 1991.

John Howard (b. 1939)

John Howard was prime minister from 1996 to 2007 — a record second only to that of Robert Menzies. But Howard's rise to the top job was far from smooth. He was first elected to parliament in 1974 and served as treasurer from 1977 to 1983.

When it lost government, the Liberal Party entered a phase of bitter rivalry between two potential leaders — John Howard and Andrew Peacock. Howard replaced Peacock as leader in 1985, but, after the disastrous 1987 election, Peacock regained the leadership in 1989. At that point Howard himself thought that his chances of ever becoming leader, let alone prime minister, had vanished. He quipped that his return to the leadership would be 'like Lazarus with a triple bypass'.

But Howard did regain the leadership, in 1995, this time replacing the unpopular Alexander Downer. Howard led the coalition to victory in 1996 and began a period of economic reforms (such as introducing the GST in 1999). Howard's political life ended at the 2007 election when the coalition lost government and he lost his seat of Bennelong. This was only the second time a prime minister had lost his seat at a general election (Stanley Bruce lost his seat in 1929). (Chapter 10 looks at the Howard government in more detail.)

Don Chipp (1925–2006)

The charismatic Don Chipp left an indelible mark on the shape of the Senate. Chipp was the Liberal member for Hotham and served under successive Liberal prime ministers from Menzies to Fraser. But, in 1977, Don Chipp resigned from the Liberal Party and rejected the major parties' attempts at forcing their members to toe the line.

A liberal democrat, Chipp pursued socially progressive policies and, in mid-1977, he helped form the Australian Democrats, which was an important player in the Australian Senate from 1977 to 2004. (Refer to Chapter 12 for more on the Democrats.)

Don Chipp famously said that the role of the Democrats was to 'keep the bastards honest'. The Democrats was a game-changing party because it revitalised the check-and-balance functions of the Senate. For that, Australians thank you, Mr Chipp.

Bob Brown (b. 1944)

It ain't easy being green — just ask Bob Brown. Trained as a general medical practitioner, Brown has been a key figure in the environmental debate since he staged a week-long fast on the summit of Tasmania's Mount Wellington to protest against an American nuclear warship visiting Hobart in 1976.

Since then, Brown has worked to place conservation issues at the forefront of the political debate. In 1983, Brown was arrested when protesting against the Tasmanian government's plan to create the Franklin Dam. He later became a parliamentarian in Tasmania and was instrumental in creating the Australian Greens.

Bob Brown first won a Senate seat in the federal parliament in 1996. His passionate views on the environment and the Greens' suite of progressive policies made Brown a controversial figure (refer to Chapter 12). Green politics would look very different in Australia without Brown.

Pauline Hanson (b. 1954)

Please explain? All right, we will. Pauline Hanson was the Liberal Party's candidate for the Queensland seat of Oxley at the 1996 election. However, she was quickly disendorsed by the party after making controversial comments regarding Indigenous Australians. She went on to win the seat as an independent. In her first speech to parliament, Hanson focused on issues concerning race and immigration, and called for an end to multiculturalism (see Chapter 17 for more on this speech).

Shortly after, Hanson created a new national party — Pauline Hanson's One Nation, which we look at in Chapter 12. Her broad accent, controversial views and bright red hair made her one of the most interesting politicians that Australia had ever seen. Hanson remained a prominent figure in the political debate and, in 2016, returned to the national parliament after winning a Senate seat in Queensland.

Chapter **17**

Ten (Plus One!) Speeches Worth Listening to Again

Speeches are one of the most potent tools in politics. The very best political speeches capture people's imaginations and lead to broader debate about particular issues. But, as they say, it's all in the delivery, and even a well-written speech can fall flat if delivered poorly. Here are ten speeches made by Australian politicians that really stand out.

Sir Henry Parkes: The Crimson Thread of Kinship, 1890

As premier of New South Wales, Sir Henry Parkes was crucial to Australia becoming a federation. Regarded as having a knack with words, Parkes made a passionate speech at one of the first constitutional conferences, in Melbourne in February 1890.

He argued that federation shouldn't be held back by disagreements over tariffs between the colonies (refer to Chapter 2). Parkes passionately argued in the speech that Australians shared the same dreams and goals, and so were united by the 'crimson thread of kinship'. His efforts in leading Australia towards a federation earned him the title 'Father of Federation'.

John Curtin: We Are Fighting Mad, 1942

John Curtin was Australia's prime minister during World War II. His actions during the war marked a shift in Australia's foreign policy. Rather than rely on the British Empire, Curtin moved to make the United States a key military ally, especially after Darwin was bombed by Japanese forces in 1942.

John Curtin delivered a memorable speech to America on 14 March 1942, broadcast on Radio Australia. In calling for military support from the United States, Curtin argued that Australia was the 'last bastion between the west coast of America and the Japanese' and that America defended itself by defending Australia.

In announcing the proposed deployment of Minister for External Affairs Dr H. V. Evatt to the US, Curtin proclaimed that Evatt would 'tell you that we are fighting mad, that our people have a government that is governing with orders and not with weak-kneed suggestions . . .'

In another emotional passage, Curtin proudly stated that 'there will always be an Australian Government, and there will always be an Australian people'. The United States came to Australia's aid following Curtin's speech.

Robert Menzies: Forgotten People, 1942

No, this wasn't a speech by Menzies listing people he had forgotten to mention in previous speeches. With the coalition between Menzies' United Australia Party and the Country Party decaying, Menzies resigned as prime minister in 1941. But, in 1942, Menzies (as a backbencher) began a series of speeches broadcast every Friday night in Melbourne and Sydney.

The 'forgotten people' speech was broadcast on 22 May 1942 and was arguably Menzies' most influential. He identified a class of people who shared common values and beliefs rather than a common socioeconomic status. He argued this middle class included 'salary-earners, shop-keepers, skilled artisans, professional men and women, farmers and so on' who were the backbone of the nation.

And Menzies believed that the middle class was ineffectively represented in parliament. Menzies later created the modern Liberal Party to represent what he termed the 'forgotten people'. The Liberal Party's focus on these 'forgotten people', whether through John Howard's 'battlers' or Scott Morrison's 'quiet Australians', continues today.

Ben Chifley: Light on the Hill, 1949

It may seem strange to include a speech by a former engine driver in a list of important speeches, but it was Chifley's down-to-earth manner that endeared him to so many Australians. Chifley quickly rose through Labor ranks after entering federal parliament in 1940. He became treasurer in John Curtin's government and, when Curtin died in office in 1945, Chifley was chosen as his successor.

His 'light on the hill' speech, delivered to an ALP Conference in 1949, is widely regarded as epitomising the philosophy of the Labor Party. According to Chifley, delivering 'better standards of living' and 'greater happiness to the mass of the people' were among the core values Labor strove for and always needed to hold on to.

In his speech, Chifley argued that the Labor Party had 'a great objective — the light on the hill — which we aim to reach by working for the betterment of mankind not only here but anywhere we may give a helping hand'. Chifley's 'light on the hill' idea is as important today in the Labor Party as it was in 1949.

Neville Bonner: Aboriginal Rights, 1971

Neville Bonner was the first Aboriginal Australian to hold a seat in the federal parliament, as a Liberal senator from Queensland from 1971 to 1983. He was a passionate advocate for Aboriginal rights and spoke of these issues in his first speech in the Senate.

In this speech, Bonner stressed the important role economic development played for all Australians and how it was particularly important for Indigenous Australians. Here's an extract from a powerful section of Bonner's speech:

Through the valour of its fighting men in two world wars and by the vigour and skill of its leaders, Australia has earned an honoured place in the world. However, I am conscious of the fact that I am the first member of my race to participate in parliamentary proceedings. I am proud that, however long it has taken, this form of participation has been achieved.

Gough Whitlam: It's Time, 1972

Delivered by Whitlam as Labor's policy speech during the 1972 election campaign, this speech hit all the right notes. Not only did Whitlam outline his plan of what Labor would do if elected to government, he also masterfully attacked the coalition's record in office.

The theme of 'it's time' was made more poignant by the fact that the coalition had been in government since 1949. Beginning with the immortal words 'Men and women of Australia', Whitlam's charismatic delivery ensured this speech gained maximum attention.

Paul Keating: The Redfern Speech, 1992

Made on the eve of the United Nations International Year of the World's Indigenous People, in 1993, Prime Minister Keating's momentous speech focused on Australia's Indigenous people. Delivered at Redfern Park in Sydney, Keating's speech was charged with emotion and recognised the negative impacts of European settlement and the failings of past governments in dealing with Australia's Aboriginal and Torres Strait Islander population. As Keating argued, European settlement 'took the traditional lands and smashed the traditional way of life'.

The importance of Keating's speech in raising reconciliation as a national issue can't be underestimated. So powerful was Keating's speech that it came third in a poll, held by Radio National in 2007, of the most unforgettable speeches (Martin Luther King's 'I Have a Dream' speech was first, followed by the Sermon on the Mount).

Pauline Hanson: Inaugural Speech to Parliament, 1996

At 5.15 pm on 10 September 1996, the little-known independent from the Queensland seat of Oxley made her first speech to the Australian parliament. Speaking as an 'ordinary Australian' rather than a 'polished politician', Hanson attacked the policies of successive governments regarding race and immigration.

Hanson argued that 'reverse racism' was occurring, with non-Indigenous Australians being disadvantaged. Furthermore, Hanson argued that Australia would be 'swamped by Asians' and multiculturalism needed to be abolished.

With her shaky voice and populist ideas, Hanson set the political debate alight. The ideas she outlined in her speech underpinned the policies of her new party, Pauline Hanson's One Nation.

John Howard: Bali Terrorist Attack, 2002

With the attacks in America on 11 September 2001 still fresh in people's minds, concerns about terrorism dominated the political debate throughout much of the decade. Unfortunately, Australians were not immune from terrorism. On 12 October 2002, 88 Australians holidaying in Bali were killed when terrorists set off bombs in tourist locations.

Prime Minister Howard made one of his most memorable speeches just after the bombings. In an emotional time, Howard's words and tone captured the solemnity of the situation as he expressed the nation's sadness for those who had been injured and for those who had died.

But the speech was also charged with a determination for justice. As Howard argued, Australia would 'mete out a proper response' to bring to justice 'those who are responsible'. This speech was measured and controlled in a time of great sadness and anger, and grave concerns about attacks from terrorists abroad and at home.

Kevin Rudd: Apology to the Stolen Generations, 2008

The election of the Rudd Labor government in 2007 marked a change in the political debate regarding Australia's Indigenous people. The Keating government had moved towards reconciliation in the early 1990s, but the Howard government had avoided formally saying sorry since winning government in 1996.

In February 2008, Rudd made a speech in parliament apologising for the policies of successive governments that had 'inflicted profound grief, suffering and loss' on Indigenous Australians, especially those of the 'stolen generations' — those children from Aboriginal and Torres Strait Islander backgrounds who were removed from their families and placed with institutions or non-Indigenous families in an attempt to assimilate them.

Rudd's speech recognised the tragedies of these policies but also looked to the future. As Rudd stated, 'For the future we take heart, resolving that this new page in the history of our great continent can now be written'.

Julia Gillard: 'Misogyny Speech', 2012

This famous speech was made by Australia's first female prime minister Julia Gillard in response to the demand by then-opposition leader Tony Abbott for the government to dismiss the Speaker, Peter Slipper, after it was reported he had allegedly sent texts that were described by observers as sexist to a former staffer.

In her speech, Gillard highlighted what she and her supporters perceived as double-standards and sexism by the opposition leader. In one of the most reported passages of her speech, Gillard argued that she would 'not be lectured about sexism and misogyny by this man'.

The speech was widely reported in Australia, and abroad, and was voted as being the 'most unforgettable moment of Australian TV history' by readers of *The Guardian*.

Gillard also drew attention to the role of gender in Australian politics in her final speech as prime minister in 2013, when she said that 'the reaction to being the first female prime minister does not explain everything about my prime minister-ship, nor does it explain nothing about my prime ministership'.

Chapter **18**

Ten Acts of Political Bastardry in Australia

How could they do that? That's usually the question people ask when they talk about the politicians noted in this chapter. People listed here acted against conventional notions of loyalty. In many cases, they were seen as traitors. But these people acted the way they did because they believed their actions would, in some way, improve the overall landscape of Australian politics. So, here we salute the ten most obvious examples of political bastardry in Australia.

The Hopetoun Blunder

Before being appointed as Australia's first governor-general, Lord Hopetoun (John Adrian Louis Hope, 1860–1908) had served as governor of Victoria from 1889 to 1895. One of the first tasks for Lord Hopetoun was to appoint Australia's first prime minister before the first federal election in 1901.

In late 1900, Lord Hopetoun selected William Lyne, the New South Wales premier, to form the first government. However, Lyne had little support because he had been a strong opponent of federation, and he couldn't form a government.

Lyne then advised Hopetoun to select Edmund Barton, who had been a leading figure in the Federation Movement (and was probably an obvious choice) and had gained the support of other politicians. Hopetoun agreed and commissioned Barton as Australia's first prime minister on 31 December 1900. Lord Hopetoun's actions were later labelled as the 'Hopetoun blunder'.

Aspiring to Conscription

Billy Hughes (William Morris Hughes, 1862–1952) played an important role in Australian politics (as we note in previous chapters, particularly Chapters 2 and 9). One of his most memorable acts, however, was one that many Labor folk regarded as political bastardry.

Having become prime minister in the middle of World War I, Hughes sought to boost Australia's military involvement. He argued for compulsory military service, which contrasted with the views of the Labor Party. So committed was Hughes that he put the question of conscription to a referendum, which was defeated in 1916.

With sections of his own party remaining unsupportive, Hughes resigned from Labor and joined the Fusion Liberal opposition to create the Nationalist Party. The question of conscription was again put to a referendum, where an even greater majority of voters rejected the idea. Hughes's actions marked him down in history as Labor's greatest 'rat'.

Fleeing a Sinking Ship?

Joseph Lyons (1879–1939) was another Labor minister who decided to resign from his party and form a new party with the opposition. Lyons served as acting treasurer between 1930 and 1931.

Faced with the financial depression that was brought on by the Wall Street crash of 1929, Lyons proposed to reduce government spending and aim for a balanced budget. The Labor party rejected this plan and argued for even greater government spending.

When Lyons wasn't given the position of treasurer, he resigned and worked with the Nationalists to create the United Australia Party (UAP). Lyons became leader of the UAP and led the new party to victory at the 1931 federal election. Lyons, of course, became prime minister, while his old party, the ALP, sat uncomfortably in the opposition benches. Lyons died in office in 1939.

Spoilsport!

Earle Page (1880–1961) was the co-founder of the Country Party and had joined his party in coalition with Lyons' United Australia Party (UAP) in 1934. Upon Lyons' death in 1939, Page was appointed as caretaker prime minister, a role he held for 20 days.

When the UAP elected Robert Menzies as leader, Page launched an unprecedented attack and accused Menzies of being a coward for not having enlisted during World War I. Unwilling to support Menzies, Page withdrew the Country Party from the coalition until dissatisfaction among his own party forced him to resign his position as Country Party leader in September 1939.

Over a Barrel

John ('Black Jack') McEwen (1900–1980) was another Country Party leader who sought to influence who its coalition partner would choose to be prime minister. Tensions were simmering between McEwen and William McMahon, who had become treasurer in 1966 after Robert Menzies had retired. As treasurer, McMahon positioned himself as a frontrunner for the Liberal leadership.

When Harold Holt disappeared in 1967, McEwen, as deputy prime minister, was appointed as caretaker prime minister. He bluntly warned the Liberal Party that he couldn't serve under McMahon because he didn't trust him, mainly due to significant differences between the two men about economic policy. As a result, McMahon withdrew his candidacy and John Gorton became prime minister. The Country Party had once again showcased its power in the coalition. (Refer to Chapter 11 for more on McEwen's influence as a political leader.)

Despite having been forced to withdraw his candidacy in the previous ballot for the Liberal Party leadership (thanks to John McEwen), William (Billy) McMahon (1908–1988) still harboured leadership aspirations. As prime minister, John Gorton faced opposition within his Liberal Party ranks about his leadership style. His opponents mobilised and McMahon once again challenged for the leadership of the party.

The divisions within the Liberal Party became clear when Gorton and McMahon received the same number of votes. Gorton, conceding he had lost the support of many in his Party Room, cast the deciding vote in favour of McMahon. In effect, McMahon had forced Gorton to vote against himself and out of the role of prime minister.

The Dismissal

Depending on what side of the political fence you're on, the actions of Sir John Kerr (1914–1991) were either timely or outrageous.

Kerr was the governor-general at the time of the Whitlam Labor government. But when the government couldn't get its budget through the Senate in 1975, the governor-general intervened. He dismissed the Whitlam government and appointed Malcolm Fraser, who was the leader of the coalition, as caretaker prime minister.

The problem with his actions was that Fraser was actually the leader of the opposition, which had fewer seats in the House Representatives than the democratically elected government. Remember, too, that Gough Whitlam had appointed Kerr as governor-general! (For much more on the dismissal refer to Chapter 5.)

The Drover's Dog

As the old adage goes, 'timing is everything'. The charismatic Bob Hawke had developed a high public profile in his role as president of the Australian Council of Trade Unions (ACTU), a role he held from 1969 to 1980. After election to the federal parliament for the Labor Party in 1980, Hawke became increasingly popular within Caucus.

With Labor leader Bill Hayden seemingly becoming less popular, Hawke called for a leadership ballot. While the result was close, Hawke lost and Hayden remained as leader. As the 1983 election neared, however, many in the Labor Party began to believe Hawke could lead the party to victory. With pressure mounting, Hayden resigned as leader and made way for Hawke. On the same day, Prime Minister Fraser called the election.

After a four-week campaign, the reinvigorated Hawke-led Labor Party won government. Believing that the Fraser government would've lost the election anyway, Hayden quipped that 'a drover's dog' could've led the Labor Party to victory. So, no hard feelings then?

Bringing out the Knives

What goes around comes around. Despite being the most successful federal Labor leader, Bob Hawke wasn't immune from intra-party shenanigans. Paul Keating, who'd been Hawke's long-serving treasurer, began a path to take over as prime minister.

Keating, who was first elected to parliament in 1969 at the age of 25, believed Hawke should resign so he could take over in an orderly manner. In 1988, the two had apparently had a meeting at Kirribilli, the prime minister's residence in Sydney, and agreed that Hawke would hand over the leadership to Keating after the 1990 election. After that election, however, Hawke refused to honour the 'Kirribilli agreement', forcing Keating to undertake a leadership challenge.

In June 1991, Keating challenged but lost, and resigned as treasurer. He continued to agitate for leadership change and six months later he defeated Hawke in another leadership ballot to become prime minister.

Kiss and Tell?

Well, where to start with one of Labor's most maligned figures? Mark Latham became leader of the Labor Party in 2003, after it slumped to its third election loss to the Howard coalition government. Latham was initially seen as being an exciting and dynamic leader. However, cracks soon began to appear in his leadership and serious concerns were raised after Labor's election loss in 2004.

Latham resigned as leader and from parliament in 2005. Soon after, he published his political diary entries in *The Latham Diaries*. The book was full of 'frank' assessments of those he worked with in politics and remains one of the most corrosive pieces of literature in Australian politics.

After stints as a journalist and political commentator (including time spent at Sky News), in 2018 Latham announced he had joined One Nation. He succeeded in winning a NSW upper house seat at the 2019 state election.

A Parade of Bastardry

Between 2007 and 2019, no fewer than five members of the House of Representatives served as prime minister. Elected in 2007, Labor's Kevin Rudd was replaced by Julia Gillard in 2010, who was replaced by Kevin Rudd again just before the 2013 election. In 2013, the Liberal's Tony Abbott won a landslide victory, only to be replaced by Malcolm Turnbull just before the 2016 election. An attempt was then made by Peter Dutton to replace Turnbull before the 2019 election, only this didn't work because Scott Morrison ended up being the prime minister.

In each of these cases, all manner of internecine battles were at play, although the inability of the failed leader to formulate a policy to deal with climate change that would either enjoy popular support or satisfy the demands on the backbench was the common denominator in each of these leadership changes.

Chapter 19

Ten (Plus One!) Women who made History in Australian Politics

Australia has been a leader when it comes to including women to participate in democratic processes. While women were allowed to vote and be elected to parliament in 1902, however, it wasn't until 1943 that the first women were actually in parliament! In the next few pages, we shine a light on the women who broke new ground and made history in Australian politics and government.

Dame Enid Lyons (1897–1981)

Dame Enid Lyons was the first woman elected to the House of Representatives. Representing the seat of Darwin in Tasmania, Lyons was a member of the United Australia Party, the predecessor of the Liberal Party.

Lyons was no stranger to the national political spotlight. Her husband, Joseph Lyons, was prime minister of Australia from 1932 to 1939 and Dame Enid had forged a high public profile during this time, especially through community work.

A mother of 11 children, Dame Enid acknowledged the significance of her election to the lower house, especially during her inaugural speech to the chamber in 1943.

In 1949, Dame Enid made history again when she was selected by Prime Minister Robert Menzies to be the first woman in Cabinet, where she held the role of the Vice President of the Executive Council. Dame Enid left parliament in 1951 and passed away in 1981.

Dame Dorothy Tangney (1907–1985)

Dame Dorothy broke new ground for women, as well as her political party, in Australia. Selected to serve in the Senate in 1943, Dame Dorothy holds the dual honour of being the first woman in the Senate and also being the first female Labor MP in the national parliament.

Serving in a range of Senate Committees, Dame Dorothy strongly supported expanding social and welfare policies across the nation. She was also a passionate advocate for education as well as increasing medical services. Dame Dorothy made these topics prominent in her very first speech in parliament in 1943.

Dame Dorothy left the Senate in 1968, almost 25 years after she first began her time in the chamber.

The seat of Tagney in Western Australia was created to recognise Dame Dorothy's contribution to national politics in 1974.

Dame Margaret Guilfoyle (1926–2020)

Representing the Liberal Party, and from the state of Victoria, Margaret Guilfoyle entered the Senate in 1971 and was quick to make history. In 1975, Dame Margaret was the first woman to become a minister when Prime Minister Malcolm Fraser gave her responsibility for Education and Social Security.

She became known as the 'iron butterfly' as some commentators drew parallels between her and Margaret Thatcher who, at the time, was on her way to becoming the prime minister of the United Kingdom and was being referred to as the 'iron lady'.

Dame Margaret was elevated to the Cabinet in 1976, making her the first woman to hold a portfolio and be in Cabinet. (While Dame Enid Lyons was in Cabinet in 1949, she did not have responsibility over a portfolio.)

In 2020, at the age of 94, Dame Margaret passed away, but left a very important legacy on the Liberal Party and national politics.

Susan Ryan (1942–2020)

The first female minister from the Labor Party was Susan Ryan, who was elected as a senator from the Australian Capital Territory in 1975.

In 1983, when the Bob Hawke–led Labor Party gained power, Ryan was given the Education and Youth Affairs portfolio, as well as being the Minister Assisting the Prime Minister for Women's Affairs.

Ryan made a major policy impact when, in 1983, she moved to implement legislation that would seek to end gender-based discrimination in Australia. In 1984, the bills passed parliament and the country had a new Sex Discrimination Act.

Joan Child (1921–2013)

Joan Child became the first female Speaker of the House of Representatives in 1986. From the Labor Party, and representing the seat of Henty from Victoria, Child was responsible for, among other things, chairing the parliamentary debates and maintaining order in the chamber.

Child also made history because she was the last Speaker to be in the old parliament house, and also the first Speaker to be in the new parliament. Child retired from national politics in the 1990 election.

In 2001, Child was awarded the Centenary Medal to recognise the contribution she had made to national politics.

Janine Haines (1945–2004)

As we explore in Chapter 12, the Australian Democrats party emerged in the aftermath of the 1975 constitutional crisis that ultimately resulted in the dismissal of the Whitlam Government. The party was created in 1977 and led by former Liberal minister Don Chipp. In the same year, Janine Haines, who had been a member of the Liberal Movement in South Australia that later became part of the Australian Democrats, was appointed to the Senate to fill a casual vacancy.

Haines left the Senate when her term came to an end in 1978. But she returned to national politics after winning a Senate seat in South Australia representing the Australian Democrats in 1980.

Having built a high public profile, the Australian Democrats chose her to lead the party in 1986 when Don Chipp retired. In doing so, Haines became the first woman to lead a party with parliamentary representation in Australia.

In 1990, Haines decided to contest the lower house seat of Kingston in South Australia with the hope of becoming the first Australian Democrats MP in the House of Representatives. The challenge ultimately failed, and Haines decided to retire from national politics.

Margaret Reid (b. 1935)

While the House of Representatives had its first woman as Speaker in 1986, it wasn't until a whole decade later that the Senate would have its first woman as President.

Margaret Reid, a Liberal senator from the Australian Capital Territory, started her time in the Senate in 1981. In 1995 she became Deputy President of the Senate and, following the election of the Howard Government, was appointed as the President of the Senate in 1996.

In 2002, after six years as President of the Senate, and over two decades in the upper house, Reid retired from national politics. She was soon appointed Officer of the Order of Australia for her contribution to the Australian Parliament and the community.

Rosemary Follett (b. 1948)

The very first head of a state or territory government in Australia was Rosemary Follett who, in 1989, made history as the first-ever Chief Minister of the Australian Capital Territory (ACT).

Follett led the Labor Party to form the ACT's inaugural government after the 1989 election. It wasn't smooth sailing, however, as her government had to rely on the support of other parties to remain in power. Just months after the election, Follett was replaced as Chief Minister by the opposition leader. Follett returned to the head of government role in 1991 and led Labor to win the 1992 election.

While Follett led Labor to its loss in 1995, she stayed on as leader of the party until 1996 when she decided to retire from parliament.

Quentin Bryce (b. 1942)

History was made in 2008 when Dame Quentin Bryce was appointed to be the 25th Governor-General of Australia. Prior to becoming governor-general, Dame Quentin had made an impact in the community through her career as a lawyer and community advocate. In 2003, she became the governor of Queensland.

As the governor-general of Australia between 2008 and 2014, Dame Quentin swore-in three prime ministers: Kevin Rudd, Julia Gillard and Tony Abbott. The swearing-in of Gillard as prime minister was the first time that both governor-general and prime minister of Australia were women.

In 2014, Prime Minister Tony Abbott announced that Quentin Bryce would be made the first dame since he had decided to bring back the honours of knights and dames that year.

Julia Gillard (b. 1961)

It took over 100 years, but in 2010 Julia Gillard became the first woman to become prime minister of Australia. Having first won the Victorian House of Representatives district of Lalor in 1998, Gillard became deputy leader of the Labor Party in 2006 when Kevin Rudd became leader.

In 2007, Gillard became deputy prime minister when Labor defeated the Howard-led coalition and sat on the government benches for the first time in 11 years. But, following growing frustration from within the party about Rudd's leadership as well as a drop in the government's popularity, Caucus members decided to replace Rudd with Gillard as party leader. In doing so, Gillard became prime minister.

Gillard managed to form minority government following the 2010 election, but was replaced as leader of the Labor Party, and prime minister, by Rudd in 2013.

Linda Burney (b. 1957)

Linda Burney has made history in Australian parliaments at state and national levels.

A member of the Labor Party, Burney became the first Indigenous Australian to win a seat in the Parliament of New South Wales in 2003. Representing the seat of Canterbury, Burney also held ministerial posts, including being the Minister for Youth between 2007 and 2008.

In 2016, Burney resigned from the New South Wales parliament to run for the federal seat of Barton. In doing so, Burney once again made history when she became the first Indigenous Australian woman to be elected to the House of Representatives.

While in the national parliament, Burney has held shadow ministerial positions, including being the Shadow Minister for Indigenous Australians.

Glossary

Act of Parliament: A *bill* that has been debated, voted on and passed by both houses of *parliament* before proceeding to the *governor* or *governor-general* to receive *royal assent* in order to become law. See also *committee stage, first reading, second reading, third reading*.

appropriation bill: A law for the allocation of government money. See also *supply*.

assistant minister: See also *full ministry*.

Australian Constitution: The document that outlines how Australia is run under the federal parliamentary system of government.

Australian Electoral Commission (AEC): The body that undertakes electoral redistributions, maintains the federal electoral roll and runs federal elections.

backbencher: A member of *parliament* who is not a minister (or shadow minister) or a *parliamentary secretary*.

balance of power: A situation where minor party or independent parliamentarians have the deciding vote on legislation. See also *hung parliament*.

bill: A proposed piece of legislation debated by a *parliament* in order to become law through an *Act of Parliament*. See also *committee stage, first reading, second reading, third reading*.

by-election: A parliamentary election held between general elections to fill the seat of a member who has died, retired or otherwise vacated the seat.

Cabinet: The collection of senior ministers who meet regularly and whose chairperson is the *prime minister*; also called the inner Cabinet or the senior ministry. See also *full ministry, parliamentary secretary*.

caretaker government: The mode of government assumed by an incumbent government when the *writs* for an election are issued, ensuring government continues but in a minimal form, undertaking no new policy decisions, initiatives or appointments.

Caucus: A body of the Australian Labor Party that includes all members of the parliamentary wing, who meet ahead of parliamentary sittings to decide on how they will vote in *parliament*.

Chairperson of Committees: The member of *parliament* who takes over the running of the parliament from the *Speaker* of the lower house or the *President* of the upper house in the *committee stage* of a *bill*. See also *Act of Parliament, first reading, second reading, third reading.*

civics: The study of constitutional and electoral systems.

Clerk of the House: A parliamentary officer assisting either the *Speaker* of the lower house or the *President* of the upper house by reading out the title of a *bill* in its *first reading* in *parliament.*

coalition: The joining of *political parties* to stand in elections or to form government as a combined force.

coalition politics: The political practice of a *minor party* supporting a m*ajor party* to form government in return for ministerial seats being secured for the minor party.

collective politics: The concept of achieving political ends through unified, disciplined action.

Collective Responsibility: A convention of the *Westminster system* that ensures the *Cabinet* is bound by its policy decisions. See also *Ministerial Responsibility, Responsible Government, Separation of Powers.*

committee stage: The stage that a *bill* passes through when the *Chairperson of Committees* takes over the running of the *parliament* from the *Speaker* of the lower house or the *President* of the upper house, and the bill is debated and voted on clause by clause and amendments may be moved. See also *Act of Parliament, first reading, second reading, third reading.*

concurrent power: Any power that is specifically noted in Section 51 of the *Australian Constitution* as being shared by the federal and state governments. See also *exclusive power, reserve power* and *residual power.*

Conference: The policy-making organ of the Australian Labor Party, both national and state.

conscience vote: A vote in *parliament* when the government decides that members may vote on a matter according to personal principle, rather than being directed by their party. See also *crossing the floor.*

conservatism: A belief in the importance of institutions such as the church and the monarchy in civilising society, based on suspicion of change.

constitution: The rulebook that sets out the institutions and systems of government. See also *Australian Constitution.*

constitutional conventions: The series of gatherings, part of the *Federation Movement*, that led to *Federation* and the drafting of the *Australian Constitution.*

constitutional crisis: A term usually referring to the events of 1975 that led to the sacking of the Labor government of Gough Whitlam by Governor-General Sir John Kerr. See also *Parliamentary Responsibility.*

constitutional monarchy: A system of government that has a parliament with the power to govern, but with a monarch (or the monarch's representative) as the head of state.

convention: An unwritten constitutional principle underpinning the *Westminster system* that refers to the operation of *parliament* and institutions of government. See also *Collective Responsibility, Ministerial Responsibility, Responsible Government, Separation of Powers.*

Council: The organ of the Liberal Party of Australia, and of the National Party of Australia, that transacts party business, both national and state.

Council of Australian Governments (COAG): The joint Commonwealth–state government body, represented by the prime minister, state premiers and territory chief ministers, that between 1992 and 2020 finalised agreements on matters of intergovernmental activity. Replaced in 2020 with the *National Cabinet.*

Court of Disputed Returns: The name that is used by *the High Court of Australia* when it deals with allegations of improper or illegal conduct during an election, resulting in a disputed outcome, a situation that may alternatively be dealt with by the *Federal Court of Australia.*

crossbencher: A member of *parliament* who is not a member of the major party of government or the official major party of opposition. See also *independent, minor party.*

crossing the floor: The action taken by members of *parliament* when they wish to vote with the opposing party, in defiance of their party direction, usually on a matter of personal principle. See also *conscience vote.*

Crown: An overall term for the British monarchy.

deadlocks provision: Section 57 of the *Australian Constitution*, which is designed to resolve disputes between the *House of Representatives* and the *Senate*, by allowing for an election of the *parliament* on the defeat of government legislation in the Senate. See also *double dissolution.*

democracy: The idea that people should be able to govern themselves.

departmental secretary: The most senior public servant of a government department who advises the minister and conveys political directives back to the department.

division: A formal vote during a parliamentary sitting when members of *parliament* are given notice via a bell rung throughout the parliament that their presence is required in the chamber.

donkey vote: A ballot paper where a voter numbers candidates in order of appearance (not of preference), still counted as a formal vote (a reverse donkey is where the numbers are from bottom to top). See also *informal vote.*

Dorothy Dixer: A question posed by a member of the governing party to a minister in order to elicit a predetermined reply.

double dissolution: The situation where a *bill* in *parliament* is defeated for a second time by the *Senate*, allowing the *governor-general* to dissolve both the *House of Representatives* and all of the Senate, and call for fresh elections. See also *deadlocks provision*.

electoral democracy: The will of the people expressed through an election of voters' representatives to the *legislature*.

electoral district: A geographic area for which citizens are registered to vote in a particular election, for federal, state or local government; also called an electoral division, electorate or seat.

exaggerated majority: An election when a party wins a proportion of seats much greater than its percentage of the vote. See also *paradoxical outcome, wasted majority*.

exclusive power: Any power that is specifically exercisable by the federal government. See also *concurrent power, reserve power, residual power*.

Executive in Council: The body formed to allow federal ministers to meet with the *governor-general*, or for state ministers to meet with state *governors*, in order to inform the *Crown* representative what the *parliament* has been doing and for the Crown representative to give *royal assent* to any bills passed by the parliament. Constitutionally, this is the formal governing body in Australia.

Expenditure Review Committee (ERC): A Cabinet committee, usually made up of the treasurer, the finance minister, the prime minister (or state premier) and possibly one or two other senior ministers, to review expenditure proposals; also known as a razor gang.

faction: An organisational sub-unit of a *political party* that operates like a small party within the larger party to use collective action in an attempt to achieve political outcomes regarding policy, ideology or leadership issues within the party.

Federal Court of Australia: A subordinate court to the *High Court of Australia* that deals with less complex constitutional matters, as well as matters of general law.

Federal Electoral Assembly (FEA): The clustering of the local branches of the Australian Labor Party geographically, according to federal electoral divisions.

federation: A system of government where the power to govern is shared between the national government and state governments.

Federation Movement: Colonial advocates of a national system of government with shared powers between the federal and state governments, led by Henry Parkes, with discussions held through a series of *constitutional conventions* in the late 1890s.

first past the post: A voting system that determines winning candidates by a simple majority of votes (discontinued in Australia in 1918). See also *preferential voting, proportional representation*.

first reading: The first mention of a *bill*, usually simply the title of the bill, by the *Clerk of the House* in a parliament. See also *Act of Parliament, committee stage, second reading, third reading*.

Fourth Estate: The media, referring to its watchdog role in keeping the other three estates — the parliamentary executive, the *legislature* and the judiciary — answerable and accountable to the people.

frontbencher: A member of *parliament* who is either a minister (or shadow minister) or a *parliamentary secretary*.

full ministry: Comprises senior ministers (*Cabinet*) and assistant or junior ministers (who hold portfolios not included in the Cabinet or who may assist ministers in the Cabinet). See also *Cabinet, parliamentary secretary*.

General Purpose Financial Assistance to the States: From 1947 to 2000 (then called a General Purpose Grant), money given by the Commonwealth government to the state governments to fund state-based programs and operations; replaced in 2000 by the allocation of revenue from the *goods and services tax* to the states. See also *Grants Commission, Specific Purpose Grant*.

goods and services tax (GST): A tax introduced in 1999; its revenue flows directly to the states as *General Purpose Financial Assistance to the States*. See also *Grants Commission*.

governor: The *Crown* representative in Australia's state governments.

governor-general: The *Crown* representative in Australia's federal government.

Grants Commission: The federal body that advises the Commonwealth government as to how to allocate funds to the state governments to ensure equity of government services. See also *General Purpose Financial Assistance to the States, goods and services tax, Specific Purpose Grant*.

half-Senate election: The staggered election of half the *Senate*, which has a six-year term, to coincide with the three-yearly election of the *House of Representatives*.

High Court of Australia: The superior court of the Australian judicial system that deals with general law and hears and resolves constitutional disputes between the Commonwealth and the states. See also *Federal Court of Australia*.

House of Commons: The lower house of the British *parliament*. See also *House of Representatives*.

House of Lords: The upper house of the British parliament. See also *Senate*.

House of Representatives: The lower house of the Australian federal *parliament*. See also *Legislative Assembly*.

how-to-vote card: A listing of election candidates for a particular seat published by each *political party* and handed out at polling booths to indicate to voters how to order the candidates on their ballot paper in order to vote for the party's candidate (in federal and state elections except in Tasmania).

hung parliament: The situation where neither of the *major parties* holds a majority in the lower house, giving the *balance of power* to *minor parties* or to *independents*.

independent: A member of *parliament* who has no party affiliation.

informal vote: A vote counted as ineligible due to any error, deliberate or accidental, in completing a ballot paper. See also *donkey vote*.

interest group: An organisation that seeks to exert influence on the party or parties that win executive power; also known as a pressure group.

intergovernmental agreement: The outcome of a meeting of Commonwealth and state and/or territory government ministers and staff of ministerial departments to discuss the coordination of regulations.

Joint House Management Committee: A state parliamentary body convened in the event of failure of a *bill* in order to reach a compromise to allow the bill to pass.

Joint Party Room: A meeting of all members of the parliamentary wings of both the Liberal Party of Australia and the National Party, either federal or state. See also *Party Room*.

Joint Select Committee on Electoral Matters (JSCEM): A parliamentary *standing committee* made up of parliamentarians from both houses and from all parties, convened following an election in order to investigate the conduct of the election and make recommendations on future reform.

joint sitting: A sitting of the federal *parliament* with both the *House of Representatives* and the *Senate* in the one chamber, provided for by Section 57 of the *Australian Constitution*, following a *double-dissolution* election in which the government is returned, in order to debate the *bills* whose defeat caused the double dissolution.

judicial interpretation: The process used by the *High Court* to interpret the meaning of the *Australian Constitution*.

junior minister: See *full ministry*.

Leader of the Government in the Senate: The leader of the governing party in the *Senate*; the most senior member of the government in the Senate.

Leader of the Opposition in the Senate: The leader of the second largest party in the *Senate*.

legislature: Generic term for *parliament*.

Legislative Assembly: The lower house of state *parliaments*. See also *House of Representatives*.

Legislative Council: The upper house of state *parliaments*. See also *Senate*.

liberalism: A belief in individual liberty being central to society, free from government interference to certain degrees. Welfare liberals see an important role for governments in ensuring access to equal opportunity; market liberals advocate freedom in the marketplace.

Loan Council: The joint Commonwealth–state government body that makes decisions about borrowing of overseas capital.

major party: A *political party* that wins a large enough share of the vote to win enough seats to give it the possibility of forming government. See also *minor party*.

marginal seat: An *electoral district* that will not be safely returned to a sitting member but could go to any party in an election, particularly a ma*jor party*.

mass party: A *political party* that allows ordinary citizens to join.

minister: See *full ministry*.

ministerial adviser: A government adviser who is not a member of the public service but part of a minister's political team.

ministerial council: The joint Commonwealth–state government body, represented by the state, territory and federal ministers responsible for a certain portfolio, that meets to discuss issues relevant to that portfolio, sometimes agreeing to common legislation so the federal system has a uniform legal approach.

Ministerial Responsibility: A convention of the *Westminster system* that ensures ministers are responsible for the policy decisions relating to their *portfolios* and the conduct of the public service department relating to that portfolio. See also *Collective Responsibility*, *full ministry*, *Responsible Government*, *Separation of Powers*.

minor party: A *political party* that receives a small share of the vote and a very small number of seats (or none) in the *parliament*. See also *major party*.

National Cabinet: This replaced COAG in 2020 and is the joint Commonwealth–state government body, represented by the prime minister, state premiers and territory chief ministers, to finalise agreements on matters of intergovernmental activity.

nationalisation: The ideology of government ownership of private industries. See also *socialism*.

nexus provision: A requirement under Section 24 of the *Australian Constitution* that the number of members of the *House of Representatives* will be twice that of the members of the *Senate*.

opinion poll: Usually a survey or questionnaire that aims to find out how people intend to vote at the next election.

original states: The states formed from the original colonies of New South Wales and Victoria (the 'big' states), and Queensland, South Australia, Tasmania and Western Australia (the 'small' states), before the creation of the territories (the Australian Capital Territory and the Northern Territory).

pairing: A practice conducted by the *Whips* (both government and opposition) during a parliamentary sitting to ensure that the absence of a member of the governing party when a vote is to be taken is equalled by an absence from voting by an MP of the other party.

paradoxical outcome: An election when a party wins government with less than 50 per cent of the two-party-preferred vote. Can occur when a party wins seats with substantial *wasted majorities* in individual seats. See also *exaggerated majority*.

parliament: The institution to which voters elect representatives, generically known as the *legislature*; in Australia, comprising the *House of Representatives* (the lower house) and the *Senate* (the upper house) for the federal parliament, and the *Legislative Assembly* (the lower house) and the *Legislative Council* (the upper house) for state parliaments.

parliamentary privilege: A protection from libel and defamation laws afforded to members of a *parliament*.

Parliamentary Responsibility: A doctrine outlined by Governor-General Sir John Kerr in his reasons for dismissing the Whitlam government in 1975, in which he argued that, in Australia, the federal government must be able to get its budget through the *House of Representatives* and the *Senate* in order to satisfy being a *Responsible Government*.

parliamentary secretary: A member of *parliament* junior to ministers, although with the same status and requirements to obey the parliamentary *conventions*. See also *Cabinet*, *full ministry*.

party endorsement: See *preselection*.

party machine: The administration of a *political party*.

party platform: A general statement of principles and goals for governing that are fundamental to a *political party*.

party political: An ABC Television broadcast segment by each *political party* in the lead-up to an election.

Party Room: A body of the Liberal Party of Australia, and of the National Party of Australia, that includes all members of the parliamentary wing, at either federal or state level, who meet ahead of parliamentary sittings to decide on how they will vote in *parliament*, though allowing all members a *conscience vote*. See also *Joint Party Room*.

party ticket: A *political party's* ranking of preferred party candidates published on *how-to-vote cards* that are handed out at polling booths.

pendulum: An assessment of the percentage of change in the vote between the previous and current election needed in particular *electoral districts* for the sitting members to lose their seats, known as the percentage *swing*, particularly in *marginal seats*.

percentage swing: See *swing*.

policy platform: The approach a *political party* takes on a particular area of policy.

political party: An association of people coming together for the express purpose of recruiting candidates for elections.

popular sovereignty: The empowerment of individual citizens to run their community.

portfolio: A specific area of policy-making responsibility given to a minister that includes being in charge of a ministerial department of the public service. See also *Ministerial Responsibility*.

pragmatism: A belief in achieving broad consensus on policy issues through dialogue, bargaining and negotiation in which ideology and philosophy are subordinate to achieving outcomes.

preferential voting: A voting system in which candidates must win a majority of the vote to win a seat, after preferences for other candidates are taken into account. See also *how-to-vote card, primary vote, proportional representation, two-party-preferred vote*.

premier: The head of an Australian state government in the *Westminster system*. See also *prime minister*.

preselection: A *political party's* selection of candidates to contest an election.

President: The presiding officer of the upper house of a *parliament*. See also *Speaker*.

press gallery: The area in the *parliament* reserved for assigned political journalists to observe each of the parliamentary chambers, and the collective term for those journalists (also known as the press corps).

primary vote: The first preference given to a candidate by voters in a preferential voting system. See also *preferential voting, two-party-preferred vote*.

prime minister: The head of national government in the *Westminster system*. See also *premier*.

property franchise: The requirement to own property in order to vote or be elected to *parliament*.

proportional representation: A voting system in which seats, in theory, should be won in proportion to the vote won. See also *preferential voting*.

public administration: The actions taken by public servants to ensure that government policy is practically applied in the relevant government departments.

public policy: A policy decision that is converted into active programs through an enacted law, policy programs, regulations or *intergovernmental agreements*.

psephology: The study and analysis of election results.

Question Time: A session during a parliamentary sitting when *backbenchers* can ask questions of ministers (usually *Dorothy Dixers*) and the opposition can ask questions of the government.

razor gang: See *Expenditure Review Committee (ERC)*.

redistribution: The process used by electoral authorities, such as the *Australian Electoral Commission*, to draw up electoral boundaries.

referendum: The mechanism used to change a *constitution* whereby a question or set of questions is put to the electorate to vote on, usually during a general election.

reserve power: The power granted to Australian *governors* and the *governor-general* to intervene in parliamentary matters under certain circumstances. See also *exclusive power, concurrent power* and *residual power*.

residual power: Any power that is not specifically noted in the *Australian Constitution* and is, therefore, exercisable by the states. See also *exclusive power, concurrent power* and *reserve power*.

Responsible Government: A convention of the *Westminster system* that refers to the way a ministry is formed in the *parliament* and how it stays in government for as long as it commands a majority in the lower house of parliament. See also *Collective Responsibility, Ministerial Responsibility, Separation of Powers*.

royal assent: The act of the *Crown* bestowing authority on an *Act of Parliament*.

scrutineer: A person appointed by each *political party* to observe the counting of votes in each electorate and report back to party officials.

seat: See *electoral district*.

second reading: The second mention of a *bill* in a *parliament*, when the responsible minister outlines its underlying policy and the reasons for the bill being introduced. See also *Act of Parliament, committee stage, first reading, third reading*.

Senate: The upper house of federal *parliament*, created with the purpose of being the chamber in which the federating states would be represented. See also *Legislative Council*.

senior executive service (SES): The pool of senior public servants from which government appoints *departmental secretaries*.

senior minister: See *full ministry*.

Separation of Powers: A convention in the *Westminster system* that keeps the key institutions of the courts, the military and the public service separate from the partisan politics that can occur in the *legislature*. See also *Collective Responsibility, Ministerial Responsibility, Responsible Government*.

Sergeant at Arms: The officer of the lower house of a *parliament* who assists the *Speaker* in disciplinary tasks. See also *Usher of the Black Rod*.

single transferrable vote (STV): A type of *proportional representation* voting system in which voters numerically order their preferred candidates, similar to the system of *preferential voting*.

socialism: Common ownership of property, primarily through a government-owned economy on behalf of the community. See also *nationalisation*.

Speaker: The presiding officer of the lower house of a *parliament*. See also *President*.

Specific Purpose Grant: Money given by the Commonwealth government to the state governments under Section 96 of the *Australian Constitution* to fund programs determined by the federal government. See also *General Purpose Financial Assistance to the States, Grants Commission*.

standing committee: A committee of *backbench* members of *parliament* brought together to inquire into specific policy matters.

Standing Orders: The rule books for the operation of the lower house of a *parliament*.

statutory authority: A public corporation set up by government and enabled by legislation to provide government services and apply government rules and regulations, but run by a board of directors and answerable to *parliament* only via an annual report.

supply: The combination of legislation that levies taxes and authorises government spending. See also *appropriation bill*.

Supreme Court: The highest court of a state or territory.

swing: The difference between the percentage of votes for a candidate in a particular seat in the current and previous elections. See also *pendulum*.

tariff: A tax levied on imports to raise funds or protect local industry by increasing the price of imported goods.

third reading: The third mention of a *bill* in a *parliament*, after it has been debated, when the *Speaker* of the lower house or the *President* of the upper house resumes the chair of the chamber to be informed by the *Chairperson of Committees* that the bill has passed the *committee stage*. See also *Act of Parliament, first reading, second reading*.

two-party system: A common description of the Australian electoral system because of the dominance of the Labor and Liberal Parties.

two-party-preferred vote: The count of votes for a specific candidate in an election after preferences are distributed. See also *primary vote, preferential voting*.

Usher of the Black Rod: The officer of the upper house of a *parliament* who assists the *President* in disciplinary tasks. See also *Sergeant at Arms*.

vertical fiscal imbalance (VFI): The concept that the federal government has financial power over the state governments, which carry the majority of responsibility for providing services.

Washminster: A term sometimes used to describe how Australia is a hybrid of the *Westminster system* of parliamentary government and the American system of federal governance (Washington).

wasted majority: A feature of a single-member electoral system when a successful candidate wins a vote in excess of the majority required to win the seat. See also *exaggerated majority, paradoxical outcome*.

Westminster system: The British system of parliamentary government.

writ: A legal document, signed by the *governor-general*, authorising a federal election; its return after the election is the legal authorisation for the election of the successful candidates.

Index

About the Authors

Dr Nick Economou has studied Australian politics for nearly all his life. He studied politics at school and at the University of Melbourne, where he completed a Master of Arts and, later, a PhD in Political Science. Nick started teaching Australian politics for university students when he was a tutor at the old Swinburne Institute (now Swinburne University) in 1985. In a couple of years he secured a lecturing position at the Gippsland Institute of Advanced Education and then, later, Monash University, where he is currently a Senior Lecturer in the School of Political and Social Inquiry.

In addition to teaching, Nick has been a frequent media commentator on Australian politics, as well as a writer of opinion pieces for a range of newspapers. He has been a contributor to numerous books and published many articles in academic journals on Australian politics. In 1999 he was the editor of *The Kennett Revolution* (MUP) with Brian Costar, and in 2008 authored *Media Politics and Power in Australia* (Pearson) with Stephen Tanner.

Dr Zareh Ghazarian is a Senior Lecturer in Politics and International Relations in the School of Social Sciences at Monash University. Zareh has published widely in the field of Australian politics, in academic as well as non-academic outlets. Zareh is a leading commentator and regularly provides analysis on Australian politics in the media.

His teaching and research interests include public policy, political parties, elections and civics and citizenship education. In 2015 he authored *The Making of a Party System: Minor Parties in the Australian Senate* (2015, Monash University Publishing) and in 2021 edited *Gender Politics: Navigating Political Leadership in Australia* (UNSW Press) with Katrina Lee-Koo.

Dedication

Nick dedicates this book to Lydia, his very first Australian politics teacher.

Zareh dedicates this book to Tony and Nadia.

Authors' Acknowledgements

The authors would like to thank the staff at Wiley for their assistance with this book. For the first edition, we would particularly like to thank Charlotte Duff and Bronwyn Duhigg, who thought of us as potential authors and who actually got us to get on with it. We also thank Kerry Davies for her incredible patience and editing skills.

For the second edition of this book, we pass on our gratitude to Lucy Raymond for inviting us back and for her patience and guidance on the project. We thank Charlotte Duff for her wonderful editing skills and fine eye for detail, as well as Chris Shorten for his patience.

We would also like to thank David Mayer, who not only helped with drafts and advice, but also has been a great mentor and friend. Thanks also to Kate Seear, Marina Cominos and Ben Whiteley, and all the others who inhabit the 11th floor of the Menzies Building at Monash University and put up with us running ideas past them and supported us during the various stages of production.

Publisher's Acknowledgements

Some of the people who helped bring this book to market include the following:

Acquisitions, Editorial and Media Development

Project Editor: Tamilmani Varadharaj

Acquisitions Editor: Lucy Raymond

Editorial Manager: Chris Shorten

Copy Editor: Charlotte Duff

Production

Graphics: SPi

Proofreader: Penny Stuart

Indexer: Estalita Slivoskey

The author and publisher would like to thank the following organisations for their permission to reproduce copyright material in this book:

- **Cover image:** © Alex Cimbal/Shutterstock
- **Page 35:** National Library of Australia/Photo by Loui Seselja, nla.pic-an24526893
- **Page 37:** National Archives of Australia
- **Page 39:** Andrew Chapman
- **Page 94:** National Library of Australia, nla.pican24355082
- **Page 101:** top, © Image Disk Photography
- **Page 101:** bottom, pp. 105, 107, image by permission of the Parliamentary Education Office, www.peo.gov.au
- **Page 102:** © Alison Farrant
- **Pages 257, 261:** AEC, copyright Commonwealth of Australia, reproduced by permission
- **Page 296:** © Bruce Petty

Every effort has been made to trace the ownership of copyright material. Information that enables the publisher to rectify any error or omission in subsequent editions is welcome. In such cases, please contact the Permissions Section of John Wiley & Sons Australia, Ltd.